A MAN OF LITTLE FAITH

SUNY series in Contemporary French Thought

David Pettigrew and François Raffoul, editors

A MAN OF LITTLE FAITH

MICHEL DEGUY

With Two Essays by

JEAN-LUC NANCY

Translated, edited, and with an Introduction by

CHRISTOPHER ELSON

STATE UNIVERSITY OF NEW YORK PRESS

Frontispiece, illustration by Alain Lestié

untitled acrostic for Michel Deguy's 80th birthday,
by Jean-Luc Nancy

Published by
State University of New York Press, Albany

Printed in the United States of America

For information, contact
State University of New York Press, Albany, NY
www.sunypress.edu

Production, Eileen Nizer
Marketing, Kate Seburyamo

Library of Congress Cataloging-in-Publication Data

Deguy, Michel.
[Un homme de peu de foi. English]
A man of little faith / Michel Deguy ; translated, edited, and with an introduction by Christopher Elson.
pages cm. — (SUNY series in contemporary French thought)
Includes bibliographical references and index.
ISBN 978-1-4384-5359-0 (hc : alk. paper) 978-1-4384-5358-3 (pb : alk. paper)
ISBN 978-1-4384-5360-6 (ebook)
1. Faith—Philosophy. 2. Belief and doubt—Philosophy. 3. Religion—Philosophy. I. Title.

BD215.D4413 2014
210—dc23 2013048559

10 9 8 7 6 5 4 3 2 1

Meteor tracing furious ellipses
Impalpable bump of worlds in rebound
Cast pebbles, coaldust, silex, micas and gypsums
Humouristic reports, sobs and zounds
Entrained by the pure avidity of saying
Luxuriant all and one like the other
Drawing on his lyre ingenious before us
Enharmonic with cadences of reason
Grave and gay in turn in the well-milled throat
Ulcerous from the saps that its conjugation
Yearning like a gluttonous muse there pours out

—Jean-Luc Nancy, from *Deguy le Grand* 8

CONTENTS

TRANSLATOR'S NOTES

It is a privilege and an adventure to translate Michel Deguy, to attempt to bring his vigorous inventivity and erudition in the original French to life in an idiomatic, comparably layered, and still comprehensible English. This often seems like an impossible exercise, balancing inspiration and peril, one where difficult choices are necessary on every page. Deguy's inventivity is that of the extreme contemporary, an already "*future* rigor" where the writer of vigilance works ceaselessly to safeguard the linguistic relics of our cultural past at the same time as he seeks to enliven today's words, which are always at risk of falling behind today's things and phenomena, keeping both sides open in a continuous retranslation for future uses and astonishments.

1. Neologisms. I have an absolute respect for Deguyan neology and a commitment to rendering it each and every time, even at the cost of occasional awkwardness. "Things change more quickly than words" and culture has been "vampirized" (CPAC, 195 and back cover). Neologisms are sharp wooden stakes in the toolbox of Michel Deguy, Vampire Hunter.

2. Something that may not be immediately apparent to the reader of only the English text is the degree to which I have respected *but not absolutely* the expansive, exigent syntax of Deguy's phraseology. Sometimes the precise preciousness of his sentences has been attenuated here, sinuosity abandoned in favor of a straightened-out stretch, his prosody's rhythmic elongation across the bar lines given more limited measures.

3. The quantity and cumulative, signifying density of allusions in this as in any other of Deguy's works adds a further dimension to its translation, as well as posing basic editorial challenges. How not to overload the text with parenthetical references or footnotes? I have attempted to find the right balance between useful information and excessive disruption of the text's flow and appearance.

On the same heading, the French poetic tradition is massively present here as elsewhere in Deguy's corpus and I have aimed for a balance between compactly indicating author names or/and the titles of works cited by Deguy and the inclusion of a few recapitulative notes gathering together a brief account of the place of Apollinaire, Baudelaire, Mallarmé, Rimbaud, and others in *A Man of Little Faith* and Deguy's other works.

4. A *Man of Little Faith* is a multilingual book before any translating takes place. There are many citations and expressions in Latin and in Greek, along with a few quotations left in their original English, German, or other languages. Like his late friend, Jacques Derrida, Deguy proceeds from the conviction that any language is always already more than one, always relating to itself diachronically and relating to its others geopoetically in full consciousness of the necessity of translation and a lucid reflection on its conditions of possibility. His 1978 text "The Compass Rose of Languages" (JMUSA, 88–98) is a fine illustration, in a kind of textualist mode, of the poet-thinker's acute awareness of the necessity of relating one European language to its others.

5. Wherever Deguy has played with a biblical or philosophical citation in Greek or Latin, I immediately give a rendering in square brackets to help the reader avoid mistaking a more or less significant alteration for a familiar reference. Explanation or translation of unaltered quotations in the original languages is treated less systematically, sometimes given parenthetically, sometimes incorporated into endnotes found on the same page, sometimes not provided, if the context is sufficiently rich.

6. The *comme* of comparison. One of the most important challenges for a translator of Deguy is to find ways to convey the density of his thought of comparison, a reflection that is both poetic and ontological in its implications. The French *comme* condenses the senses of English "like" and "as" or German *wie* and *als*. Deguy has worked on and with its ambivalent two-sidedness virtually since the beginning of his career. The cumulative richness of these years of poetic and philosophical reflection on *comme* is present in the translator's mind at each occasion of choice. In the subsection "Escence" (*infra* 30–31), Deguy makes it clear that he privileges the *like* over the *as* but cannot escape from the undividedness of the comparative and the definitive, the proximity in *comme* of the open multivalence of *like* and the identitary risks of *as*. "The work of reason, which always still awaits, is to scrutinize the obscurity of a difference which is reducible to that of '*as*' and '*like*,' [*en tant que*/ *pareil à*] which in French comes down to the homogeneity of the *comme* where this difference cannot be heard" (*infra* 118).

A crucial decision must be made with respect to Deguy's tendency to substantify the adverb or conjunction "*comme*" in order to treat comparison theoretically: *Le comme*, when it is used analytically as a conceptual operator, will be treated in English translation as a compound common noun, "the like-or-as," despite the possible awkwardness of that expansive choice—I think the reader needs this occasional reminder; this will not be the case in expressions like *l'ontologie du comme*, which is translated as "the ontology of like," suppressing the implicit definite article and condensing the two-sidedness of like-or-as for the sake of elegance. (Sometimes too it is a matter of rendering an impossible pun like "*le comme-un des mortels*," which I tend to translate as "as-oneness of mortals.")

In handling the presence of *comme* in the poems or passages of quasi-poetic condensation, I feel unbound by any such general principles and guidelines, treating each case as a singularity.

Semblance and *semblable* are key terms related to comparison and to the *ontology of like* that are frequently employed by Deguy in *A Man of Little Faith* (see, centrally, *infra* 66–67). (Baudelaire's "*le semblable*" presents a related conundrum for English renderings [cf. *infra* 30, 38].) I generally opt for the English words "semblance" and "alike" but sometimes, as the contexts demand, will vary these choices when the term or terms are repeated in a development—"similarity," "likeness," and "appearance" are occasionally deployed to bring out the steps in a reasoning about comparison.

INTRODUCTION

TO CONSERVE WHILE LEAVING BEHIND

Michel Deguy's Palinody

We must ensure that the palinody which disenchants in its descant not "purely and simply" lose that which it overthrows. The chant of palinody draws the superstition of chanting incantation along to its very loss. And after having brought about the loss of those beliefs and illusions which the singing of the song entailed, it then accompanies their transfer into. . . . ? Leading opinions on to their loss, drowning them in song, means that one may take them along with oneself; one can make them dance until they drop from exhaustion, overturning them, reversing them . . . into what?

How to retrace that movement?[1]

What is finished is only just beginning.[2]

Michel Deguy's *Un Homme de peu de foi* appeared in 2002 and was his thirtieth published book. As its opening pages make explicit, the volume must be situated, as Deguy's work has always situated itself, in dialogue with "our aporetic times" (*infra* 112). This *palinody*, a complex, quasi-generic term that Deguy (1930–) himself gives to his book and that is examined and clarified throughout this introduction, stands in translation as an exemplary statement for English-speaking readers of that correspondence with our time. It prolongs and extends some of Deguy's essential propositions on poetics, ontology, ethics, religion, and cultural theory while opening up new angles and forms of reflection that we see confirmed in the work that has followed.

A Man of Little Faith is the first and principal part of an unintended diptych. Unintended because the second volume, 2004's *Sans Retour* [With No Return], was produced from the circumstantial energy of polemic, after a ferocious and indeed *ad hominem* attack was leveled at Deguy and *A Man of Little Faith* by Benny Lévy. Lévy is a fascinating figure, a clandestine immigrant to France from Egypt and a radical student activist in the sixties, Jean-Paul Sartre's personal secretary in the last years of Sartre's life, a left-wing materialist who underwent a late conversion to Judaism, a return to the faith of the fathers under the influence of Emmanuel Levinas. In the epilogue to his book *Etre juif Etude lévinassienne* [Being Jewish/Levinassian Study], he was virulently critical of some of the propositions of *A Man of Little Faith* (although some of his remarks indicate clearly that he had not read the whole book) and Deguy responded rapidly and with commensurate intensity in his *Sans Retour*; complicating these matters is the fact that Benny Lévy's death was to coincide more or less exactly with the appearance of his book and, consequently, Deguy's response to its "execration" could elicit no further echo.[3]

Un Homme de peu de foi and *Sans Retour* take part and take a place in what Deguy has identified in some recapitulatory texts as a significant strand of his overall body of work, one that he calls the "combat within the 'exit from religion.'"[4] That terminology is closely identified in the French intellectual landscape with Marcel Gauchet, whose work on the "disenchantment of the world" has had a profound effect on the philosophy, history, and sociology of religion in recent years. Deguy has made explicit in various places the connection of his vocabulary of a departure or an exit from religion with Gauchet's work but Deguy uses the term a good deal more allusively and nonsystematically than does the author of *Le religieux après la religion* [The Religious after Religion].[5]

In *Dis-Enclosure. The Deconstruction of Christianity*, Jean-Luc Nancy devotes a chapter, "De-Mythified Prayer," to the poet's sense of the a-religious dimension of prayer.[6] At the heart of Nancy's group of interconnected studies, he states that Michel Deguy has elaborated "one of the most acute formulations of what is brought into play, in my view at least, by a 'deconstruction of Christianity'" through his reflections on such formulas and concepts as "demythified prayer."[7] Nancy admires Deguy's tenacious work of poetic reflection on and translation of tradition; he underlines in particular Deguy's "approach to a remnant or *relic*, as [he] likes to put it, freed, dis-enclosed from the religious edifice, impossible to put back, but the bearer or the worker of a requirement that will not be dismissed."[8] This introduction will begin to show how Deguy's palinody both does and does not participate in an exit from religion, whether in the sense of Gauchet's arguments or understood more broadly, and how what Nancy calls "the more or less tightly knit systematization connecting these themes"[9] in *A Man of Little Faith* and *With No Return* makes of the "little faith" a more complex matter than an apparently decisive exit from religion. It also begins to address how Deguy's account of *laïcité*, a term that always resists a reductive translation to *secularity*, might correspond to or with each of those sides, both the exit and the no-exit, while proposing in its poetic orientation and progression something other still.

The direction of a more extensive elaboration along those lines might be suggested with a reference to Charles Taylor's foreword to the English edition of Gauchet's *The Disenchantment of the World A Political History of Religion*. The Catholic thinker of multiculturalism and secularity there poses the question of a certain irreducible character of faith and an associated tension within Gauchet's thought. Taylor is skeptical that a meaning-centric account of higher religious cultures and their evolution toward an exit from religion, such as that described by Gauchet, could ever be adequate to the richness of religious experience or the human realities to which it points. Faith, for Taylor, is not just about a need for sense-making meaning that can forever be taken to a higher level of theoretical detachment and explanatory coherence for a human world leaving behind its transcendental backdrop; the phenomenon of faith corresponds to something both elusive and irreducible:

> . . . can the new departures in faith, of Buddha, of Jesus, or for that matter of St. Francis or St. Teresa, be understood simply in terms of the hunger for meaning? If the basic aim is just to make sense of it all, why is it that *karuna* or *agape* are so central to those traditions? Can the evolution at this level of detail be accounted for simply in terms of the structural tensions of "religion"? If so, then the explanatory primacy of these structures would indeed be vindicated. Faith would be merely a "dependent variable," flotsam on the sea of a postreligious age. But perhaps these mutations can only be explained by suposing [*sic*] that something like what they relate to—God, Nirvana—really exists. In that case, a purely cultural account of religion would be like Hamlet without the Prince.[10]

This concern with what to do with the "flotsam" of faith affords a useful perspective on Deguy's deep unease, expressed in these pages and elsewhere, with the culturalization of religion and his clear statements about the risks of an insipid carrying-on or replacement of religion within or by literature: "And let not the religion of literature replace the literature of religion! We want no lethargic ersatz" (*infra* 73).[11]

Deguy's diptych is decidedly not about a return to faith, that much should be beyond debate or misreading, and his painstaking and technically demanding work on quasi-transcendence understood within a regime of impossibility makes the postulation of "something like what [faith and religion] relate to," in Taylor's expression, an even more complex object to locate and to think. But in situating Deguy's perspective on the possible character of the "little faith" or of the paradoxes of "religion without religion," or "the sacred without the sacred," it must also be understood that the culturalization of religion and the relay of religion by some sort of sacralization of literature are, for him, very likely just the other side of today's shrill, intensifying orthodox fundamentalisms.[12] Neither of those widespread perspectives or attitudes would be adequate to the most radical implications of the evidence and experience of an exit from religion. Neither would be sufficient to capture the remainder of the truths of religion and faith at the moment when they are being left behind with difficulty—preciously or desperately conserved as identitary cultural manifestations or violently reaffirmed in theologico-political reactions.

The poet-thinker's ongoing work on revelation and profanation, on ineffacement, on theologemes, on the Fable, on the Great Code, on relics, stakes out a different perspective, neither the "cultural account" of a Gauchet, nor the reasonable, conservative yet resolutely secular objections of a Taylor, offered from within faith. Deguy's poetics of demythologization, making revelation anew out of profanation, refiguring, and revivifying the relics of tradition, do not constitute a simple refusal of faith, and are most certainly not a rationally over confident refutation of its reality either. The essentially poetic acts of Michel Deguy are proposed with urgency as a program of paradoxical artistic and cultural duty. They take up from another angle the challenge posed by the object(s) of faith, one repressed by Gauchet, we might say, following the concerns of Taylor and of some of those writing on Deguy and religion in the essential critical collection *L'Allégresse pensive*,[13] and they do so in the light of Nancy's already cited and very perceptive evocation of what is moving in Deguy's writings, of all that may be considered there "as the bearer or the worker of a requirement that will not be dismissed." Deguy's response to this requirement of the relics of religion and faith, a requirement that will not and cannot be easily dismissed, is framed within a space of rational and empirical skepticism and historically alert late cultural anxiety. But "making revelation out of profanation after having first made profanation out of revelation"[14] does not simply set aside the experiences of religion and faith as imperfect moments or secondary effects of a humanizing, empowering, or progressive evolution. Deguy sees all of the counterfinalities of such developments, of such an "exit," too, and he takes them on himself in his "willing suspension of belief," in the anxious singing of his palinody, his ode against the grain. All of Michel Deguy's exits are "exits without exit."[15]

The selective and distorted reading of *A Man of Little Faith* by Benny Lévy notwithstanding, Deguy's corpus has attracted keen and illuminating literary-critical and philosophical attention, as Nancy's essay in *Dis-Enclosure* and those gathered in the appendix here attest. Despite such serious and substantial reception, one would not be exaggerating much to say that we are just beginning to take properly the measure of Deguy's work, its effect, its sources, and its connections, just now situating him adequately within the currents and relationships of the French poetic and philosophical scenes of the past fifty years. He has been in a hurry, as Jean-Luc Nancy points out in his affectionate and penetrating essay, "Deguy, the New Year!" and international scholarship, as well as his French peers, is catching up, still, perhaps inevitably, a step or a half step behind.

At the heart of the difficulty of an adequate critical and intellectual-historical appreciation of Michel Deguy lies the multiple, mixed, or hybrid character of the thought, the works, and the engagements of this protean figure. "One must always be doing two things at once. At least!" he joyfully and playfully proclaimed on the jacket cover of *Jumelages/Made in U.S.A.* [Twinnings/Made in U.S.A.].[16]

Deguy is well aware of the demands of his plural project, of its ambitions and its challenges both for himself and for readers and scholars; he has written of the "insurmountable difficulty of the situation he confronts,"[17] although he was characteristically not speaking there of himself but of a generically impossible-to-pin-down kind of writer very much *like* himself: "the thinking poet who tries to make poetry and poetics interpenetrate and to sanction that poetic thought as a mode of thinking not unequal to philosophical thought."[18] We necessarily return frequently here to the fundamental poetry–philosophy relation as it cuts so powerfully and so variously through the work of Michel Deguy, who, for none other than Jacques Derrida, is an utterly singular instance of a new and far from stable type, indeed one not yet invented, but which Derrida marks out in a deep exercise of interpretation and naming through a playful and provisional trilingual syntagma: the *french* [*sic*] *Dichter-Denker*. In the context of his reflection on how to name and how to name Deguy, he takes up and considers with friendly admiration

> the name of a poet thinker given over to the vocation of so many languages, wanderer, guest, inventor, geo-grapher and teller of new continents and, we will come to this too, the poet of promised lands, configuring them through many transports and

> translations such that he bears the name of *french Dichter-Denker* well, it is comely on him, it fits him so well but so as to make it migrate right away, like a word that is given, embarked in advance for other places, other maps and charts, flying toward the destination of future genealogies and given over to idioms to come.[19]

The *french Dichter-Denker* is a name that suits Deguy well and that locates him within a tradition of poet-thinkers and within the tradition of their meditation by Heidegger, but also in a future, in an unnamed and unnameable futuricity. *The poet that I am seeking to be . . .* And the thinker, just as well. Deguy's reading of the contemporary condition disallows any stability or self-satisfaction—figural, conceptual, politico-ethical—pushing the thinker-poet to renewed invention at every turn, in every turn of thought and of language.

Near the beginning of his comprehensive and ambitious study, *Différence et Identité: Michel Deguy Situation d'un poète lyrique à l'apogée du capitalisme culturel* [Difference and Identity: Michel Deguy Situation of a lyric poet at the apogee of cultural capitalism], University of Geneva Professor Martin Rueff makes a strong judgment about the importance of Deguy's oeuvre and situates it in terms of the double character of his abundant corpus, declaring it the most significant body of work to have emerged in French poetry in the past fifty years. His reasons for that judgment have to do with the universality of the oeuvre's ambitions and with the very refined and sustained critical reflection that it proposes on what is quite likely the fundamental theoretical problem of our era, the thinking of identity and difference:

> . . . if there are, among the poets of his generation, some poets who are more immediately lyrical or more traditionally poets, if there are, beyond a doubt, more avant-gardist poets than Michel Deguy, there is not one who is more important, more decisive. If Michel Deguy's poetry counts more than any other within the French poetic creation of the post-war years, it it not only because of its own lyrical power to which nothing is foreign (*poeta sum, humani nihil a me alienum puto* [poet am I and nothing human can be alien to me]), from the destiny of one man right up to the adventures of thought and of forms; nothing is alien to it because of its incandescence and its magnificent inventions, this is also the case because Deguy's poetry and the poetics which doubles it make of identity and of difference their object, their stake, their terrain and their question. No

one before Deguy had so unanimously, so poetically questioned identity and difference.[20]

American writers and scholars, too, have noted the strikingly comprehensive character of Deguy's oeuvre in analogous terms. Kenneth Koch puts it in terms of an "adventurous disjunctiveness," whereas Paul Auster notes Deguy's "determination to carry poetry into uncharted territory."[21] Koch further remarks:

> rather than choosing one strand, or line, of poetic subject matter and style, as have some of his talented contemporaries (Du Bouchet and Bonnefoy, for example), Deguy seems to me to stay in the center, as if he were unwilling to miss anything, didn't want to give anything up, not any way of life or any of the "old privileges" of the poet: being able to rhyme, to tell stories, to write long poems, to mix poetry and prose, to be precise and intellectual, to be ecstatic and lyrical, to write about anything he wants.[22]

Nothing human, nothing from the poetic tradition and nothing from its beyond, can remain foreign to the contemporary poet of difference.

In his preface to the anthologization of Deguy's *Gisants* in the Gallimard *Poésie* collection, Andrea Zanzotto, the late great Italian poet, wrote of Deguy's overcoming of sterile generic oppositions, of his participation in the post-structuralist and textualist experimentations of his time while sacrificing nothing to mere passing fashions and, most tellingly, of Deguy's poetic approach to a reinvention of "philosophicity."

> All of the apparatuses and the little textual machines that characterized a period of French culture are present. . . . But they are nevertheless constructed with a sense of form—measure and tension—which remains eminently and viscerally literary.
>
> Another contradiction with respect to Derrida, for whom the persistence of a "genre" gap between poetry and prose seems to remain central: the unformalness [*l'informel*] of Deguy's writing, conscious of the impossibility of passing over the limit, even if it were in an unstable balance open to the "poetic," a chancy circumstance that today constrains the identification of a different "philosophicity."[23]

Leaving aside the possible "contradiction" with respect to Derrida on these matters, Zanzotto puts his finger on the formal and generic demands of Deguy's project and on the very slight room for maneuver that he has, notwithstanding the quantity and range of his writings. He respectfully acknowledges Deguy's capacities for operating on and beyond the limits of genres and modes of thought and writing. The translator into English of the 1985 volume *Gisants*, Wilson Baldridge, writes in very much the same vein of Deguy "keeping vigil over the medium of difference through poetical invention beyond conventional distinctions between philosophy and literature."[24]

At some inevitable risk for oversimplification, one might advance the following impossible summary of the unity of Deguy's stance and its varied productions: There is no more significant poetic and theoretical writer of vigilance today than Michel Deguy. His productive energy and broad engagement with our contemporary moment come from a sense of the intellectual and artist's uniquely acute responsibility, a responsibility drawing on two sources, two inspirations, philosophical and poetic, ever relating them in the questioning of responsibility itself, ever seeking their already-relatedness through that motif and others, constantly reinventing those sources in a complex interweaving of innumerable theoretical and poetical propositions and acts.

Deguy's work indeed began under the sign of watchfulness more than fifty years ago. The opening poem of his first Gallimard collection, *Fragment du Cadastre* [Fragment of the Cadaster] in 1960 was entitled "La Vigie" ["The Look-Out" or "The Watch-Keeper"]. Thirty-odd years later, in an interview for the France-Culture radio program, *Le Bon Plaisir*, writer and filmmaker Claude Lanzmann spoke with a palpable gratitude of waking early and knowing that Deguy was already at his desk, keeping a poetic watch that ends the night, a thinker in the posture of a look-out, gazing out over the contemporary. "In the morning I go out with bouquet gestures/ To gather/ . . . Disjointed essences in the spectacle,/In order that the fire of relation burn more alive," says the poetic voice of "La Vigie." Vigilance with respect to the relations in being, a poetic gathering that permits a stronger articulation of identity and difference within a vocabulary borrowed from philosophy but clearly not constrained by any priority of that mode of thinking; we have in germ here in this early text clear indicators of the main directions Deguy's prolific poetics has taken ever since, and of his conviction of the rightness or necessity of this orientation: "None a more obstinate haunter . . ."[25]

Deguy's poetics of responsibility, which he has called with greater or lesser insistence a po*ethics* since the late 1970s, is rooted in large part in his reading of Baudelaire. As *A Man of Little Faith* shows, Deguy's relation to the whole of poetic modernity is a powerfully lucid and engaged one. He addresses himself to this tradition, citing Apollinaire, Rimbaud, the surrealists, Mallarmé, Char, Ponge, Bonnefoy, and others in these pages, but the most constant spur to his poetic reflection is the author of *Les Fleurs du mal*:

> I receive poetic responsibility from Baudelaire. I get it from a *flower of evil*, and not from a hymn to a great river in Germania. It is a clausula, that of the distych which completes the hundredth *flower*; that flower whose admirable incipit intones:
>
> *The great-hearted servant of whom you were jealous:*
> What could I reply to that pious soul
> Seeing from her hollow lids the tears fall?[26]
>
> Men are pious. Poetry, whose pronoun *I* Charles Baudelaire takes on here, is the pious impiety which *must* speak to the pious souls of readers.[27]

Coming as they do right after a retranslation of the famous Hölderlinian formula from *Andenken*, "*Was bleibet aber, stiften die Dichter*" (which Deguy translates as "What remains, the artists give it again"), so crucial to his conception of poetry and his theorization of tradition, these lines from 2005 emphasize both Michel Deguy's awareness of the vitality of the Heideggerian–Hölderlinian paradigm and a precautious privileging of other currents of modernity.

Pious impiety, the palinody within and *after* Baudelaire—"after" both in the sense of an historical anteriority and in the sense of an art-historical tradition, a figuring within a line of inspiration and imitation—can provide the conditions for the translation, the reinterpretation of relics, and for some sort of faithful infidelity to them. Turning his own new translation of Hölderlin away from the general emphasis in most existing versions upon endurance, upon dwelling, and foundations, reorienting it instead toward the gift of the unpredictable usage of the remainder says much about Deguy's ontology of *comme*, the ontology of like, and much about the distinctive note that poetic piety can strike.

This poetic piety, which plays out as an omnivorous and responsible reflection on identity and difference and, we shall see, as an impassioned defense of earthly habitability and attachment, has been profoundly nourished in Deguy through his long familiarity with Martin Heidegger's philosophical corpus. Notwithstanding a certain precautious distancing in the movement that *From Hölderlin to Baudelaire* evoked in 2005, there is no question that the poetic responsibility evoked relative to Baudelaire also plunges its roots deeply into Heideggerian themes and texts, including most especially those texts that Deguy translated as a young writer and with respect to which he has continued a dialogue of speculative differentiation.[28] The Heideggerian *Seinsfrage* haunts the pages of *A Man of Little Faith*, one can point to the amusingly grave pages devoted to reading Heidegger while on vacation in Fiji (*infra* 44 seq), among others. Fundamental to the enduring Heideggerian influence in Deguy is the question of a responsibility, both a care for and an ability to respond to Being's call, a call and a response that are prior to any of the subsequent and more or less crucial theoretical differentiations on metaphor or ontological difference, for example, which Jacques Derrida, Jacques Taminiaux, Philippe Lacoue-Labarthe, Philippe Verstraten, and other patient, insightful readers have outlined as constitutive of the Deguy–Heidegger difference.[29]

> The responsibility Heidegger's thought demands us to take—through which it obliges us and exercises a compelling attraction on our thoughts—is the responsibility in regard to being, of which our languages maintain the understanding and the expectation—and maybe they maintain themselves only through this countless extension. By dint of hearing "being," being re-observed, re-examined, plumbed, mentioned, capitalized, put between quotation marks, we become responsible (able to respond), we have to respond, that is, to say how it sounds in our understanding, "how we hear it."
>
> Experience consists in the understanding—gracious in that it could have left it ununderstood—of being accorded its given, its "there-is." Having become recipients of the given, *données*, we respond by interrogating the giving. Language speaks to itself about being; it speaks of being by speaking of itself, and vice versa, the antedosis, the original chiasma, i.e., before all beginning. Each one, being and language, has been changed into the other; can exchange with the other. "The exchange of a reciprocity of proofs": this beautiful Mallarmean formula expresses the given's way of being as a general relation: and could, for example, translate the *mimeïtai* which according to Aristotle is the word describing the relation of reciprocity between *phusis* and *techné*.[30]

Deguy has more recently spoken of a "Heideggerian disposition upstream of the post-Heideggerian (or an-Heideggerian) system."[31] Jacques Derrida devoted some of his important essay on Deguy, "How to Name," to working out that an-Heideggerianism relative precisely to this and related passages of *La Poésie n'est pas seule* (some of which were translated into English for the Cambridge Press volume, *Contemporary French Philosophy*, as "Motifs Towards a Poetics"). According to Derrida, Deguy achieves a unique relation to Heidegger through another variation on faithful infidelity:

> out of a concern for rigorously assuming the responsibility to which Heidegger calls us, and which is ours before him, and that

> which engages us in relation to languages, facing the work of thought and of poetic writing, the legatee's attestation contests and protests in the very movement of reaffirmation.[32]

The proximity of poetry and philosophy, the whole "metaphorics" of proximity progressively and cumulatively explored by Deguy and Derrida, occasionally in very explicit reference to one another, were also presented as a lifelong subject of reflection to students of Deguy in the *classes préparatoires*. Some learned this lesson very well.

In an eightieth birthday tribute to Michel Deguy, philosopher Barbara Cassin, editor of the extraordinary *Vocabulaire européen des philosophies*, affirmed that "it is as a poet that [Deguy] is a philosopher," leaning heavily here on the richness of the French *comme*, the *comme* of like-or-as so profoundly meditated for years by Deguy,[33] affirming with or after Deguy that sensitivity and attention to figurativity must in consequence inform all of the modes of truth-saying; she insists on the normalcy and the justness of that proposition:

> The metaphor, Michel Deguy taught me/us this right away, is nothing that comes along afterwards, it is *photophore*, normal light; the "*comme*" is a healthy regime, nothing that is compared is being dragged along behind, but we speak, as it were, from comparant to comparant, in an immediate appearing with and before [*comparution*].[34]

On his side, the distinguished historian and thinker of medieval philosophy, Alain de Libera emphasizes the famous Heideggerian image of the separate peaks and Deguy's deconstruction of it through a rereading of the abyss:

> *Denken und Dichten*. Deguy translation: Thinking and making an oeuvre. Right away he set the bar, and high. It was necessary to work, to make works. Philosophy and poetry, neighbors through the abyss, but indiscernible there where (and because) thinking, speaking, utterance is made. In brief: holding onto epiphany.[35]

Holding onto epiphany. Deguy taught budding philosophers, writers, translators, and scholars *the figurativity of existence* in the wake of a century of ontology and phenomenology thought and expressed in continental Europe by Husserl, Heidegger, Sartre, Beaufret, Char, and so many others.[36] And he did so in a singularly striking new way, preparing ongoing reflections on the nature of metaphor, on the varieties of reason, on the possible post-phenomenologic relations of poetry and philosophy. This is an unshakeable legacy for a certain part of a certain generation of French thought, as Cassin's and de Libera's recent hommages to their teacher show.

How to think the poetry-philosophy relation in terms of the nuances of like/as, the *comme* of comparison and the *comme* of *as* and *as-if*, rather than across an abyss of isolated, identitary difference, an unbridgeable chasm of *as-such*, wonders Cassin? "The answer to that question, so badly posed that no one dares to pose it that way (but then how might we pose it?), the answer is clearly: thought has need of both of them, my captain, o my captain. And what of philosophy, if it may be held that it is different from thought, does it need both? And poetry in general, does it need the two?"[37]

These are quite strikingly the very questions posed in their own way by three fraternal readers of Michel Deguy, namely Philippe Lacoue-Labarthe, Jean-Luc Nancy, and Jacques Derrida. Their neighboring essays from the 1996 collection *La Poète que je cherche à être* respond to that colloquium's organizers' request to reflect on the nature of the poetry–philosophy link in Deguy. A brief account of them here will further point up the place of Deguy on these issues within his generation of French thought and will better prepare the reader for the tone and modes of his poetic deconstruction which she or he will find throughout *A Man of Little Faith*.

A reading fully tracing out the multiple angles of approach and interconnection found in these three essays as they situate, read, and think along with Michel Deguy is beyond the scope of this brief introduction.[38] Maintaining the focus on faithful impiety, the development of palinody's possibility through the insights of Lacoue-Labarthe, Nancy, and Derrida will be emphasized through their interest in a related generic term, the *threnody*. In Deguy's works of grieving (to be distinguished radically from the work of mourning, as Jean-Luc Nancy does so clearly in "To Accompany Michel Deguy" *infra* 189–199) there is a preparation, a prefiguring and a precondition, of the singing-away-from-faith at the heart of palinody.

PALINODY AND THRENODY

Deguy wrote *A ce qui n'en finit pas* [*To That Which is Never-Ending* (or perhaps more strikingly and very aptly *Ever-Ending*)] after his wife Monique's death from cancer in 1994. This unpaginated, unprecedented text sought not to mourn her in some act of psychic reintegration and recovery but rather to carry grief forward into thought, sustaining it, watching over it in order to exceed the personal experience in the name of its truths. The propositions and modes of what Deguy called in a subtitle, *threnody*, touched and fascinated three of the major philosophers associated with the movement of deconstruction, who were also all friends of the writer. It is revealing to connect what they had to say about Deguy's threnody in 1996 with the development of the palinodic mode in Deguy's subsequent oeuvre. In the case of Jean-Luc Nancy, his second essay in our appendix to this volume, written ten years later, takes up the question of the Threnody once again, after the Palinody. There he relates them in their intertwined nature as foundational tonal and generic aspects of Deguy's later oeuvre, showing, in Nancy's deeply personal way, the interdependence of their meanings within and for Deguy's life and work.

There was to be in fact, astonishingly, a second extended song of grief in Deguy's oeuvre, entitled *Desolatio* (2007). In it Deguy writes in the same insistent, fully risked way of his strickenness; this second time following the death of his grandson, Raphaël, the loss of his sister (also named Monique), and the passing of "the friend" who is never named but whose resting place is situated by the texts themselves in Ris-Orangis (it is Jacques Derrida). Under the sign of this triple loss, Deguy extends the never-ending character of the meditation upon grief. The poignancy and courageous self-exposure of the 1995 volume are equaled or surpassed in the second threnody: "How can we (how dare we; how can we manage to) survive those whom we love truly; without whom we are not; with whom we have been among living, lively, convivial company; men; human men?"[39]

In *A Man of Little Faith*, there are several references to *A ce qui n'en finit pas*, and Deguy situates his a-theism in these pages in terms of the 1994 "encyclical letter" as he ironically terms it (*infra* 38); *splendor veritatis, the truth of splendour*, in a reversal of the well-known papal encyclical's title. Derrida had admiringly evoked "this threnody whose breath and inspiration one day made a church and its priests tremble while Monique Deguy, who was no longer there, was still there, absent so near to us, infinitely far from us."[40] The words that Derrida recalls, in "How to Name," are the following ones, spoken by Deguy during his eulogy for his late wife and later reproduced in the threnody:

> For a long time now, I must say it, I have not believed in all of this, which is so magnificent, *splendor veritatis* and my soul is afflicted, at the moment of saying with you adieu to Monique; and so, many here will say ADIEU to her better than I.[41]

This singular, agnostic eulogy anticipated the multiple tension found in *A Man of Little Faith*, one that might be condensed in four terms: 1) a real and heartrending regret at faith's passing; 2) an exercise of thought consisting of keeping belief suspended so as to draw everything possible from its loss ("a willing suspension of belief" is the simple statement of this far from simple attitude); 3) a lighter, at times even flippant, autobiographical account of withdrawal from religious practice and the Roman Catholic sacraments; and 4) an occasional broad and scathing anti-religious outburst, taking on any and all believers, and especially any public acknowledgment or manifestation of religious faith, expressed in a sometimes strikingly vehement fashion:

> I want to be able to detest the Orthodox of Jerusalem as much as the Taliban, the kippa outside of the synagogue as much as the head-scarf in school, without passing for an anti-Semite; want to be able to respect just as much the secular atheist of Tel-Aviv as the agnostic intellectual from Cairo. (*infra* 139)

If the dimensions of this introduction allowed, it would be important to explore what kind of *laïcité* Deguy is aiming to define through his exposition and analysis of a faithful unfaithfulness and its compatibility with what sometimes surfaces, as above, of a complete refusal of the religious, one drawing on a radical republican refusal of the manifestations of any particularities of faith and community. In *A Man of Little Faith*, this is expressed in terms of a refusal of communitarianism. It would also be important in this light to make even more explicit the risks of the exit from religion, a departure that might in fact be integral to the exit from the *logos* that Deguy fears as a destiny of this culture. This destiny is one that he seeks to avoid or transform in and through his work and particularly its appeal for a *translatio studiorum* for our times.

Two quotations will serve for now to present these related dimensions of a hesitation that runs as a fine but real thread in the weave of Deguy's a-theological thought. First, the consequences for thought of the loss of faith:

> But it may be that it is impossible for a pensive, reasonable humanity to think decidedly without "God." God was in the sentences of humanity's thought, of thought. It is made of a mixture (a bit like knowledge in Kant is a mixture made of concept and intuition "mixed together" by the imagination). Just as etymologies passed through fine analyses, through high-precision philological detectors, are always found to be full of the religious. They can be neither integrally integrated nor dis-integrated. Operating upon justice, pardon or the guest, without writing God; without thinking of God. In such a way that what is coming—a humanity, a discourse, entirely without God, well, that would be something other than humanity. The end of God would be the end of the world, and in this sense, God will have truly created the world and finished off the world through his last Judgment.[42]

Such a possible destiny of atheism is a determining aspect of a totalizing, annihilating risk to humanity. This is one of the *End(s) in the World* of which Deguy's recent book by that title worriedly speaks.

Second, there are consequences in lived terms of the dissolution of the link or the linking (*ligio*) functions of the *religio*, a dissolution that implies, for Deguy, the loss of important and enriching ways of human being-together, ways formed and conditioned over centuries by the interplay of theology, sacred texts and figures, liturgy, and social relations:

> There was someone; there was a person; no one else; which means "himself"; yourself and no one other. You were no one else; my dear being, my being.
>
> Thinking is thinking of you. Or instead, thinking of you was thinking. And I do want to believe that love and the person, that relation, that existential, will have been Christian, our way of loving. The fashion of loving and the hashed-over theology of the god-person grew up together, educating each other mutually; and our love was courtly and Christian, and "charity" contributed to that, and the injunction with respect to the "neighbour," and all of that.[43]

Although here the "someone" in the first paragraph is oriented referentially by the lost grandchild, how can we not hear in it also a version of the anxiety about God, God as integral to thought, to social possibility or good sociability, and to culture? This writer is a thinker haunted by the loss of belief at the very same time that he resolutely affirms such a loss as being *with no return*; a thinker-writer gambling all on the effects of the palinody in a work determined to combat both the culturalization of religion and the irreversible exit from religion, with the nihilistic potentialities of the "death" of God.[44]

Lacoue-Labarthe, Nancy, and Derrida all remark with seriousness and sensitivity on the immense challenge of reading and attempting to respond to Deguy's writings on grief and grieving: "Reading—with difficulty, I admit it, with pain—reading the "threnody" and knowing, as I advance in my reading, because I am left voiceless, that we can really never paraphrase Deguy again, nor even, perhaps, make phrases after what he has done . . ." (Lacoue-Labarthe)[45]; "I haven't got the heart to go too far in recalling without decency (but silence also would be bound up with indecency) . . ." (Derrida)[46]; "How not to cry and yet why cry—inasmuch as along with death there also enters into life—there has always already entered—the very simple revelation of that insouciance, that exemption from sense that also makes for the taste for life?" (Nancy, *infra* 194). But the threnody, or in Nancy's case the two books of grieving and the religious diptych, are compelling, irresistible pretexts for reflection and writing within the nexus of the four friends' mutually aware thinking.

Philippe Lacoue-Labarthe takes up a number of dimensions of *To That Which is Never-Ending* that underlie both the threnody and the later palinody. First of all, the atheistic character of Deguy's song of grief is underlined by the author of *Heidegger, Art and Politics*; importantly, this is not phrased by him in modern-contemporary terms but in ancient Greek terms: "the threnody is also a declaration of a-theism, in the Greek, Sophoclean sense."[47] Deguy's atheism is anachronic; it cuts across the traditions of thought with which he associates himself. We get a sense of what Lacoue-Labarthe means by a "Sophoclean" atheism when we read Deguy on Simone Weil and ponder his meditations on what it is to be pre-Christian (cf. *infra* 6, 99).

We also find in "Of Transport" (surely an echo of Derrida's dedication of "The Retrait of Metaphor" to Deguy) a smiling if somewhat frustrated attempt to situate Michel Deguy's use of Heidegger (ever-present as "the other" in Lacoue-Labarthe's essay). Philippe Lacoue-Labarthe wonders, early in his essay, "why is the other, precisely, he who while ceaselessly evoking poetry doesn't speak of poetry, or does so so little, why is he accepted and challenged? And why, when he is challenged, is it there where we expect it the least?"[48] We may recall Derrida's remark on this very heading that "the legatee's attestation contests and protests in the very movement of reaffirmation."[49] Both Lacoue-Labarthe and Derrida thereby locate the distinctiveness of Deguy's an- or post-Heideggerianism. The question of the acceptance that is also a challenge and of its surprising and perhaps sometimes inconsistent forms and essays opens up a cascading sequence of questions that Lacoue-Labarthe himself deems too "chaotic." He accordingly suspends their generality while focusing on what he calls an "apocope," a loss or breaking of voice in the saying of a few crucial syllables.

The question of the exit from religion is explicitly posed by Lacoue-Labarthe relative to a passage of Deguy's threnody, quite specifically in terms of the loss of the linking functions that religion provides or provided and that have been briefly discussed in terms of the threats run in any putative departure from religion. Lacoue-Labarthe radicalizes those risks, one might say, putting into play and into doubt the very possibility of *figuration* itself in the light of the loss of the *-ligio*. Examining two possible interpretations of a passage in the threnody that gives him pause, he proffers two interconnected interpretations, two translations.

One interpretation is atheological: "there is no justice, there is no 'point outside the world' "; and the other is literary: "poetry does not arrive, there is no other shore, no other side. No transport." No metaphor, no figurativity of existence, we might add. Whether from the side of religion or that of poetics, there is de-liaison, unlinking, *caesura*, in Lacoue-Labarthe's terms: "In one and the other case, an end is announced: that of the *religio*, literally, that is to say just as well that of the *comme-un*. He [Deguy] says, there where I have come to a halt: that of tragedy. "Tragedy has disappeared.""[50] Deguy's vigilant preservation of grief brings us to confront the failure of forms of representation and of catharsis. This is Lacoue-Labarthe's apocope, the stammer in which all phrasing fails.

Jacques Derrida's "How to Name" is one of his major statements on literature.[51] Despite being almost entirely overlooked by scholars of deconstruction,[52] it is one of his most important essays on poetry and poetics because it takes up the ambivalences of the French *salut*, so important in the later Derrida, and it does so within the infinitely rich metaphorics of proximity provided by his lifelong friendship with a singular poet, the *french Dichter-Denker*, Deguy. Things are said in this essay with a clarity and decisiveness that are of a unique power and distinctive significance within Derrida's enormous and varied corpus. "How to Name" draws upon all of Derrida's cumulative thought of naming, witnessing, the signature, and much else. In our more constrained context here, that of situating the threnody as it pertains to Deguy's twenty-first century palinody, it is important to note just a few elements of Derrida's seemingly inexhaustible essay.

Derrida, like Lacoue-Labarthe, is at pains to offer some clarification of the complex relation binding Deguy to Heidegger. Where Lacoue-Labarthe pulled back from the broader questions in the interests of brevity and of a focus on a certain singularly striking *caesura* in *A ce qui n'en finit pas*, Derrida forges ahead in summarizing a number of the things that separate Deguy from the Heideggerian account of poetry, using both the most recent of Deguy's books (in 1996) and some crucial earlier texts. We have already heard Derrida's assessment based on *Poetry is not Alone* that Deguy seeks to render to the *comme* of comparison its fullest dignity in thought: the "anachrony" or the "dischrony" of the *like-or-as* over which Deguy has kept watch through his many years of writing have opened up a space that is his alone.

Much of what Derrida says about Deguy comes, however, not from a direct reading of the texts where Deguy engages most openly with Heidegger but from rereading an early text about Dante, entitled "Apparition of the Name," which takes as its interrelated starting points the phenomenology of appearing and disappearing, the function of the undecidable saving-greeting (*salut*), and the fittingness or comeliness of proper names in Dante's *La Vita Nuova*.[53] The possible connection to palinody may be discerned through the thematics of the sacred and the *salut*.

In the Threnody, as in the Palinody, Deguy speaks up for an anthropomorphosis, calls for a "repatriation" of the divine powers by the human in a coming negative anthropology. Derrida is fascinated by a passage from the first book of grieving where Deguy calls for a moratorium on attributing any statements or attributes to God.

> In the singular time of this moratorium, in the abidance of this abiding, in what once was spelled in French *demourance*, Deguy will immediately draw out the atheologico-political and atheologico-poetical consequences of that which he has just retraced, namely a logical and rhetorical (hypothesis or hypotyposis) genesis of what it would be more proper to call a *functioning* of the name of God as trope.[54]

This suspension has the character of a retrait in Derrida's terms, a withdrawal and a (re)marking, and it opens up new possibilities for thinking the sacred, very much elsewhere, very much nearby. Derrida underlines in this "at least two noticeable departures, if not two ruptures, within the most enigmatic proximity, two separations with regard to this Heideggerian poetics of the unscathed, of the immune, of the *safe*, or of *salvation*."[55] These matters, so central to the late Derrida, are given a fine condensation here, in a testament of friendship at a time of grief and persistent poetic courage.

The two "departures" from Heidegger are, then, a clear refusal of Heideggerian motifs of *Heimkumft*, homecoming, return, nationalism, of any privileging of a German people (or, for Deguy and Derrida, of any particular people), and, along with that firm refusal of *return*, a strikingly un-Heideggerian turn toward a respectful consideration of "Christian onomastics" or more precisely, in Derrida's reading, a pre-Christian, pre-religious relation to naming that nonetheless remains sacrosanct in its poetic source.[56] With this, Derrida has identified two of the key characteristics of the palinodic modes and texts to come: 1) the little faith is to be *without return* and it can admit no exceptionalism; and 2) the man of little faith shall maintain a relation to the sacred without the sacred, in its withdrawal, and to the apparitions of all the names that figure and favor possibly or potentially renewed relations as relics of former belief, now willingly suspended.

Jean-Luc Nancy's two essays found in this volume are different in character than those of Derrida or Lacoue-Labarthe. Nancy's sequence of three essays on Michel Deguy, if we include, as we must, "Demythified Prayer" from *Dis-Enclosure*, provides the fullest engagement with the two books of grief and with the palinodic diptych. As the last of Deguy's three friends still alive, Nancy's "accompaniment" of Michel Deguy is also, then, an accompaniment of Derrida and Lacoue-Labarthe, as innumerable traces in these essays show. We see how Nancy's celebratory enthusiasm for Deguy's oeuvre is initially tempered and enhanced by a compassion with respect to the immediacy of grief, then how, over the ensuing years, it becomes heavily inflected by an intense desire to share grieving more directly, to share its common burden, while thinking in common.

A few of the most relevant and stimulating motifs of Nancy's accompaniment of Deguy are: an understanding of the Deguyan poetics as an ontological poetics characterized by a "caring for presence in passage"; an attentiveness to the prose/poetry difference that is likely almost as central as the poet/thinker relation; "the so-recent and so-ancient" conversation with Jacques Derrida, engaged around a limited number of motifs common to all the friends of deconstruction, most centrally *salut* and consolation; a fascination with the music of grief and with the impossible singing that underlies both threnody and palinody like a sob of sense in discontinuity with itself or like meaning's withdrawal in a stammer.

In 1996, Nancy wrote, in immediate temporal and emotional proximity to Deguy's threnody, of the ever-renewing character of Deguy's corpus: "today threnody and prose, yesterday a great rhetorician, a poet always of circumstance but never established in that state" (*infra* 170). This permanent self-disestablishment of Deguy *as poet* fascinates all serious commentators of the work but few have captured as finely as Nancy does here, and indeed in all three essays, the interplay between poet and poem in their consequential ontic play:

> Deguy parasites and dis-assures the poem—that is to say the work and the substance, the thing itself of the poem, the hymn or the epos, the formed and closed song. He chooses instead the poet. The poet is not the subject of the poem. The poet is not substance but displacement, he is not subject, but he is to come, the to-come of the "it" that there is. [*l'à-venir du "il" qu'il y a*]
>
> For a long time poet and not yet, never . . .[57]

Nancy locates the situation of this headlong, displaced lyrical subject in the terms of a proximity, perhaps slightly different from the one that sets poet and thinker in relation. He knows with Deguy that the ontological poet is a poet of no return, of the very much elsewhere *and* the very much near to hand:

> poet, the one returned from what is most ancient, which is making no return, but which comes again, ancient as new, the ancient new. Deguy can say then: "What you are seeking, that is near, is here—and is not that."[58] (*infra* 175)

In the paradox of that proximity/distancing, which has consequences for a relation to the presencing of otherness and for the relation to a past and a future, Nancy writes, "the poet is the one who finds the words to propose the multiplied turn of being's *like*" (*infra* 181)

Such a poetic task, taken on by Deguy, is a work, even a steady job, according to Nancy:

> There we have our job, the poetic making, the service of aid that we must attempt to provide. Caring for presence in passage. Not at all shielding it from passage, but passing along with it, discreetly, almost furtively. A furtive eternity, that is what we are lacking, that is within our reach. Passing beneath a silence of words, speaking beneath the passage of a silence. Immortals elsewhere, very much elsewhere, right here. (*infra* 176)

What the focus on the grieving, lamenting side of *poetic making* brings into clearer relief is this motif of caring for presence. In recent writings, Deguy attacks the bland and moralizing character of Anglo-Saxon philosophies of care,[59] but what Nancy has in mind is both more modest and more ambitious. It has to do with the fundamental poetic relation to appearance and disappearance, even with the possibility of a new poetic phenomenology.

Deguy's threnodies and his palinody allow Jean-Luc Nancy to think

> the somber and ineffaceable flash of *having been there* . . . what is not a survivor, not a revenant, not a phantom, not a shade, that is what is not of here and which, in that precisely, *is here*, outside of space and time, it is of this *outside-with* that neither philosophy nor religion speak, even while nothing else concerns them. No word says it, but a chant is being addressed. Without rest, a threnody, a *cantus firmus*, a *cante jondo* rises up, in music or in words—poetry, yes, if you will, but first of all, call and lament, first of all the tone which makes heard *here* the resonance of *there*, of that outside. (*infra* 198)

Not philosophy, not religion, but only poetry brings this relation to something like an *outside-with*.

Much in Nancy's three essays turns upon the perception of the addressed song or chant, in its emotionally syncopated, hiccoughing inadequacy, its impossible primacy and its resonant advance toward the outside of grieving:

> They make us sing, our dearly departed, they make us hum the *lamentate* in which our tears say nothing but the saying nothing, nothing but a speaking which is a crying and a crying which is a sob, if the sob is nothing other than the shaken-up voice, tripping up in the throat and giving up on speaking, the cry-

> ing like this renunciation and this giving-up like a consent to desolation, to its stammering. (*infra* 198)

Nancy's stammering sob, consenting to desolation, the hiccup that is also a musical notation or ornamentation, a *hocket* (*infra* 198) for the hearing of another's music antiphonally along with one's own, might well be linked to the apocope that centered Lacoue-Labarthe's meditation on Deguy. The apocope, the cutting-off of syllables, letters, or other elements of utterance in the choked stutter of grief, was related by the author of "Of Transport" to both a "diminution" of being-there and an encroaching prosiness and flat literality of the world. This implied also the severing of the ties of the religious and of the *comm-unity* of comparison. However, both for Nancy and Lacoue-Labarthe, the linking up of the stammer understood as antiphon, the apocope understood as a new possibility of prose, might point also to renewed possibilities within the "sadness of disproportion itself" (a formula from the first threnody that both philosophers cite).

> "Tragedy has disappeared": the retrait of the tragic, as [Deguy] says, with a formula borrowed from Derrida, that of metaphor ("in retreat like metaphor"). The retrait—of the caesura just as well, we will have understood this, from the "point-outside-the-world"—is not pure and simple effacement. The retrait retraces, effacement does not efface itself.[60]

What is this impossibility of a self-effacement of effacement? It points us again toward the resourcefulness of palinody.

THE PROJECT OF INEFFACEMENT AND THE RELICS

In Deguy, we find a powerful theory of tradition and transmission. It is articulated in *A Man of Little Faith* through a metaphorical language of sacred relics, a language that is a further development and a new take on what are for him longstanding reflections on profanation and revelation. The master term underlying all of this is a characteristically Deguyan double negation: *ineffacement*. The section of *A Man of Little Faith* entitled "The Future of an Illusion" brings this out. Immediately before the first occurrence in Deguy's corpus of the expression, "the precious relics," we find this passage: "how can we make ineffaceable that which has become unbelievable? that is the function of literature—one of the modes of the Hegelian overcoming (*Aufhebung*), coming in "relief" or in loss-preservation, that is "metamorphosis." Literature reemploys mythologemes and theologemes (the Great Code, said William Blake and Northrop Frye)" (*infra* 74).

The term *ineffaceable* refers to a line of thinking begun more than a decade before. *Arrêts fréquents* [Frequent Stops], one of Deguy's telling titles gleaned from the semiology of the contemporary city, a found profane object awaiting revelatory activation through its condensation as an *art poétique*, lies at the source of the thinking of ineffacement. In the numerous verbal-conceptual variations of the term in the pages of *Arrêts fréquents* we find also the possibility, or what we might even call the infrastructural necessity, of the relics; they will be carried as a possibility by the oeuvre for about a decade before their explicit re-emergence in *A Man of Little Faith*.

"How to make revelation with profanation after having made profanation with revelation?"[61] The question is simple but doubled up and it redoubles in intensity through one of those abyssal twists that Deguy likes so much ("falling and, in falling, to fall" being another example that he has used and re-contextualized for years).[62] In *Arrêts fréquents* it is a question of "all that has been profaned,"[63] a non-totalizable totality corresponding to the ravages of what Deguy calls the "cultural culture." What is sought by the poet is another kind of profanation, running counter to reductive totalization, one that might preserve and reactivate the full richness of imaginative language, the general fable as it is expressed in "theologemes and mythologemes" and taken up in poems. This further twist in profanation seeks within disenchantment itself the resource for renewal:

> True profanation reenchants the world, once sacred, now abandoned, and procures within the "hopeless" itself the "illusion of joy," known as such and paradoxically maintained as an illusion, that is to say *the game of love and of chance* [Marivaux]. It is a matter of a metaphysical change which profanes the sacred, disenchanting, then, by putting back into the game and into composition the figures and the fables in the milieu of language.

By recentering figures and fables in and on language, literature and its thought can entertain the ambition of a second enchantment, which is not that of a return, to reiterate that fundamental trait of the Deguyan argument and sensibility, but rather *a promise of a promised land*, according to an expression that the author used a great deal when he was elaborating his theories of the cultural and of the sublime and which persists in more current modulations around the relics and around ecology and ecologics.

In this vein, Deguy could speculate in *Frequent Stops* that "A great Work delivers us from archaic metamorphoses . . . for a last, staggering transformation, but which one?"[64] a question that is partially answered later in his own reflection: "The work through its passage, (re)opens a translation:

a relation to the earth, a promise of a promised land. The sacred will be with us until the end of the world—as profanation."[65]

The work, which is a work of art, in the usage that Deguy makes of it here, needs to be understood in three ways: first, as a life-work (or an attempt at mortal proportion); second, as a *worked* and meaning-filled work (a product of refined and sublimely hidden technique in contradistinction to purely spontaneous expressivity and its aleatory products, so valued by contemporary aesthetics); and, finally, as a work of memory (bringing with it a "duty of memory," certainly, to evoke a common theme in our current consideration of the past, but a work of memory that also must imply, according to Deguy's most recent books, a "duty of thought"[66]).

The relation to the earth through the work is also recalled and foregrounded here and it has its place, a central one, in the later phases of the project of ineffacement. The attention of the poet-thinker gets slightly but significantly displaced from its initial focus on the "promise of a promised land," the promise of another world in this one, a "diplopic" vision, not so distant perhaps from that of Northrop Frye in his *Double Vision*; in Deguy's case it is the double vision of a slight transcendence glimpsed within the very impossibility of transcendence. The emphasis of this movement shifts in later works from the language of fable and of myth (of course renewed in and through metaphoricity) moving toward heightened concern for the vulnerable, "exhausted" earth (*infra* 91 and *passim*), a concern that has grown with each of Deguy's books and that attains its most focused intensity in 2012's *Ecologiques*. There it also finds again a rich connection to Baudelairean pious impiety.

PIETY AND ECOLOGY

The piety which the hundredth flower of Baudelaire's *Fleurs du mal* illustrates and to which it seeks, in Deguy's reading of it, to commit us, becomes, in the latter's extensive reflections, a piety oriented toward earthly dwelling (and we should hear in that formulation an expression or a soft echo of the possible confluence or harmonization of the Baudelairean and Heideggerian currents in Deguy's thought). In *A Man of Little Faith* we get a modulation of the general poethical disposition of concern and vigilance with respect to Being and the related project of inflecting a pious impiety for our own times, our own dangers and distresses. In these pages and in other writings from the early twenty-first century, the author of *Choses de la poésie et affaire culturelle* [Things of Poetry and the Cultural Affair] delimits the menace and the possible remedy with reference to threats to our sense of and capacity for earthly attachment:

> The heart of the matter can only be said "in poems"—of language, music, painting, stone. What is the heart of the matter? Today I will call it *attachment*.
>
> What is threatening today also threatens poetry. I often call it "the cultural." How can we resist this Threat, if not by renewing our attachment—to the world of the earth, to the literature of our languages, to the tradition of poetry? (*infra* 36)

The threat is what Deguy calls *the cultural*. The substantification of the adjective "cultural" as a noun, "the cultural," is a coinage operated by him in his essays of the 1980s, particularly "*L'Escalade*" [The Escalation/The Climb]. It allows for making visible, "the solidarity of events which in appearance are very different" and "the elevation to the rank and to the appellation of "cultural" of this generality." Significantly, this is achieved through neologism, inasmuch as "the names do not change as quickly as the objects," that is, the profound transformations underway in our time use an outdated language, which Deguy has characterized in this context as a *vampirized* language.[67] The emergence into regular usage within his work of "the cultural" was one of Deguy's decisive neologizing moments.

In his most recent book, *La Pietà Baudelaire*, Michel Deguy elucidates the connections between earthly attachment, the threat of the cultural, and the aesthetic and emotional logics of the palinody that underlie both *A Man of Little Faith* and the subsequent works. "Where does the world stand; where are we with respect to its *habitability*? Ecological anxiety."[68] After *Ecologiques*, *La Pietà Baudelaire* is in its turn and in its way thoroughgoingly ecological; Deguy there gives us a Baudelaire-ecologist for our today, transposing and transporting him in a poetics for our time. *La pietà* constitutes a further elaboration of the theory of tradition, of transmission, and of translation found in *A Man of Little Faith*, a *translatio studiorum* under the threat of catastrophic failure, under the threat of the impossible, a translation of studies or of culture which links tradition to habitability and dwelling to culture in a way unique to Deguy among contemporary thinkers of tradition, of ecology, or indeed of crisis:

> An operation of transfer then. If our time, the course of which is being determined by another "end of the world" than that of Baudelaire's fifteenth *fusée*, an end of the world that I call cultural, following the downward slope of the "apogee of capitalism" (Walter Benjamin), the transfer transmits the remains or the *relics* that the palinody of his Christian faith, or piety/pity; *pietà*, allows Baudelaire to gather together in "the aim of mystic nature" and that, in our turn, we transport, transforming

> this past into its loss: continuing deposition, or profanation, of mystical tension.[69]

In a paradox highly characteristic of Deguy, the habitability of the world would depend upon our capacity to imagine well its ending:

> An artist, painter, musician or poet . . . has the responsibility of figuring the end of the world, let's say of envisaging it . . .
>
> For us the end of the world—of this world that was one characterized by the plurality of its worlds—is called globalization. What Valéry called "the time of the finished world," which for him was beginning at the end of the XIXth century marked by the Spanish-American war, is for us *ending*. The time of the finished world is finishing up, on the condition that we accompany this formulation with a worrying paradox: "what is finished is only just beginning." . . . we pass from the expression, "the end of the world" to this one: "an end of world."[70]

Our world is the world of *La Fin dans le monde* [The End in the World (punning with the homophony *faim/fin*, end or hunger in the world)]. The end in the world is unending; depending on the context, Deguy can turn this circulation and recirculation of ends in the direction of either autobiographical survival or historical and cultural endings.

In Deguy's resistance to "the cultural" there is an affirmation of the power of image and logicity, the logicity of poetic image, "image" taken in the broadest sense but conceived of logico-poetically, as something embedded in the thought of vernacular languages, approachable through language, a conception that he repeatedly and explicitly opposes to the unthought generalization of reproductibility, to the radical transformation of the character of images in the era of their boundless proliferation, and to the generalized *screenization* of the real and its concomitant veiling of the world or worlds. Deguy's early geopoetics of attachment became an ecopoetics of unending world-endings in the conviction of a need for continuing resistance to the mutations underway, a resistance that can only come from language's deeply sedimented poetic resources.

In *A Man of Little Faith* Deguy speaks of the need to oppose a thought and a practice of "the other inclination (toward the other world, always there, a-globalizable, the world whose "like itself" depends upon comparisons, that is, upon the "logic" of the poem)" (*infra* 35) to the totalizing threat of the cultural. In the Dublin interview from December 2012 found in the appendix, Deguy speaks explicitly of the dangers of an "exit from the logos" and of an ejection from an "ontology of like," an ejection and an exit that are already quite far-advanced.[71] To recall another key term from Deguy's theoretical lexicon, this forced exit from the logos is no conceptually or practically productive "exit without exit." Never losing hope in the promise of the aporia, Deguy intensifies his paradoxical resistance:

> I am proposing another exit than those, another world of transcendence than the one which is pushing these transgressions—another movement of the *trans*. Toward a writing, that is to say a thinking, that is parabolic, if the parable is at once a fable and a launch-pad, the genius of imagination and the curve of a figuration which transmits, one which confides in survivors an interpretable promise of a relation to the promised-land that is forever inappropriable. And why now? In the urgency which is commensurate with the challenge of the growing threat, in other words, because the stakes are more serious: the stakes of meaning.[72]

In our interview appended here, Deguy reemphasizes the radical difference of the present mutation, one without precedent. The questions it raises are not to be considered as discrete theoretical problems but rather as an immediate dilemma. This lived and living concern for earthly habitability proceeds from an urgent necessity that can only be grasped in terms of the "logic" of the poem and its capacity for attachment, a logic that Deguy considers from the time of *A Man of Little Faith*'s insights to be an "eco-logic." The question of faith in Deguy and the whole sense of his unfolding body of work must henceforth be grasped in terms of those stakes.

NOTES

1. *Le poète que je cherche à être Cahier Michel Deguy* ed. Yves Charnet (Paris: La Table Ronde/Belin 1996) 317. Hereafter cited as PQCE.

2. Michel Deguy, *La Fin dans le monde* (Paris: Hermann coll. Le Bel Aujourd'hui 2009) 8. Hereafter cited as FM.

3. Deguy, *Sans Retour* (Paris: Galilée 2004). Hereafter cited as SR. Benny Lévy, *Etre juif Etude lévinassienne* (Paris: Verdier 2003). In the Postface to Benny Lévy's book Deguy is held up as a great exemplar of the hypocrisy of secularized or vestigially Christian intellectuals who seek to deny or denigrate the specificity of Judaism. Deguy is cited as operating, without integrity or honesty, a singularly uninteresting and biased account of Jewish exceptionalism ("un exemple d'absence de probité" 118). In these passages at the end of Lévy's book, which mirror a scathing reflection on the mid-century Catholic novelist François Mauriac at the beginning of the book, there is a palpable sense of resentment toward what he regards as the Parisian intellectual establishment (Deguy's echo of Péguy's title, *Notre jeunesse* arouses

his ire) and a sense that a mere poet has no business trying to think through matters that should be reserved for Masters of Studies, presumably like Benny Lévy himself. Indeed, what Deguy perhaps took greatest exception to in *Etre juif's* hyperbolic and dubiously partial charges was the repeated use of "the poet" as a perjorative epithet by Lévy. Deguy's *Sans Retour* responds to some of Lévy's most one-sided criticism of *A Man of Little Faith* but also uses the violence of the posthumous attack and the impossibility of a real conversation as an occasion to develop further the theoretical and autobiographical connections between Poetry and Studies, between "philosophical conversion" (SR 12) and "ignorance" (SR 55).

4. Deguy, "Ouverture" in *L'Allégresse pensive* ed. Martin Rueff (Paris: Belin 2007) 51, hereafter cited as AP. The same passage is used by Deguy in his introduction to *Donnant Donnant Poèmes 1960–1980* (Paris: Gallimard coll. Poésie 2006) 19.

5. For Deguy and Gauchet see "Retour ou Sans Retour?" an interview with Lucette Finas that first appeared in the *Revue Littéraire* at the time of the release of *Sans Retour* and was collected in the *Grand Cahier Michel Deguy* ed. Jean-Pierre Moussaron (Bordeaux: Le Bleu du ciel 2007) 196–200, hereafter cited as GCD. The quotation in the title of this introduction, "To Conserve While Leaving Behind," is found there. Cf. Marcel Gauchet (w. Luc Ferry), *Le religieux après le religieux* (Paris: Grasset 2004).

6. Jean-Luc Nancy, *Dis-Enclosure The Deconstruction of Christianity* (New York: Fordham University Press 2008). Hereafter DC. "Prayer Demythified" (tr. Michael B. Smith), the chapter devoted and dedicated to Deguy, is found on pages 129–138.

7. Nancy, DC 134.

8. Ibid.

9. Ibid., 187 n.1.

10. Charles Taylor, "Foreword" in Marcel Gauchet, *The Disenchantment of the World A Political History of Religion* (tr. Oscar Burge) (Princeton, NJ: 1997) xiv–xv.

11. See also, Deguy, "Note sur le devenir culturel du religieux" in SR 79–82.

12. These expressions and the logic underpinning them may be found in "Retour ou Sans Retour?" *op. cit.*, in GCD 196.

13. A substantial section of this wide-ranging collection of studies of Deguy is given over to the religious diptych. Under the heading *Sans Retour*, seven thinkers and writers, from the philosopher Jean-Michel Rey to the novelist Natasha Michel, from the theater director and professor Denis Guénoun to the anthropologist Lucien Scubla of the *Centre de recherches en épistémologie appliquée*, take up the pertinence and urgency of Deguy's concerns from an array of methodological and lived perspectives. AP 297–381.

14. What appears to be the first occurrence of this recurring expression is found in AF 89.

15. An image and an expression which appear early in Deguy's work, cf. "Husserl en seconde lecture," the first-ever published critical text on Jacques Derrida in *Critique* 19 no.192 mai 1963 434–448, and which became central in formulations of his poetics in the 1980s, cf. in particular, *Gisants* (Paris: Gallimard 1986) translated as *Recumbents* by Wilson Baldridge (Middletown, CT: Wesleyan Press 2005) hereafter cited as GIS and REC. "Path that leads to nowhere/Without exit is the apex/Showing us that the exit is/That there is no exit/—hence no exit beyond the

paradox/ Of the exit without exit" (REC 185). Deguy's thinking of the "exit from religion" is to be situated within the general economy of that paradox.

16. Deguy, *Jumelages* suivi de *Made in U.S.A.* (Paris: Seuil 1978). Hereafter cited as JMUSA.

17. Deguy, "Motifs Towards a Poetics" in *Contemporary French Philosphy* ed. A. Philips Griffiths (Cambridge University Press: 1987) 60. Hereafter cited as MOTIFS.

18. Ibid.

19. Jacques Derrida, "Comment Nommer" in PQCE, 182. This translation is from the forthcoming *In the Name of Friendship: Deguy, Derrida, Deconstruction* eds. Christopher Elson, Garry Sherbert (Amsterdam: Rodopi Editions Chiasma collection).

20. Martin Rueff, *Différence et identité: Michel Deguy, situation d'un poète lyrique à l'apogée du capitalisme culturel* (Paris: Hermann coll. Le Bel Aujourd'hui 2009) 41–42. Hereafter cited as DI.

21. Kenneth Koch, "Introduction" in *Given Giving: Selected Poems of Michel Deguy* tr. Clayton Eshleman (Berkeley CA: University of California Press 1984) xv. Hereafter cited as GG. Paul Auster, "Introduction" in *The Random House Book of Twentieth Century Poetry* ed. Paul Auster (New York: Vintage Books 1984 [Random House 1982]) xlv.

22. Koch, GG xvi.

23. Andrea Zanzotto, "Préface à *Gisants*" tr. Philippe di Meo, in Deguy, *Gisants Poèmes III 1980–1995* (Paris: Gallimard coll. Poésie 1999) 11.

24. Wilson Baldridge, "Translator's Preface" in REC xviii.

25. Deguy, "La Vigie" in *Fragment du Cadastre* (Paris: Gallimard 1960) 7–12. The first broadcast of "Le Bon Plaisir de Michel Deguy" on France-Culture was December 10, 1994. It is consultable at the *Inathèque* at the Bibliothèque nationale de France, document no. 822693.

26. The translation here is my own. A comparison of several English versions of this and other poems from the *Fleurs du Mal* may be found at the useful site http://fleursdumal.org/poem/168 (retrieved January 2, 2013).

27. Deguy, *Réouverture après travaux* (Paris: Galilée 2006) 56. Hereafter cited as RAT.

28. Deguy was one of the second generation of French translators of Heidegger, having come under the influence of Jean Beaufret in the late 1940s. He was the leader of the team that produced *Approche de Hölderlin* (Paris: Gallimard 1961) and remained associated with the larger circle of French Heideggerians around Beaufret, contributing a text, "Le Principe," to the Beaufret hommage, *L'Endurance de la pensée* (Paris: Plon 1968) 145–148, and participating in the seminars with Heidegger and René Char in the later 1960s. Deguy may be seen at the Séminaire du Thor in *Soixante-deux photographies de Martin Heidegger* by François Fédier (Paris: Gallimard coll. L'Infini 1999) and he is cited and interviewed in *Heidegger en France* by Dominique Janicaud (Paris: Albin Michel 2001).

29. A few of the most helpful essays that have as a central preoccupation an attempt to situate Deguy's specificity relative to Heidegger are: Gisèle Berkman, "Raisons de Michel Deguy" in AP 247–277; Jacques Derrida, "Comment nommer" *op. cit.*; Philippe Lacoue-Labarthe, "Du transport" in PQCE 158–163; Jacques Taminiaux,

"Remarques post-heideggeriennes sur la phénoménologie poétique" in AP 217–234; Philippe Vestraten, "Lecture d'un poéticien par un ontologue" in GCD 202–213. See also Rueff, DI, especially 39–41, 54–55, 215–217, 311–313, 345–348.

30. Deguy, MOTIFS 56–57.

31. Deguy, RAT 111.

32. Jacques Derrida, "Comment Nommer" in PQCE 198.

33. See also "Translator's Notes," point 6.

34. Cassin, *art. cit.*, G8 60–61.

35. de Libera, *art. cit.*, G8 91.

36. This decisive expression, the figurativity of existence, emerges in Deguy's books from the second half of the 1960s, *Actes* (Paris: Gallimard 1966) and *Figurations* (Paris: Gallimard 1969). The notion is deeply related to the formula "the ontology of like [*comme*]" and its variants, some of which we hear in the December 2012 interview with Deguy found in this volume and indeed in some of the formulations of Jean-Luc Nancy's essay "Deguy, the New Year!" (*infra*). Cf. Elson, "Michel Deguy et la figurativité de l'existence" in *Poétiques et poésies contemporaines* ed. Daniel Guillaume (Cognac: Le Temps qu'il fait 2003) 189–201.

37. Cassin, *art. cit.*, GG 61.

38. Some of that fuller reading is carried out in *In the Name of Friendship*, with its strong focus on Derrida's essay, "How to Name."

39. Deguy, *Desolatio* (Paris: Galilée 2007) 71. Hereafter cited as DES.

40. Derrida, "How to Name" in PQCE 188.

41. Deguy, ACFP 23.

42. Deguy, RAT 213.

43. Deguy, DES back cover page. I present in this note the first paragraph in French rather than overburden the translation with multiple parenthetical explanations of the play on *personne*: "*Il y eut quelqu'un; il y eut personne; personne d'autre; ce qui veut dire "lui-même"; toi-même et personne d'autre. Tu étais personne d'autre; mon être cher, mon être.*"

44. On these matters, Denis Guénoun has written forcefully of a choice between two atheisms in Deguy's oeuvre, "L'un des deux athéismes," AP 309–321. In the same section of *L'Allégresse Pensive*, Lucien Scubla puts forward grave doubts and what he takes to be a refutation of what Deguy is seeking to achieve through a *translatio* of religion through poetry and poetics ("Michel Deguy et la Sortie de la Religion," AP 359–374). Much more would need to be said about this.

45. Philippe Lacoue-Labarthe, "Du Transport" in PQCE 158.

46. Derrida, "Comment Nommer" in PQCE 202.

47. Lacoue-Labarthe, "Du Transport" in PQCE 160.

48. Ibid., 159.

49. Derrida, "Comment Nommer," in PQCE 198.

50. Lacoue-Labarthe, "Du Transport," in PQCE 160.

51. Cf. *In the Name of Friendship: Deguy, Derrida and Deconstruction*, eds. Elson and Sherbert, forthcoming with Rodopi Editions Chiasma Collection.

52. An exception is Martin Hagglund who takes it up in his reading of Derrida's atheism in *Radical Atheism: Derrida and the Time of Life* (Stanford: Stanford University Press coll. Meridian Crossing Aesthetics 2008). It is the contention of

my colleague Garry Sherbert and myself that he oversimplifies Derrida on *salut* in "How to Name" with serious complications for his overall representation of Derrida's putative radical atheism. This is addressed in considerable detail in our forthcoming *In the Name of Friendship*.

53. Deguy, "Apparition du nom" in *Actes* (Paris: Gallimard 1966).

54. Derrida, "Comment Nommer," in PQCE 188.

55. Ibid.

56. I am paraphrasing very dense and difficult matters. Here is the passage where Deguy's Dantean, Latinizing, soteriological, post- or pre-Christian onomastics are auscultated with real delight by a Derrida searching for just this kind of difference with respect to Heideggerian paradigms: "the inscription of this *salut* in *salut*, in the memory or the promise of a poetic event of Latinity, is even less Heideggerian in its operation of writing and in its historical determination because to the sin of Latinity is added another sin, even more serious in the eyes of a certain Heidegger, that of the interest shown, at least in this passage, for that which links poetic naming, and therefore *salut* in this place, namely the *Vita Nova*, to a Christian onomastics. Not that Deguy's atheological poetics would be secretly Christian, that is understood, not secretly Christian even at that moment, but this poetics has for us the interest of situating the place where sacrality, the sacro-sanctity, the untouchability, and even Christian soteriology, like others, all draw from a source that is first of all poetic. They proceed from a poetic sacro-sanctification of *any* naming. It is a matter of returning to the eve of nomination, to the first name [*le prénom*] or to the first coming of nomination. Pre-Christian moment, I will say, a moment which is loaded down and which is bent with all the ambiguity of the 'pre.'" Ibid., 189.

57. JLN note. *Poèmes* 27.

58. JLN note. ACFP 106.

59. See Deguy, FM, 38 seq.

60. Lacoue-Labarthe, "Du Transport" PQCE 163.

61. Deguy, *Arrêts fréquents* (Marseille: Métailé 1990) 89. Hereafter cited as AF.

62. Beginning with "Tombant et en tombant tomber" in *Interdictions du séjour* (Paris: L'Energumène 1975) 14–15.

63. AF, 91.

64. Ibid., 27.

65. Ibid., 92.

66. "We should speak of a duty of thought, not of a duty of memory." Deguy, SV 196.

67. Deguy, "L'escalade" in *Choses de la poésie et affaire culturelle* (Paris: Hachette 1986) 195 for the solidarity of disparate phenomena and the need for a new naming. Back cover and *passim* for the disparity of names and things, for the lag of words, and for the vampirization of culture by *the cultural*. Hereafter cited as CPAC. Other crucial texts in Deguy's elaboration of "the cultural" include: "Nouvelles notes sur le culturel" *La part de l'oeil* no. 12 1996 31–41; "Du culturel dans l'art" in *La Raison poétique* (Paris: Galilée 2000) 137–150; "Retour sur le culturel" in RAT 249–269; "Identité," in ECO 143–176. Martin Rueff's book *Différence et Identité* takes as a starting point the "situation of a lyrical poet at the apogee of cultural capitalism," with its echo of Benjamin and Baudelaire, and a lucid engagement with the logic of

the cultural is to be found throughout its pages. The section entitled "Le Culturel" DI 59–98 is the most extensive explication of the neologism and the most sustained engagement with its thinking to be found in Deguy criticism.

68. Deguy, *La Pietà Baudelaire* (Paris: Belin coll. L'extrême contemporain 2012) 19. Hereafter cited as PB.

69. Ibid., 22–23.

70. Ibid., 76

71. In his book, *La Pietà Baudelaire*, published in December 2012, he takes up this conception of the threat as follows: "I am engaged in a discussion with many contemporary poeticians on the question of "representation," as they call it, by which they often mean that of "metaphoricity," on which they do not wish the poem, writing in "poems," to depend. I take the time to consider this because it is a decisive matter today; and most of our young contemporaries are ready to leave writing (we can hear their preparations for departure) precisely in order not to owe any accounts to "metaphor," they argue; or to "the analogical," if you prefer: Make way for the Exit! Exit from logicity, if we understand by this word, neither Aristotelian "syllogicity" nor the calculation of propositions by modern logic, but more simply and archeologically the *languagy* linguistic complexion of thought, the "in-logos" of our language element. Exit into other "mediums," as they say: the medium of "imagery" in the photographic-iconic sense, or the medium of the body ("my body")." PB 119.

72. Deguy, DD 13.

A MAN OF LITTLE FAITH

Michel Deguy

To the memory of Monique
to Sylvie, Arnaud, Nicolas, Marie-Armelle
to Raphaël, Aurélia, Timothée, Etoile
to Martine
to those I love

So Peter got out of the boat and walked on the water and came to Jesus; but when he saw the wind, he was afraid, and beginning to sink he cried out, "Lord, save me." Jesus immediately reached out his hand and caught him, saying to him, "O man of little faith, why did you doubt?"

—Matthew 14, 29–30

This text is of little faith, reader, and of slow exodus, it tells of the country left behind. In my childhood and my youth, God was Jewish. The great story and the "great code" for my faithful infidelity were, and hence will always be, evangelical. That was when the weeks were "after Pentecost," or "in Advent" and when christophoric readings from the Ordinary heaped invective upon "men of little faith."

Then the slow revelation of the Holocaust and the establishment of Israel among the nations were to be major events of our generations, in the course of the seventy years that have passed. Finally the massacres of September 2001, and all through that autumn, were bloody hinges opening the gates of the twenty-first century, they still reverberate with the groaning. Not a day goes by, at the moment I'm writing these lines, that the newspapers do not offer a platform and a possibility of speaking to the abjurations and the intestine hatreds of the religions of the Book, to the zealots of the unique god (all three of them), between and within themselves, a platform for intellectuals who are passionately for or passionately inimical to holy Lands, be they mystified or demystifying.

*

Palinody, treason are the words that I use.

I like the word *palinody* because it is the chant of the other way (ode; *palin*). *Palin* retraces our steps, upstream: Could *against the grain*, a famous title [Huysmans], be its translation? But it is *anew*. For we do not retrace our steps as we do in extended space. The opposite, the contrary, is not a symmetrical movement that cancels out, it is not the retro movement of a winch handle. But it is *logical*, that is to say it is in thought or in "duration" as Bergson calls it. A movement that opens up contrariety, invents other meaning, the meaning of meaning; the depth of "metalevels" as today's anthropologists like to say. For our life is thwarted, contrary: Self-defeating is the proper name of its being. The hegemony of Parmenidean Being is broken, Reiner Schürmann used to say. "Nothing is simple," does not mean that the incident of "complications" comes along, aleatory, but rather that the complex intensity of being is in itself (if I may say!) a torn tearing; a turning turnabout. Not in the sense of "I'm going to turn back" but in the sense of "that's turning me inside out." It's an overturned overturning.

As for treason, Judas is treason. Faceless Judas, forever secret, closed-up. His "psychology" does not interest me. Paul too is a traitor—traitor to the synagogue. We are always traitors to something. He had to betray. It was necessary for him to betray what he was, and had been, in order to be—or to "become" in Goethe's expression, attributed to Pindar.

*

There is no life without *conversion*. The Fable often exalts its paradigm in the guise of suddenness, rupture, or the miraculous; the conversion of Miguel Manara, for example, or of Rancé.[1] But any existence turns more or less slowly upon itself: it is the passage from one age to another, from "youth" to "old age."

Now the *doxa*, tenacious, incorrigible opinion, simplifies matters and analysis must, here as elsewhere, protect or restore complexity, that is to say the paradoxical truth of things: the unilateral character of the identifications of values, and here the belief that youth is good, old age is bad, blinds the intelligence, and thereby unleashes a worsening (*non video meliora: deteriora sequuntur*! [I don't see better things: follow the worse; Ovid]).[2] We must know how to envisage the negative of youth and the positive of decline in order to appreciate the twisted character of conversion in its general and in its modern sense.

Conversion brings with it a more or less intense degree of reflection and a more or less intense consciousness of the reversal in which it consists. And Socrates's lesson—his pressing interrogation and his harassing "irony"—consists precisely of awakening and exciting the self-consciousness of (non) wisdom; of believing-I-know and of believing-oneself-knowledgeable-and-wise: You think that you know but you do not know, because you don't know that you don't know. You do not know, still do not, are not knowing-who-you-are, not *sophos*. You do not know yourself; and yet the "oracle" had enjoined us: Know thyself.

*

Aging is nothing other than growing wise—or it is nothing at all: nothing of value. So, what is wisdom? It is judgment. The secret lies in judging. The conflict of generations, a "gap which widens," and there is one, between adolescence (youth) and senescence, not so much one of near-sightedness as it is one of "sapescence" or "sapience" (what else could we come up with?), "sapientiality," "sophogenesis" (it is indeed about this becoming-*sophos* where old Socrates, Socrates the essentially old one, confronts the youth, the essential youthfulness of his interlocutors), this generation gap is a mode of contrariety—insurmountable, constitutive, to be arranged and adjusted then, because there will always be youth and age in symbiosis, in adversity, in "tension," as we say, in the enantiomorphy of two ages that must knit themselves together, coming across one another, defying one another, coming to terms with one another (because we have "grown old together" says M. Teste [Paul Valéry]). And what is this sapience? The sophos "knows that he knows not." The secret lies in that matter, that area to be explored, the field of the old laborer. For of course Socrates knows a lot, he is nothing less than he is ignorant. Yet while immensely knowing, and continuing to learn right up to the last minute, he knows not. Not that he knows nothing; but he knows that he-knows-not. In this way he becomes capable of judgment; justness and justice are his business. That is what old Alain suggested with his fables of twisted bonhomie, like this one: the good judge is the one who sleeps during the proceedings, in such a way that he would awaken fresh, lucid and ready, a good judge at the moment of the verdict.

Youth thinks it knows; today we say of it that it is intelligent. Yes, voracity, rapidity, invention, solution of difficulties. ("The mathematician has no genius after thirty," they like to glorify themselves, making their own legends.) An affair of IQ.

High IQ. Gifted. But that is not the question. The quotient of the intelligence is nothing other than that which the questionnaire measures. Circularity. But what is it that the questionnaire does not measure in the pure ignorance of its youthful, questioning excitement?

It would be necessary to take up the whole business of judgment lying behind Kant and Arendt. The hastiness of judgment, of course; but especially the brilliance of judgment. What is that brilliance? What are its axioms? And there will always be confrontation; and the "youth" will always be stronger, more carried away, more murderous. That is his genius.

And Socrates must resist, even if they hardly listen, because youthful anger, youthful suspicion and youthful power have definitively bested the "gerontocracy." Judging has been put out to pasture.

Growing old. Without giving in. A mutation with no concessions, how is that possible? Or, to say it through a brutal transposition of this melody: Where do we stand with the Revolution? It has disappeared.

This is surely a good, if we are able to understand where it has gone; Revolution has disappeared, which is to say that it *had to* disappear; the good is how there must no longer be any Revolution in the youthful sense of a revolution in capital letters. That is to say again, that we must conceive of a transformation (of societies; of mentalities; of intelligence; of "history") without Revolution, without capitalization, without idols. "Great age, here we are!" [*Grand âge, nous voici!*] we ought to say, borrowing the poet's expression (Saint-John Perse [*Chronique*]). A great age of the earth, a great age of humanity. But, that's just it, how can we make comprehensible all of these formulations that the aforementioned youth puts down to our aged bumbling, and how can we get them accepted?

*

When submitted to analysis, the *conversion* about which I am speaking shows its doubleness. It consists of the twisting back "upon oneself" of two movements; the paradoxical conjugation (or co-version) of two versions. The modern age of anthropomorphism, this "modern age" or the phase underway of humanity-becoming-historical has as its originality (making a "new origin" in the Cartesian sense, a "change of axes") that of inverting, or reversing the two movements or vectors in question. What are they?

The opposite of Manara's model, in other words, is unlike the classical imagery of conversion as a religious or spiritual conversion, it is a matter of wisdom, of a becoming-wise that would reverse the polarity, and for which we could perhaps use again (serving ourselves yet again to it) the model of the pre-Christian Socratic conversion to wisdom (the consciousness of not yet *being sophos*).

One of the stitches of the thread (or: one of the components of the reversing or converse movement) is loss of faith, or the passage from credulity to unbelief, from belief to atheism, from gnosis to agnosticism (from believing-I-know to knowing-I-don't-know, from believing-belief to I-don't-believe-I-know and to knowing-I-will-no-longer-believe) . . . I mull over the well-known formulas, translated and retranslated for us a thousand times or more, in order to serve up Socratic conversion once again for an analysis of contemporary authenticity; in a new light, that is to say without anachronism, without thinking that I'm providing a commentary on what Socrates thought, he who was not at all "irreligious" in the modern sense, and not at all pre-Christian, for good cause, nor post-presocratic for that matter. (Only Simone Weil can be "pre-Christian.")

That version is quite clearly the opposite of the movement that we usually understand as conversion: it goes *in the other direction*.

Secondly: on the contrary, the other component goes in the same direction as, or *resembles*, the Manara model. This is the movement of going from stupid to wise, from naïve to conscious, from violent to reasonable, from arrogant to *sophos* (in the sense of Socrates who really had to admit that he was, in his negating way, *sophôtatos*, since the god could not have lied about it). In brief, from young to old.

This conversion is conversion to the truth of age, the consciousness of getting old; an inclination and a consent to taking on one's age; entering into the thought of the end.

So paradoxical thinking divides and splits the unilateral character of the *doxa* touching on conversions, such thinking reverses the generally admitted values (young = good; old = bad), not turning *a* into *not-a*, but splitting them, making them bifid, *amphibiologizing* them, revealing those components that thwart one another, forming the contrariety that is constitutive of a thing (here, a state, an age); *and* the contradictions of two things between themselves, things of the same nature (here, two phases of the time of living, being young and being old, adolescence and senescence), such that neither is unequivocally "bad," while inverting their intense adversity, all the while preserving it.

*

In the end is there only failure? I catch myself here wanting to place in exergue Mallarmé's, "failures, all of us are failures" [*"ratés, nous le sommes tous"*] a remark that I have already quoted too much.[3]

Yes, only failure, on the condition—here too—that we thicken up the thought of failure, that we give it consistency, relief, internal complexity, endoconflictual complexity if I dare say, like the Baudelairean *duellum.*[4] Any thought divided against itself will be true.

There is no conjugal life—and any life is conjugal seen from a certain angle—with its perpetual mutiny, its heterocidal impulses ("everyone kills what he loves" [Wilde]), its erosion, its general hostility, its defeats (look at that old washed-up boat, coming apart on its way to washing ashore as a wreck), which is not heading for the dénouement of washing ashore . . . at its destination. Is washing-up a wash-out? Almost. A slight difference remains decisive. Perishing is in the becoming of any divided thing, and any thing is divided in itself.

Failure, as we call it, is one of the modes of bringing to completion; one of the exits from emergency, one of the possible achievements. We have failed and that was in the course of things. So we might simplify the schema, following the inevitable usage ("He failed his exam," etc.) as though with an effective empirical limit, a real term *beyond* which there is "something else" and "again." Or we might refine its enigma, as the logic of the insolvable, the paradox of the aporetic exit, the infinitization of the confines of the end, as "ex-termination," and that just is modern thought of the end in general.

*

At a certain distance between my view and what there is to be seen, on a certain scale of appreciating things, of "judgment," the things in question may be discerned and set apart, they might be "relatively" spread out, through clear and clean distinction, as common sense has it in its reputedly Cartesian expressions. On a finer, more microscopic scale, within the tight tissue of the antagonistic differences in "life," the vertiginous is simply inextricable. To be neighbors is to neighbor through the abyss and the abyss is present everywhere, it runs through everything in the finest detail. The abyssal, abyssality, comes forth, it appears and plays hard, getting right to the very bottom of things, and does so explosively! In the vicinity, and for the neighborhood, heterogeneity surges up. More often than not it is unbearable, or, as conversation has it, "that's impossible!"

On the scale where universals are in play (eg, "human rights"; aren't you made of flesh, like me, and a mammal and a mortal and loquacious and conscious?), we will agree, we already agree. But on another level (according to the most frequently exploited metaphorical cliché, which itself makes for empty language, the cliché of "levels" . . .), "at the level" of detail, on the level of the private, of the everyday, of singularities in infinitely local particularities "on the ground" (another pulpy cliché), the ditches and the graves get dug, repugnancies are fuming: and this is why "people in their concrete needs" will feel and believe themselves ever more "ignored by politicians," by "philosophers," etc. (despite the ever more pitiful efforts of demagogic attention, "suspect," quite foreign to abstraction). The mechanism of this illusion is implacable because it is constitutive. Abstraction grows along with the concrete, but the latter will have nothing of it. Nonetheless our task is to increase the power of abstraction some more.

I

PALINODY

I will not tell of how "I lost faith," for that very old loss, which in a certain manner has always already happened, is a long story right from its beginning, and, still under way, will always have been present—and I will say, it is the truth of treason, the slow palinody or movement of becoming oneself—instead I will tell of how I stopped practicing, ceased the gestures, reversed the Pascalian attitude and gave up "kneeling first."[1]

I had promised my wife that I would help her raise the children as Christians and I continued to frequent the Church as a family, to count myself in the assembly—to be part of the *ecclesia*, of the "parish," because we know that that is what counts in "Christian life."

And so I received the sacraments, even if less and less assiduously. It was through "confession" that the real break occurred. A priest from Saint-Sulpice, an impressive ascetic, a learned and persuasive preacher, a holy man whom I admired, received me to hear my confession in one of those small pieces of furniture (or small buildings) called confessionals, sentry boxes in worked oak, two- or three-seaters, which are no longer in use in Christendom, not since the famous Council, but the monuments of which, humble or disproportionate, little houses or edifices of marble, grottoes in the stone or transportable woodwork, a recess for Orgon or Tartuffe, condense the dark coolness of Churches for the purposes of tourists in Catholic Europe, and sometimes even for the plots of sacrilegious black and white films. This is a heritage that cannot be sold even if we might imagine that, like Egyptian necropolises, they might, brought together in certain neighborhoods give shelter to those who have none. . . . Invited, I was saying, to decline my faults under the routine rubrics, so it was that at the moment of penitence and absolution this priest came to pose the question, "And now do you feel WORTHY of the next Eucharist?" He did not underline "worthy" and I didn't hear the quotation as a threat. Inattentive, then, or less scrupulous than when listening to philosophical texts (this is, I quickly understood, the point where the holy man was lying in wait for me, knowing me a little, he wanted to humble my young philosopher's vanity), believing that I was replying as might be expected, as if he had asked me if I would take communion on Sunday and if I were faithful to that sacrament, I murmured that yes, it seemed to me, I was worthy. Then the skinny sacerdote, in whom I took real pleasure, enjoying his unconventional Sunday messages and seeing in him the cheeks of Bernard or Dominic rather than those of Savonarola, fell upon me! "How can you claim to be worthy, he cried, when we all repeat, striking our chests, DOMINE NON SUM DIGNUS . . . ?" etc. He had found fault with me, opened a trap door to catch me out on the sin of inconsistency. Me, the young teacher, suddenly a bad student . . . I never recovered. And I never returned.

There is no transcendent but there is transcendence; movement; being carried away; movement, momentum, *élan* in French, *ormê* in Longinus: the invention of an overlook, of the sheer and steep (*upsos*), of the point-from-which.[2] This is what gives meaning, makes meaning, in the sense of a sense.

There is no justice, says the *vox populi*. It may be true that there is none on the mode of a high, fixed instance or institution, from which justice might be rendered, there is no more immanent justice than there is distributive justice; but there is justice: provisional, expedient, that which judgment tries to render, as if from a point of view that is both outside and inside the system: its cornerstone. There is the difference between just and unjust that the judge in each one of us exercises in a disagreement.

There is no need to hypostasize any Instance, I am saying, neither out of idolatry nor from conventional habits. It's the end of reactionaries; suspicion reigns with regard to hypotyposis. Suspicion of the Other . . .

How to make up for this lack of a third party? That is the problem of Justice. The incurable absence of the Other, the impossibility of a third, of Mediation, perhaps even of the mediator.

There is a difference between wrong and right. I make myself stronger if I can prove it, but stronger for my other (who has put himself in the wrong with me, I can prove it!). And so I cannot stick with Pascal's ninth *pensée* ("none can err in the side that he looks at"). I'm right, even in the other's place I would not have acted that way—but, as now even from my own position I will and can demonstrate—one *had to* act. But it is not possible to show this to my other; it would be pleading for oneself: both judge AND accused, the same. The other cannot be the judge, because he is wholly in the wrong, he is *in* his wrong. And the other-than-any-other, or the third-party, has ceased to be recognizable, or: has gone missing. Or "God is dead." How can we make more third-party again . . . ?

If I were a visual artist, one of today's artist-installers, I would be inclined to believe that there is only one "installation," and it is that of the *Cave*. A primitive scene to be represented, a fable *par excellence* of enigma: the Cave.

To install is to try to hold up the high from below (how else, the young Platonist might say, *pôs allôs?*), *as if* everything came from the high, hung down, depended from the Most-High. I give you the Church as installation: an upended cave, represented and overturned, or the Cavern become Cupola.

Let us follow this movement: it is *épi-strophê*, "conversion," one that a didascaly in the text of *The Republic* signals; a famous bit of stage direction: *tis lutheiê* "that someone comes to be delivered" . . . an inversion of the *zoon logon échôn* as *logos zoon échôn* [the being possessing language as language possessing being].

Everything depends on a conversion, on a moment-movement of anthropogenesis (thousands of centuries of the animal getting upright in the grotto, giving itself a vociferation, becoming a voice, then a prelogical language, then . . .), which overturns itself yet again as an anthropomorphosis (*tis lutheiê*) and comes out into the bright sunlight, lifting up its eyes toward the sun, and acting as if everything were connected by the high, the unwatchable source of light, and as if everything built began with the summit, a "creation," a word made flesh, *logos en archê, logos zoon échôn* [in the beginning was the word (John 1:1), the word possessing being].

That is as-if [*comme si*]; we need to act as if "heaven had formed this mass of miracles"["Psyche," Corneille; "The Young Fate," Paul Valéry]. From the invention of the sun by Akhenaton or Plato, right up to the sacred Books of the Fable that we have taken upon ourselves responsibly.

That's the world turned upside down, someone might say. The world only holds together if it is upside down, walking on its head. Conversion to inversion is a (new) start. Conversion to reversal, a fictioned, wanted, "created" conversion. As if. From which comes education, which allows us to climb.

And so representation re-generates; it invents this ascension with an overturning, it hangs up this high-from-on-high and from which all might fall back down. Does the Dantean itinerary have a relation to this schema? Descent to the center of the earth, reversal, ascension . . .

I will reverse a saying of Auguste Comte's (or was he quoting Clotilde de Vaux?) about which an old prof would sermonize for us in philosophy class in the middle of the twentieth century: "He is unworthy," etc.; and I will propose this inverted version: "it is worthy of a (great) soul to spread the news of the trouble which it feels." Now not an hour passes without thinking of death, at night too I feel it, and in the strange pronominality of the French verb *se mourir*, which intimates its coming; thinking about death is not thinking death, but it predisposes us to that thinking; struggling thoughts open the possibility of thinking; a thought that might hit the mark, just so.

Often I have taken up the argument—first formed by the reading of Pseudo-Longinus the Sublime—that the testamentary character of a work of art means that it must be sealed by being folded back upon itself. And perhaps it is best if the complex seal is its crypt. But often a "last word" sums up the work's promise, which is not necessarily a promise of happiness.

Too pompous sometimes, last words, as with the bass rumblings of Auguste Comte, or the low Napoleonic roar that "leaves to the reigning families the horror of [his] last moments," and that I have attempted to transpose as follows: "I leave you these lines in the event that my name [. . .] should happily reach your shores [. . .]."

In the stoic bath, I open the veins of my trouble, to make a little spiritual blood flow. Never will I understand. Never will I forget you. But after this "never," in the end it is forgetting that wins.

The earth does not age. I set off in order to love it with my eyes once more; I will not say for the last time. For this time I hope to roam it ever more and surround it with care, with even later lines.

I find it as I did in the time of *Histoire des Rechutes* [1968].

The masts over the launch site
Will still be those ash trees where the sun
Beats down, coining vernal worth
Now, now, gaiety, Do not cry
The sunstroke of the field peels away in poppies
This is the earth with its independent swervings
And its dancer's handkerchief which still lays down the law

Look at the mass of marvels

The beloved of the sun the other side of the clouds
The pavement of no bird: when it opens ajar
Earth is at the bottom of a loss which abounds
The sun there lowers green ladders

The virgin ocean, the green virgin peak, the virgin dawn, *Norvirgin* fjord in Skjolden, the standing stones of Larchant or the god on the corner in Sounion.

How would I know if I am down here if I am not from here? How would I know I am here if I am not really of down-here?

Where does the struggle between earth and humanity stand? The billions will not manage—to destroy it? It's Pamphilus's dream, cleaving the air of the Pacific (one night it was midnight at the crossing of the Equator and of the Date Line, and the 23d of December was reduced to minutes) or of Siberia, Baffin Land, or the Himalayas. "That is of another order," and the enormous is intact.

There will, however, be that other phase of ravaging and of installation; new billions taking the blue expanse by assault. Or rather they might turn away from it; neglecting it for what they call Space, for empty homogeneity where earth is no longer seen from the sky. A few will make their getaway, *cosmanthropes*, specialists in "deterrestration" as Lyotard said, they will "represent" humanity.

*

But this old body, now known under the name of *Body*, *unexquisite corpse* [in English in the original], eroded, denerved, a smoothed crust, crappy-cracky, naked more and more, sinewy slackness, neither flesh nor fish, blemished, *dermaticized*, ocellated eyepieced grumbling moth-eaten glassy . . .

> Remember the object that we saw, my soul
> That beautiful summer morning so sweet!
> At the turn of a path an awful carcass
> On a bed sown with stones
> [Baudelaire, "*Une Charogne*"]

> *Havel havalim*
> Says Qohelet
> All is *Havel*
> Wind
> [Ecclesiastes]

*

The last dwelling. It is as if it were forever. Enlarge the emblem of the world, dilated like the fresco of Judgment, the divine freeze-frame in a book by Claude Simon. This one: the silenciary's taciturn condoling in the last room of death, when, all hatred extinguished, the hands are stacked up, faced with sweats, the lips are resealed, horizonal, whispered co-misery hushed, the mantillas of wrinkles shudder. I am sad unto death. I hear the seven last words.

Or our Titanic dream: isn't it to wait together for the end, the everyman-for-himself of souls? The Noah-esque ark finally dark, slowly, the deluge fills it, drowns it, *Vredens Dag* [*Day of Wrath*, Carl Dreyer]. Lord we are perishing, the pious side by side, joined at the zenith; there will be a tomorrow for no one, sings the song; even asymptosis is exhausted, this is infinity.

*

"Believe that it was to have been very beautiful" [Mallarmé]

Adieu my heart adieu my life

CONFITEOR

With a furious gesture against purists and purifiers, the intellectual pushes back the binomial of pure and impure; a case of deconstruction. Hunting for purity! Prefer the impure! Very likely, but . . . Taking the part of impurity, of "métissage" which has such a good reputation, requires the play of the dyad of the pure and the impure and the conceptual convolutions of the pure: a pure precipitate in the chemist's retort (here in an alexandrine verse by Mallarmé): "*Un sens plus pur aux mots de la tribu*," [a purer sense for the words of the tribe] "*Ses purs ongles très haut* . . ." [her pure fingernails on high]. Central purity! (Lucette Finas)

"Me and Evil," I'll take the thing by the arm, by heart—my badness, my casuistic of evil. *A Touch of Evil* [in English in the original]. You who claim to be touching truth with your phrases, *tu quis es*?

I was the worst, I was criminal. But how? The good–evil mix is so intimate, so subtly impure, unanalyzable, as were the wheat and the chaff of the parable—the way that I drove her to her loss, to that destiny which without me would have been better, that is my only certainty, and by "me" I mean this poison of good intentions, of good wills, of generosities, of alibis, in a word evil, like an evil potion for her, and her life by my life slowly infected; I was horror without realizing it (Freud's UCS: set a course for the worst!), a fatal mixture whose dose each time was composed by no murderous nastiness, but depended on circumstances, like a pharmacy that would only become mortal through the unpredictable contribution of an invisible vapor surging up, or like a good driver who "loses control," and to all witnesses it seemed as if there was no harm in acting the way he did: "the excusable evildoer" would have been the title to which I was entitled. But with age and thought, that is to say, a more intelligent catharsis more and more detached from one's violent "amour-propre" (Jean-Jacques would have said), more detached from his self-satisfaction, the exorcist at last of his own instinct for preservation becomes more capable of discerning the intimate mustard seed, the impurity in a mixture of good quality.

One evil can hide another—the homonymy of *mal* even helps with that. A theory of the middle ground, of compromise, of a-little-bit-of, and consequently a theory of taste, demands clarification of impurity.

As for youth, let it be judged!

The hand does not see (*non despicit*); sight does not touch (*non comprehendit*). The high view, staggering, foreign. The compassionate, helping, healing hand.

It is because I am infected with the same evil as you are that I understand you; understanding the primal wrong, our nature, as we often say, and what would have to be done to oneself, against oneself, in order to heal from it, what homeopathy would be required.

And when we say of so-and-so, a remarkable person with a rich destiny, that he is a *real bastard*, that is what we mean: knowing him better, knowing him right up to the *defect* of his being, the flaw, or the poor "fit" of his assembly, through which the evil shines, the evil that he has done, his wrongdoings, to which we bear witness, because *even he* was the cause of some evil, we know him almost as well as we know our self.

LOVE STORY

A writer is someone who wants his love letters to be read. Everyone writes love letters; any subject prefers his own I love yous throughout his existence. The writer, a doubled-up subject, wants to show his love.

How does the love story end? That's what "others" (that is to say us, we in our turn) want to know. Myth stages how-it-began; and philosophy with respect to its "end" wonders about the end of the Love Story. Yet it cannot end, that was the definition of love, or if you will, its principal attribute; its locution, its analytical predicate may be heard in the expression "stronger-than." What is love? Love is stronger-than: for example, stronger than its end. In any case stronger than absence (cf. *Peter Ibbetson* according to R. Queneau). I can love someone who isn't there. The "dream" is the site of encounter. Stronger than death: this is Marivaux's *faithful woman*. I can love what does not exist: God for example. Women whom we call "religious" are "married" to the Being who is lacking in existence.

I can love in nonreciprocity, in a lack of equality; unrequited, as we say, with no return. This is the case of the love of parents for children.

Love is stronger than its fatal end. For, necessarily, it must end badly, since death *is*. *Stronger-than* signified then: stronger than its end.

Certainly if I look back upon my writings, again in the quietude of autocitation, having spoken mostly of love, like most people, I can see which perspective I might then draw, which love story:

This or that page tells of the hesitation, the multivocity of addressees, of the you who is addressed as "you" . . .

Another (following Sappho) tells how the preference that love is leads to the incomparable through comparison . . .

Yet another strikes at and smashes up the figure of Aphrodite by remembering her for us, up to our time (I was about to say remembering her right up to Twombly and his "Aphrodiqu'iconolasty").

Another, by way of Lucretius, seeks to say how love tells of that of which it actively deprives itself in order to be-like (like an "act of devouring" for example); or, another page worries about the plural of the attachment of beings among themselves, tells of the multiple modes of love, and for example, that of friendship or the difference of parents and children; or the figures of love not shared, in that expression Arendt used about Auden, where I understand: a figure of one who has not loved enough, or rather of one who has not been loved enough . . . ; or of the struggle of imaginations; in the growing split between the technico-scientificity of genitality and the iconodulia of advertising's publicitary presentation of sexuality.[3]

But it is instead on the motif of the *duellum*, as the *flower of evil* has it, that I am fixed this morning; on the enigma of "everyone kills what he loves" (Oscar Wilde ["The Ballad of Reading Gaol"]), grief and fault.

I will consider again what I thought about in my threnody (*A ce qui n'en finit pas* [To That Which Is Never Ending]): fault, or the death sentence.

Because "in life," as we say, the duo is not that of blame and of death but of you and of me, of she and me; *my* fault and *her* death. She began to die in that time when she discovered, little by little, my treason, my mediocrity; when she lost her faith, her belief in "my love," in "me" as adorable. She told me so then. Her disappointment separated her body and her soul; she began to "give up the ghost." Her disbelief revealed decline, mine, *ours*. My fallibility, my fault, my being ever-so-ordinary. Being was rent in two, everything fell away. She no longer believed in *us*; she left the earth.

Speaking this way I know myself as a criminal; I recognize the mortal fault: "all men kill the thing they love." I understand then in my way the "mortal sin" of Christians. The common sin committed. The original sin, that is to say the fact of being a human; which is to cause to die. The crime committed *by existing*, by loving (as Nietzsche's version of Anaxamander has it, or the Oedipal version); which cannot be repaired by the Christian "love one another" (it is too late! Impossible!), and isn't that always too local; at once after-the-fact and sporadic, unable to modify "this world." Neither pardon nor confession.

NEGLIGENCE

In a poem of (great) youth, the lyrical *I* calls himself "you," a kind of "indifferent" you. Much later, at the end of the threnody, he denies this indifference. Now I will pronounce the sentence: it is one of negligence.

In French, negligence is culpable. I have recounted this in *Recumbents*, but by imputing it to "her." "Negligent you neglected me." One of the secret passages from my life to my life is negligence.

A turn through etymology doesn't really help me. *Nec-lego*; with negation affecting the *legere*, the reading/retreat. . . . The affectation of not gathering oneself peacefully? I slip into the sonorous aura of the vocable, its stretchable, seducing anapestic inflection. I will stage the negligent as a drawing, like a Dürer print, accompanying Canto 4 of *Purgatory*:

> *La vi traemmo, ed ivi eran persone*
> *Che si stavano all'ombra dietro al sasso*
> *Com'uom per negligenza a star si pone.*
> [. . .]
> *Gli atti suoi pigri e le corte parole*
> *Mosson le labbra mie un poco a riso.*
> (vv. 102–106 and 121–122)

> Thither we drew; and there were persons there
> Who in the shadow stood behind the rock
> As one through indolence [*negligenza*] is wont to stand.
> [. . .]
> His sluggish attitude and his curt words
> A little unto laughter moved my lips.
> (Translation Henry W. Longfellow)

I am now going to aggravate further the sufferings of the negligent one.

In what bowge does the negligent one belong? What is his hell? Taciturn, acedic, the negligent one turns away. Anticipating the "fatal outcome," he hastens the inevitable along. "So what?" That's his motto. What would have happened to the negligent one if he had not demonstrated such negligence? That is the question. What did he not care enough about? From what did he pull back a little too soon, withdraw a little too confidently? "He disdained not to see . . ." On the poop deck, "this balcony tossed upon the sea," rather than at the prow, that is where I once put him in a poem.[4]

The fantasy of forgetting the decisive argument. I know (I believe that I know), that this happens to me from time to time, out of laziness, just when I have thought well, just gotten to the bottom of a question, and if I fail to note down the thought, then I forget it with no hope of ever finding it again; I *lose* a key.

For example: "one day" I discovered in the night, I'm sure of it, it's always in the night, a "decisive" reading of Mallarmé's sonnet, "The Virgin, the vivid . . ." [*Le Vierge, le vivace,* . . .]. One day (one night) I "understood" the difference of man and woman, how one was not the other, but *like*. Another time . . .

And with the decisive readings forever lost, I return in my meandering to the vicinity of amnesic loss.

And I have nearly forgotten the very subject of this "fantasy of an irreparable forgetting of a truth."

CUTTINGS

We had gotten pretty used to living.

As if servitude was never to cease.

This is death speaking: "I am beautiful O mortals like a dream of stone." [Baudelaire, "*La Beauté*"]

Not double, but *dual*; this is the case.

The soul is like a foreign body in the body.

"The quantic sea of virtual particles has a repulsive gravity." (*Le Monde*, June 29) . . . Only astrophysics still speaks like Schelling.

Natura . . . sive Deus [Nature . . . or God; Spinoza]—if you wish.

Paul Valéry's "to be awake" [*Variété I*] refers us then to "life is a dream"; less a nightmare than a soft, cottony dream where the expression "nothing was real" means "nothing was real enough"; life is a dream, or it threatens to be merely a dream, and vague, because we are not sufficiently attached to it, or we have not sufficiently attached ourselves to it; the links are too loose, too superficial, not those of "real" love, of "real" pain, etc. So, if we return to the thought of Charles Baudelaire in "The Painter of Modern Life" we find the idea that being *awake*, is to discover *more in the same*; not "another world" but a more lively one. A *terrible* attachment, thanks to which "I have lived."

GIFT WITHOUT EXCHANGE

I would give anything. I would give "everything." But why? For you, for us . . .

Does this manner of speaking tell me anything about the thing of which it speaks? Does the gift, does what the gift is, uncover or reveal itself? Everything is owed to you at that moment, life and happiness and if I wished, if I was in a third-party status in that relation between you and smiling Being, I wouldn't stand in the way; I promise.

May I take what is there, everything, as my witness, as a stake? But everything is not within reach, within sight, under wishes, lying beneath words. I give them to you, they are not mine. "Consider the lilies of the fields . . ."; they are yours.

You will perish and I can do nothing for you; I would give anything that you might increase, might heal, might understand, and that . . .

In order to be capable; in order to change this glaring lack into a gift. Giving one's life for . . . A gift of a fable, a gift of a flower. But what I am means that I have nothing. I cannot give you beauty, being ugly. I cannot give you knowledge, knowing nothing. Yes, yes, I know: to love is to give what one has not.

*

It is the request that is generous. I am thinking of those two friends; one is illustrious and whatever he does, whatever he is, he cannot not condescend, like a King in other times, even with his brother, saying "Rise!" The other loves him but is not a king.

Yet it is he who gives *by asking*; the counter-gift comes from the monarch, who gives "infinitely" more than he can receive, but it is in response. Which one is *obligated*?

There are always then already at one and the same time the two movements. One is in the other, and each one precedes the other—and follows the other. In this way *everything is possible*. It is vain to seek an order, a chronology of the before, or the gift, or of the after, the counter-gift. The gift was to hope to receive.

It is the afterwards that is in the beforehand. The exchange, or chiasma, is at the origin—before the beginning. Primordial.

*

To make others laugh, that is giving. I can fulfill you with laughter, for one moment, with a word. Like the fool beside the king, who changes something awkward into a joke. Making you laugh. A fool's story, told by a buffoon, signifying nothing—*droll*. Making much disappear.

Already through the homophone . . . I absorb the obstacle, the obstinacy of identity into words, for laughs. I draw it in, I take it away, I get the laughers on our side.

*

("He's got to come around" . . .)

It is not loyal to wait. To wait for the other to show some signs of interest in order that I might give (myself) (again). To open up, to tell stories, etc. Generosity does not count on reciprocity; it hopes to unleash it; but at bottom generosity does not expect reciprocity; it doesn't depend on it.

One must ceaselessly be the first to provide. Without accounting, without return, without vindictiveness of any kind; outside of any laws of alternation (ie, without exchange). Outside symmetry, outside sequentiality (outside of the theater because this must be outside of dialogue? With no reply?).

The gift exits exchange understood as succession (Watzlawick's sinusoidal). The gift leaves expected exchange in its wake; it is primordial expulsion, something that exchange cannot regulate: the damned part—or the blessed one?

Spouse: you must not say: "I won't say anything because you aren't saying anything"; do not refuse to speak on the pretext that the other isn't speaking to you. Each one says that at the same time. Everything depends on the Other who is not even simply "in a third-party position."

Time is the possibility of at the same time.

*

The gift of the given never ceases to abound. The given does not stop "giving itself"—without a donee? Or goes more or less unnoticed by a commensurate receiver. The donee loses the capacity or perhaps does not find it . . . that would be the receiver's essence. (And so it goes with the "romantic" poet receiving and giving to others, "passing" like the Roman fountain in Heidegger's paraphrase. *The cup is full.*) Or, following the thought of rhythm as a general "possession," a shaky welcome for that lack of measure: the "cup," [la coupe] this time in the sense of prosody, overflows, fails.

The *gift* is not received. Perhaps it is not receivable. It never ceases arriving "because" there is no reception in adequate measure (*adequatio*). Is this the idea of "grace"? (Devotion murmurs: "If you knew the God-Gift!?!") There is suspense. The gift is suspended. We are hanging on its every word.

But why do we need the *gift*, such a thought of the given, rather than just taking things flatly, positively, taking them "as they are while *being merely that*," taking them as merely that; as it seems indeed they are. What need is there for this business of "grace"? Can I not live without it? And indeed *one* does do perfectly well without it . . .

The *present* is not received. That is the false humility of Peter on Mount Thabor (if I take any parable as an apologue) or of Martha in the kitchen. Transfiguration will do just fine without me. What is going on can certainly happen without "me." . . . (This is a thought that makes death more acceptable.)

To think all of that without a giver, without "god(s)," is this even possible? Translating *phusis* as "it gives," superfluous. Overflow. With no receiver. ("It is not principally a matter of man," said Heidegger.—without humanism?)[5]

CASE OF EQUALITY

The risk that equality runs is the risk of missing out on hospitality. Equilibrium gets blocked. In equality, the impulsive movement of the self, getting out ahead of the self, is aborted, forbidden. Can a host be a host within strict equality? Or a guest a guest? Taking some risks of my own now, I wonder if a certain feminism, for example, permanently on guard, does not make the first movement impossible, the movement that the gift makes in passing itself on. "I'm still waiting—he's the one who started it by not getting started."

For gracious life—hospitality—does not worry first of all about equality, it takes right off into dissymmetry. And in order for any inequality to be tolerable today, it is necessary that it not be imputable to "me." Some sort of "it's-beyond-us" must be posed to render things tolerable. Religion managed this, interiorizing "sacrifice" ("giving one's life for those we love"), taking things at their figure (no longer at the letter) and "profaning" sacrifice, deritualizing it, that is "substituting" a "spiritual" renunciation for a real victim and a real putting-to-death.[6] Can art compensate for the "cultural"? In which art is exhausted.

Inequality or dissymmetry, that is, when one accepts taking the first step. The permanent praise of spontaneity in the current *doxa* is a sign of this. Spontaneity "disarms." That is its title. *Sponte sua.* The axiom of the scoundrels confirms this: "Never follow the first movement, as Talleyrand said, it's the right one." More proof that Pascal's *habile* is still and always will be a *demi-habile. Does it remain true* that the axiom "always follow the first movement, it's the right one" would be the right principle of spontaneity? Or "nature," Rousseau might have said. But this is uncertain. Because culture or second nature has interposed itself forever: the first movement is one of suspicion, fear, one of clashing . . . Unless? There are two "first movements."

With Marivaux—I mean in the theater—no one can make the first move anymore. No one gives in.[7]

What is *giving in*, that becomes the question.

Many prefer to be alone so as not to enter into the duel, they always feign to be easy to get along with. What are the situations?

Love has no why
You too you ask
You ask why
Love has no why

It is not pleased with its athelia
Why me rather than you
We can ask it of death too

And if I reply with predicates
it makes a portrait of you where
you say you don't recognize yourself
Do we love a portrait,
are predicates loveable?

I was thinking of talking to you about your siren-being
Which veers on me and runs to opposites
About your bolting your despairanto
Your dedications to violence, to carefreeness

At the bottom of you as of me
we can't get over being loved by you
Why me you you me why
–this taste

OF THE AUTHOR

There is (an) I; but it is not "me." And yet the two are blended, they are inextricable. "I" can mistake myself, others too, who say: "That can't really be *him*!"

He-who-says-I, a subject to, and of, enunciation, an instantiated pronoun, gets delegated: *in place of what* is he set, that is the question.

The relation of the *I* to the body is problematic. The latter represents it poorly; leaves too much out. It can never manage to make the *I* heard or understood, nor to fulfill it.

What do we mean by authenticity if not that manner of being-well-together, perceptible to others, which is of a triple nature. We can assure ourselves of this whenever we consider the botched alloys when, for example, the preoccupation of the idiot ego is joined to an obesity and to a usurpation of what is "mine" encumbered with and by a self that the *I* vomits up.

ESCENCE

"Old age is a shipwreck." [Chateaubriand/De Gaulle]

Very likely, but saying it this way is not sufficient. It is a matter of what it is to go under, to founder; SOMBRER in French. (*Essombre*: 1260. Obscurity, dark place. *Subumbrare*: 1860. To go under while under sail; to disappear like a shadow into the waves which swallow up. *Assombrir*: Mirabeau. The sky grew somber.)

To founder in slow motion, that is the *escence* of aging. But to teach others about near-sightedness in general, about the going-under, about the growing-somber, is that really worth it?

He says: I'm still breathing.

*

If becoming is to enter into the essence ("become what you are," through *escence*), the French translation *estre* attempts to translate Heidegger's transitive *wesen* (untranslatable transitivity). Perhaps thought might propose the opposition of the other movement, that of being-like, or "assimilation," on the condition that we might understand in this word a becoming-alike and not at all a return-to-the-same: outside of any superstition about essence-substance. Identifying oneself is myth, but how do we demystify? It is not a matter of becoming more and more an incomparable *same*, ever more an identitary one*self*, but of becoming a "oneself *as* another." (Ricoeur)

So it is less a matter of entering (in German) into the thickness of an *als* (as) than into the generosity of a *wie* (as-with, like), or even of scouring the very bottom of the unknown (and the bottom of the misunderstanding favored by the homonymy in French of "like" and "as" in the *comme*) for an undividedness of *als* and of *wie*; a "secret family relation" (of adoption)? Is this the work of "deconstruction"?

Inasmuch as A will not become B (woman will never become man, nor the inverse; the Jew a Roman, nor the inverse) in the "literal" sense of the identity of "to be"; and above all not by becoming more and more A (A *als* A) or B (B *als* B), the future (possibility) is bound up in becoming-like: A *wie* B, B *wie* A.

Because it is not about an empirical common character, the *homoïon* of their homology will be constructed: a constructed, intelligible third term will (perhaps) be that to (within) which they will both be "comparable," and wherein they might take each other by the hand. My likeness, my brother, my sister [*Mon semblable, mon frère, ma soeur*]; semblance is not the resemblance of blood relation, the familial family air. We must invent what brings together, what *as*-sembles: inventing the case of semblance.[8]

Between no-longer and not-yet, the balance is not equal. The past hangs on but grieving it is a less powerful remedy than the coveting of the psychotropic future. *Libido vivendi; expectandi; captandi.* The heart does not go more than three generations back. But no one can console himself for not knowing the rest of the story. *Moriturus vos non salutat* [those who are about to die *do not* salute you; Suetonius].

The fascination of that-which-is-not, in the mode of not-yet, this species of non-being that we think of as irresistibly called to be; we despair at being someday deprived of its imminence. The imminence of a possible real of the future whose victory would rise up like the pyramid of K2. (I've been reading stories of Himalayan climbing and the K2 offers its comparant, its figure, to this schema that I am trying to retrace.) The drunkenness of the last meters in the anaerobic zone, one step, than another, into survival. "Like a piece of existence cut off from existence itself," says, extraordinarily, the alpinist Pierre Béghin. Further still, perhaps, is the last door, then the door opens, which no one yet has tried nor even glimpsed. The one beyond which I no longer die, I am no longer dying in the present. Like Dante, I will pass living through the gates of death, of the House of the Dead. But Dante chatted with Ovid or Lucian amidst the daisies. That was a dialogue with those who had been and not a dialogue with what will be.

Why not come to terms with dying? I certainly come to terms with their deaths. All of them without exception: Pliny the Younger along with the Older, Flora the Roman with Jeanne La Lorraine, Caesar or Garibaldi, and all the way up to Mallarmé, Borges, or Lenin whom I almost knew, Dante along with them, and I could go on. All are dead and it makes no difference. I don't really cry about Christ or Mona Monroe. They are no more. I don't weep over Hölderlin or Vico, nor Emerson nor Lao Tzu, nor Francis, nor Pasolini. Or those tears are verse tears. We reshelve the book of the billions of dead. Those from all the human tribes massacred by death, like the Indians in the book by Robert Marteau.[9]

But I do cry over the children of my daughters' sons whom I will not "see." *Super flumina novae Babylonae sedemus et flevimus* [By the river of the new Babylon we sat down and wept]. The extendable character of my love will be limited: the expansion of infinite things will not be infinite. That which does not depend on us will always crush that which does depend on us.

We can never get enough of that about which we say: "It's always the same thing": the phenomenal ecstasy of being, the rising up of the summit, the clearing of the clearing, the transfiguring heaven of the Thabor or the great sweep of the blue wall of K2, the senseless asymptosis of sense, the promise of unhappiness, the apathy at the heart of the pathetic, the eternity of the the anemomene void . . .[10]

Our attachment is insatiable. The wait could last forever. It doesn't matter if evolution is creative; it is the future as such, posterity avid for afterward, the day to day, that is good. The idea of progress is an alibi for the desire of repetition. Banal recurrence ($n + 1 < n + 1 + 1 \ldots$) reasons. Husserlian protentation leans out over the void and considers it. One instant more, Madame Death. The living present is the secret. The Italian invention of perspective made death back off—over there.

I waited in the field.

ATTACHED

The plurality of indifferent worlds, or barely neighboring ones, safeguarded the earth, without those worlds having to take any particular care. It is the advent of a single world that threatens the earth. Will the earth and the world be able to love one another, to reunite, to find their undividedness? Or will the world, in coming to an end, deterrestrate us?—such that every mortal, installed as if in the center, might immortalize himself in the fabricated capsule of a hotel with six billion rooms. It is eugenically that man will inhabit this earth.

*

What has occurred? Not merely the equalization, not merely the monotonization, the real-time character of the intercommunication of any locale with any other locale, but also the dislocation, the deglobalization, the co-location of something that has occurred following after rapprochements (this is the major word of poetics), the unpredictable rapprochements that prepare us for the Baudelairean plunge into the depths of the unknown, surprising all of our precautionary measures, I would say, to dissonantly echo a current dominant discourse while making allusion to Heidegger's late and oh-so-strange oracle—"Only a god can save us"—where I mean simply that what is salutary does not submit to our domination.

What there is of a gaze in thought needs to be turned in that direction: with-a-view-to and with-respect-to that which cannot be mastered or possessed. The echography for the *ecoumène* (Augustin Berque)[11] cannot avoid having recourse to technological echo-graphy, for example, to high-definition photography of the earth seen from the skies or from space, but this serves to turn over our view of that view just for an instant to the sole end of "disinterested" enjoyment.

The splendor of the Earth (seen from above and hence technologically) adds nothing to its commercial value and in no way increases the sales price of our patrimonial land. Earth is not for sale. This shownness shows us what takes place in beauty and truth. That changes nothing.

Attached in every way, and each and every time by love, by obligation and by constraints, we are something other than tied up or tied down; through attachment we measure that from which we could never tear ourselves away, that which never stops revealing itself and holding on to us. Homer's Ulysses is nostalgic; we know him to be attached to Ithaca; Dante's Ulysses is with no return, but if he leaves everything behind, if he leaves the road—which attaches one place to another, says the dictionary—he does not leave behind "this mass of marvels," nor the enigma of the transfer of being's funds onto the world's account. We prefer this world to any other; that is its privilege. We have to *go here* without turning back, without return; that is the task. And we would accept death provided that we still had a living eye, a phantom's view of down-here from beyond the grave.

*

This is the song of a Robinson, but a Robinson of today. The shipwreck of Outis/Ulysses is that of any tourist-bather. Attachment can be recounted in this experience, from the deep waters to the deep earth, anterior to appropriation, before any rights to anything. This is the trial of stripping-down.

When, swimming toward the shore, I find my footing like Ulysses or Robinson on the edge of the earth, on the salty margins of the two elements, it is anywhere on the Earth, anywhere in the world. Taipi, let's say, or this summer in Sardinia, last year in Brazil, or five hundred years later. I do not land as a first occupier, I am naked and new, the son of Deucalion, the equal of the barely clad men who bathe here, those who are from here. There is no confrontation with the stripped-down natives; the young Pheacians are not customs officers; we are together, escaped, survivors, welcomed; in the moment of a lightning stroke when the elements shine forth, Earth is for all.

Or rather it is not the Earth that is for all equally; it is each one of us as *outis*, no one, who is for the earth, on earth. Upstream of any "right" for each one to situate himself where he wishes, short of any appropriative covetousness, I stage in this primal scene the moment of attachment stripped bare by its hosts even—in relation to which the moment of right is secondary.

I wish to tell of one of the orientations of showing the world again in a new light. If what has been globalized is characterized by uniformization, by conformity to the images of products, then the other inclination (toward the other world, always there, a-globalizable, the world whose "like itself" depends on comparisons, that is, on the "logic" of the poem), that inclination is attracted by the abyssal diversity that needs diversification, by plurification, by a-touristical inaccessibility: for example, the other night the spectacle (yes, it is a "spectacle" and a televised one, but isn't what is important what words can make the spectacle say, what discourse and exchange can take away from the spectacle, whether it be seen or on the screen?), the view, I'm saying (once again the Earth seen from heaven) of an omphalos of green water at six thousand meters elevation in the Andes, an eye of mournful water, said Rimbaud,[12] surrounded by men exhausted by the effort of going up to see this biotope which is as much etymological as it is scientific: there we had the two perspectives, the two gazes, that of the learned-technician and that of the poet-athlete. The world is what is never through revealing itself to a *-logy*. Does its world hostility still endure, resist?

Poetry is triple: as an experience it is that of being gripped before the beauty of the world *here*—this water table, visible and invisible, which makes the arts communicate among themselves. As something vernacular, it is the exercise of the imagination considering things according to the figuring schematism of images. Insofar as it is *conscious* of its use of words and learned in language, it is the *great game* in words with words.

The heart of the matter can only be said "in poems"—of language, music, painting, stone. What is the heart of the matter? Today I will call it *attachment*.

What is threatening today also threatens poetry. I often call it "the cultural." How can we resist this Threat, if not by renewing our attachment—to the world of the earth, to the literature of our languages, to the tradition of poetry?[13]

—We can wonder how such a reasonable guy (far from being a fool) can devote himself to "poetry."

—Precisely! The relation of poetry to what is reasonable, that is the point. Its relation to versimilitude, to wisdom, to *artefiction* through knowledge of procedure, its relation to jurisprudence. . . . Deflation, the end of heroic furor, the end of self-arrogating bluster.

And not a return but a going; going on into the enormous country where all is hushed, hushed in "a little," hushed in "only . . ."[14]

Man is the being who tramps his own transcendence. [L'homme est l'être qui pâtit sa propre transcendance.]

The Panamanian poet Edison Simons, who died in Paris in 2001, relayed this strange sentence to me as a thought of Maria Zambrano's. I quoted it in *L'Énergie du désespoir*, which I published in 1998. It is a strange thought, and probably an error of translation, or of transmission, since *pâtir* in French is not transitive.[15] But that's just it: this "error" can make a real contribution to the difficult thought of transcendence. By picking up a value of transitivity from its neighbors *souffrir* [to suffer] or *endurer* [to endure] and getting a little gospel air from *paître* [to graze], its anagram, *pâtir* comes to absorb the active into the very heart of the passive, and that will help us think transcendence.

Immanence and transcendence have gotten too disjointed, falling away from one other, each one to its own side, if we dare put it that way, like a somnolent pleasure-seeker and a dreamy bigot, each to his own. In terms of anthropology, normal and normative intelligence lacks an instance of quasi-transcendence, an epistemology of "metalevels." "[The history of social systems] is the history of efforts deployed by humans to turn against transcendence which they engender in spite of themselves and in order to liberate themselves from its too-cumbersome power."[16]

Let us consider an example that takes the form of an argument for Europe: the *federal* would provide precisely that intermediary instance, within reach, a supplement of substitutive "transcendence," "between" the familial-municipal (the "community") and the humanitarian universals. An opportunity to be seized! In the same way that federal law is respected without suspicion in the American space, above the local (the norms of Arkansas or Missouri) and yet short of UN global norms (where's that? wonders the hayseed from Ohio)—the fear of the FBI is the beginning of citizenship—so it may be that a European legality and an imagery of "from the Atlantic to the Urals" could educate a consciousness of the common good and the general will; a whole concrete-abstract horizon at the right distance between the interests of my clan and the generalities without obligation or sanction concerning Humanity. The "planetary village" is a slogan or an illusion, and "globalization" is an alibi for the cold monstrosity of Large Groups. Europe must be *made*.

An entity is harmful when it is an idol of credulousness—"superstition." So it goes with imaginary transcendent things and with Transcendence capitalized in bogus, second-rate ideologies and aesthetics of propaganda. The Invisible, the Unsayable and other *asilus asinorum* [the refuge of a jackass; *asinus asinorum* Spinoza]. But transcendence is not to be leveled or dismasted or disarmed; rather it is to be rebuilt, to be "deconstructed," as they say, provided that this be done learnedly, subtly. That is to say transposing, recovering it as a *good*, through the *as-if*. Conserving the same, minus the superstition; a subtraction or diminution and a restitution. Take this political example: like the monarchy in Europe, especially in England and Spain, as a reasonable institution, a "constitutional" one, without the cult (objection: but doesn't its persistence rest precisely upon popular credulity, a form of belief?).

Let's not make a clean slate of the past! But . . . but what? Neither restoration nor rehabilitation ("cultural"); the *as-if* is not a facsimile. An intelligent simulation? One which *knows itself* to be a simulation.

The operation would be carried out for the Revolution. What would *that* give: revolution minus Revolution?

*

Making revelation again out of profanation, not so long ago I proposed that as a "poetics."[17] Meaning or sense would be the product of an operation: that of making two containers communicate, one profaning, the other revealing: meaning lies at their confluence, making life bearable. Making some things come down, making others rise up is another way of putting it. Like this:

bringing down mythemes and theologemes into the profane, as schemas and emblems: a "simony" of figures. A meaning-this for the use of our immanence; a "falling-back-upon." A traversal of figuration (a trans-figuration) in the direction opposite to Paul's: then you will see in riddles; in a mirror; in comparison.

The kingdom of the earth is like what this fable of the Kingdom says. And so, I went into the Church on January 20, 1994 to tell of my abandonment, my overturning, in my encyclical *splendoris veritatem*.[18] Invert the comparison: then you will see in riddles, in a mirror, in comparison. You will discover what things are like: resembling that which they resemble. So *be* it: it *is* like that which it *resembles*. A poem in reverse flight; poem, reverse the parable, chase the temple from the haggle.

. . . and *making others rise*—for example, underscoring lexicalizations in the text; reanimating stereotypes by bringing them into play; awakening what is latent in order to make some more lucidity, something patent, something manifest. Locution, proverbs, ways of saying, all of these turns, are there, in reserve. And thousands upon thousands of quotations. Calling things to testify in their light. Dormant fables, paraphrasable condensations, all of the *letter* where the *spirit* lies, as with Aladdin's lamp. The "proper" *shall be* the total expansion of the figurativeness of that letter.

"My fellow, my sister . . ." [*Mon semblable, ma soeur*]

What they have in common is to be alike, that is, to not be the same. They are in common [*comme-un*]. Complexity is knotted in this paradox.

What makes their identity is their being-alike: a being (I was saying) which in its being is-like.

They resemble one another in their human semblance. They go face to face. My friend my sister. They make like. Their semblance is their difference.

Human semblance used to be defined by resemblance to God. Humans were one like the other because they were "images of God." What does this say? What is the third term today, if humans are to be alike by resembling it? Face to face, facing what? If I could manage to find what our semblance resembles, I would know.

*

Now, what is style? Allure, manner(s), fashion, air, stamp, *et alia:* just so many synonyms or nearby meanings which the answer to our question would have to dissect. "I recognize him there, we say, that's really him; it's in his style." Said another way, it is this "family resemblance," or family look, which makes the different registers correspond wherein a complex, enveloped singularity, an individual, for example, expresses himself. (I will not discuss the concept of expression here.) Resembling "oneself"—which is nothing other than that resemblance! A being is what he is by resembling without being able (no one is able) to isolate THAT which he resembles. So a "unique and its property," would be summed up, condensed, and symbolized (Leibniz would say) by one's way of writing, of course, as by one's way of dressing, of moving, of eating, etc.; one's way of writing, insofar as writing is a modality of thinking-speaking. Style is what causes all of these "traits" to resemble one another, through homology. (I will not cite Buffon.) Through the enigma of the *homoïon* which cannot, I've said this, be abstracted from the expressive zones that it brings into relation. A proper, a *oneself*, then, is only presentable in the mode of the *like-or-as*, to be glimpsed through a series of "a like b like c like x," lodged (logical) in the "family" (Wittgenstein) of its airs and resemblances. To be is to have an air of something, to have a look; to have a look is to be like.

Natives of Eden, that's who we are. Impulsive life engraves "the original print," imprinting its first comparants, putting in place the *analoga*; the secondary figures-in-waiting to serve the fable about which the second, adult, existence, "disenchanted" but intelligent, will write.

A naïve belief is attached to privileges: for example, to the inside-outside difference experienced in body-and-soul, such that the power of comparison can use it to tell the parable or the "riddle" of our life.

A veiling or a first structure that will follow unveiling in parables . . . *The kingdom of life is like* . . .

Yet all of the intraworldly comparants are unable to give a figure to what nonetheless needs to be told. Namely, death as a reduction to nothingness. Any thought that feels and endures anguishing "nothingness," any thought that experiences what is feared, will attempt to "represent this to itself." From out of this fundamental discrepancy between the saying and the sayable proceed all of our words about the "unsayable," about silence and the *nihil*. And ceaselessly, from age to age, "authors" set off again to make their assault: seeking what in a yawn might swallow up being, the self-engendering of truth.

“Everything is full of soul(s) . . . !” [“*Tout est plein d’âme(s) . . . !*” Victor Hugo, *Contemplations* XXVI. Deguy adds the plural.]

Are they animists? The narrator believes it.

Our quarrel? Hateful anthropomorphism.

I call poetry (hold on, I wanted to write *poèse*, poesis, because of *noèse*, noesis) . . . I call poetry that which maintains the view of the soul and of its souls as an as-if after having de-canted it (“reduced” it: a poetic phenomenological reduction)—and then put it back into play. That is to say in comparisons, attributing nothing to things. I put this not so long ago as an “hypallage” (the writer, even if he is called a poet, *does not believe* in what the hypallage says. The hypallage troubles the distinction between the letter and the spirit.)

The line that separates the two sides—the side that believes in heaven and the side that believes in “heaven”—is this line an abyss? Is that separation homologous with the one that will not allow us to confuse, according to so many, philosophy and poetry?

But, to turn things upside down, and counter to the *doxa*: the poem is less credulous than philosophy.

"*KEINE RACHE MEHR*" [NO MORE REVENGE]

They will not avenge *him* because he is dead; the HE has disappeared; his pronoun is defunct for any verb in the present or in the future. Language keeps up superstition, because it keeps him in being, he, saying that he *is*—dead. It preserves his image from the waters of death. Yet *he* has died. Language must then struggle against itself; thought is what struggles in language with language. Against its cult of the dead.

The spirit of vendetta rests upon animism, the inextirpable superstition of the "soul of the dead." In this belief the infernal chain gets linked.

Yet the soul is not immortal; there is no other sojourn of the dead but in our survivors' souls. No wandering soul that "cries for vengeance." There is nothing to be rendered unto the dead but the piety of our memory. There is found what we owe to one another, among ourselves. Survival is our business. It is a matter of surmounting beliefs.

But in place of general superstition, what can we "put," or propose to those multitudes who are "modernizing"? What to put in that place, in the cold hearth, where there is no longer anything; what can be substituted for the nihilism of covetousness that occupies that place?

The unchaining of vengeance is unleashed in a chain reaction. How can we break the chain of the ancestors, break with the Manes, leave the dead to bury the dead, refuse the inheritance of vengeance through the voice of a scribe?

Let us be done with vengeance and make the *americanothrope* withdraw. We need to invent another alloy.

"ECCE HOMO"[19]

The great self-portraits of the major Western painters, from Dürer to Van Gogh, from Rembrandt to Picasso, do not merely remain, *aere perennius*, but they are the most famous icons, the best loved works. We might say that at the same time as they represent the painter, they also represent painting: they give a face to painting. "Prosopopeia" of painting. But why does painting need that?

Velázquez, Chardin, Cézanne . . . What a beautiful project he had to paint himself! It is temptation itself. All have desired to scrutinize, to pick out, to grasp resemblance. Resemblance or semblance? Human semblance, *semblability* [*semblabilité*]. Here am I, I resemble a human being. *Anch' io son pittore*. "It's me" and I am like you. I can prove it to you. And yet am I not that, all the while that I am. My eye (my gaze) says yes and says no. You will not have me. I have not had myself. I begin again. The *I* of the me hides itself in showing itself. Showing oneself is the gift. *Giving one's own* sight for those one loves . . .

In the comedy of the eighteenth century the lovers give one another portraits: the medallion is a decisive proof of love; this is generalizable: love one another; exchange your self-portraits.

An unknown young man. Self-portrait in a turban; with a cigarette-holder, with brown gloves; with a boil; as Arcimboldo. Young man as an old man (I have looked at myself, I did not recognize myself, I fell into a replay/meplay [*je me suis pris au* je], fell into the fountain, into the mirror with its tain; I lost myself; then we grew old together).

The self-portrait is the masterpiece. They are forever recognizable, each one by its name; even more famous than Johnny or Marilyn in their photos; so famous that any visitor salutes them, prefers them; Albrecht, Vincent, Pablo and the others . . .

Of whom is Christ the self-portrait? This artist's-impression, composite sketch (millions of icons in Russia, hair in two painted hemispheres, sharp black beard, disproportionate black eyes, disproportionately thin nose, like the Greenwich meridian), a portrait with no model of the Saviour in every chapel (as of the suspect in all of the police stations) . . . "In his image" does not refer back to the face of God. What does that resemble? The man, a painter, is thereby reduced to seeking His resemblance in his own mirror.

Without a model because there is no model. A self-portrait of the painter as Christ, or of Christ as Piero, as Dürer. We say that it is God's portrait that is looking at us. *Ecce homo*? INRI. *Ecce deus*, "son of man."

*

"The face is revelation" (Levinas). Of what?

The face, the visage, is the surge of human-semblance; or much more weakly, of "resemblance" between this one and that one and between portrait and model. From appearance, some resemblance might proceed. Semblance is the source of resemblance, not the reverse, even if the road to semblance, Aspect, passes through resemblance. When something horrible "disfigures" appearance, horror pushes us away from it. For a long while "leprosy" was the occasion for this.

It is through the face as face (where we must grasp that the face is like the face and hence a face) that man *presents himself*, arrives, is there as a likeness.

Human means alike and so "brother," following the famous apposition in Baudelaire's poem.

Whatever its factual character may be (empiricity that has become scientific at the end of the historical era, and the examination of which is entrusted to techniques of heredity), inasmuch as it is clear that the literal sense of fraternity is consanguinity through an attested engendering by one and the same mother, fraternity can only have a meaning, and I mean a future, as the French Revolutionaries clamored, if it says the same thing as fellow-man, son of man (and not of the monster or the god or the devil). We must or should enter into the truth of the figure (in the "age of the spirit"!) at the very time when knowledge as scientific knowledge minimizes the figure, makes it seem futile, or denies it, or refuses it, or casts it into suspicion . . . The spirit of the laws (justice) and literature are there to heal this schism, to stitch together the two sides that are splitting apart, at the risk of losing sight of the figuring meaning of scientific "propriety." *Memento quia homo es et in (hominis) vultum reverteris.* [Remember man that you are *man* and to *man* will return. (Genesis 3:19 *dust*)]

Of course it is childbirth in general that makes fraternity real and possible, and, if we may say so, produces and ensures the existence of fellows and thus of semblance, "*il a assuré sa semblance*," we can say in French to say that someone ensured his descendence or his heredity (until, someday, *cloning* . . .).

Semblance is the same thing as being like. (These turns in French follow a line of thought, an "isotope" which is translatable—let us understand by that, to be translated. I do what I can within French grammatical and terminological networks in order to produce signification and sense, which seek for, and open up, their translatability—their conductivity—and which seek and open up their translation into other languages: not that the thinkable in its working would be Spirit already-there before languages, but rather in reverse: spirit, something of spirit, if there can be any, will be the "translation," or the result of all this.)

Being-like, then, a verbal turn, says the same thing as being-alike. The identity of this ("human") being consists in its being-alike, its being-like. A being is "*mon semblable, mon frère*" in being who he is. It is *semblability*, or fraternity, that makes his being, his being quite himself. My Neighbor, as we call it in a Christian context, in his being, is precisely alike. Making being (procreating), is making semblance, making a being that in its being is like another. Respect is the gaze (*spectans*) that turns to consider this, and that devotes itself to that very thing: the aspect of the other as the same in its alterity.

Of appearing, there is only the face. When a human appears, it is a being. Being appears face first. The philosopher would say: ontology is phenomenological and the phenomenon *kat'exochen* [pre-eminently], is the face. Semblance *is*, can only be, if there is a face and a singular one. (What animal has a face?) The other is another face.

We might say that the portrait, and more intensely, the self-portrait, plunges its gaze into that perspective: recognizing itself—for my likeness, double, fellow. Tightening up semblance, seizing-it-as-itself. If there were only one man, he would have no self-portrait. One cannot think up an Adam, before Eve, painting his self-portrait. There is no narcissism of Adam. But barely has his body given birth to Eve and he has to paint her: an image of the third party, a mediator whereby they ensure themselves of their semblance and their resemblance. Adam becomes Narcissus at the fountain after he sees Eve, after being seen and being painted as an Eve, and perhaps in order to return to himself. Did Marivaux dream that? With whom, with what, am I in being? "With myself." (A being which in its being, in order to be alone, must be WITH.) But like that to which (to whom) I return for having been nearer to my other.

I pause for a moment over the strange figure of Joseph. (Without forgetting . . . "Joseph *and his brothers*," Joseph the Egyptian, readopting his brothers . . .)

Joseph, the non-biological father, as we say today. Is he the god?

Is the figure of Joseph there to make distinct the viviparous character of *Homo sapiens* on the one hand and the divine paternity-filiation, an "operation of the Spirit" on the other? I was going to say, the thought of a humanity of humankind, circulating among men, independent of effective consanguinity: a holy family, that is to say an "adoptive" one. The adoptive father and the adopted son transmit themselves through exchanging human semblance: a super-natural trans-semblance [*transsemblance*]. This *transsemblance* which makes it so that the guest or the host, the absolutely unknown,[20] the Other whom we put in capitals, can be my likeness, my double, my fellow-creature, because he might be my brother, and reciprocally, the Other whom I adopt right now (Joseph the Pharaoh, an unknown host for his brothers), in his unknown being where his face is revealed and mine too. The face is the entry-into-presence of being-no-one (*outis*) and is all the more alike because he is no one, and reciprocally. The face of the unknown is the hoped-for revelation. "A god may save us . . ."

We are in the Fiji Islands. Santa Claus is all red, it's thirty-five degrees Celsius under the coconut trees. It is on the other side of the world, but it is the world. Over on this side, people ask me "which France" I come from. There is Caledonia-France and Polynesia-France. But France-France, where is that?

Before sun or after sun, I read the Arendt/Heidegger correspondence.[21] The belief in Being, a simple and extraordinary thing, fills up these pages, these years. It is the ether where the phrases of prose alternate with poems. The poem is less intimidated by Being. Being has its seat there. Poems of Being. Reverence of Being. *Salut* to and in Being.

Belief that suddenly vacillates, fleeing from me. I have taken Heidegger along to Fiji. Has the history of Being followed? No. I fall without. Where is that? Last night in the dream there was an end of the world as an end of the cosmos; it was like a corner of the cosmos that was exploding, a fracas of stars, the destruction of all *Lichtung*; an anontological event, in a causality with no relation to a "destining of Being." A power that swallowed up all of that History.

It is Heidegger who will have made possible and made it such that "Greece," as Platonic and Aristotelian thought, might return, might recommence, take the initiative once again, and be put back into play. "Forever future vigor." "One last time." As though the medieval and then the Cartesian had not entirely consumed her, wilted, rejected, translated, assimilated, exhausted Greece. She is "always there," an unknown readily available for a returning-to, a stepping-back, a reintrocession back before the Scholastic and Roman centuries. As if she hadn't given birth to theologies, cosmologies, ontologies. Here we go again, "phenomenologically." The book, the course most cited in the correspondence is devoted to the *Sophist*.

We are in the Fiji Islands. We have parted the Pacific and kept our feet dry; in one night. Humanity here is divided; side by side, face to face. There are masters and possessors, Australians and Occidentals. And there are the servants, the Fijians. The two populations, each in its own way, haunt the blue, white, green edges of sand, water, palms; where, in a certain way, neither of the two is at home. Island of Reason. Colony. Between the two are active Trivelinos, come from away, the Indians of India. The colored Hinduistical idols and the crosses of Christian sects don't mind being neighbors. A marble Mormon monument dominates the port of Suva.

The history of Being, untranslatable, untransported, will not have arrived here. Almost nowhere, finally. Non-globalizable. What the thinker calls for will not have happened; no salvation; "it will have been" for one world only, the world of Being. Fewer and fewer beings, absolutely and relatively, will be its figurants. Fable, *Errinerung* [remembrance/recollection], the last "great narrative" of the West—few will have "interiorized" it. And even if it is indifferent to that history of which humans are the subjects, or even the objects, the fact that it does not concern humanity undergoing globalization puts it outside of sense. It is not even the "decline of the West" which makes destiny, global destiny. The last god-which-alone-might-save-us will have been the Christian one.

A memory of that history, as the philosophy of the West, then a (re) thinking of its unforgettable thought, will have interested a lot of Europeans. Scarcely a handful among the Ango-Saxons, masters of the world, who will instead have fought against it or ignored it. Already less and less "understandable" in the Great Library, just one among others for the Head Librarian (Borges) it is no longer shareable as a truth becoming a world for all. Its knowledge, if indeed there is one, will soon no longer be propagated, neither in terms of *Wissenschaft* nor in a "cultural" transposition.

Loss of faith, the unbelieving disbelief which rises with age, infected with misology and misanthropy, can such loss make it there: striking, then taking the whole inspiratory apparatus, depriving us of air—aria, allure, being? Affecting the faith in Being?

The disgust for self, the suspicion of one's own "fatal inability" [Rimbaud, "Angoisse"] to keep together the relation to what is most beautiful, most grand, most difficult—everything that the Master called the Simple—I fear this. The milk of kindness turns, sours in derision. . . . The bad *nothing* of the expression "all of that is nothing" separates itself off from being.

Janicaud speaks[22] of the the "brilliant stylization" of the historial-destinal schema that "Heidegger exposes to the danger of extremism." Perhaps he is touching there upon the secret risk that a moment ago made me use the verb "to turn," to go sour, as we would say of milk. A thought risks being reduced to its (dis)figuring condensation. Reduced to the shortcuts that it takes from itself to itself. The thought is irreducible to them and it would be necessary for those of us whom we call readers, those who follow its path, to resist the very insistence on not resisting the stylization in which it consists, in which any thought "stenographs" itself, as [Jean-Claude] Milner would say. But, out of breath in the van, we murmur: "Ahh! There he goes again with his Being and its Outpour . . . !" That kind of reaction is the wrong kind of acting-out, a mental one; it's really a suicide. It is an *Elenchia* [*Elenchie*] (if I dare to neologize with the Greek *élegcheïn* [reproach, opprobrium]), a reproach that "sends packing" the useful expedient of the compendium within which the thought itself had first of all expedited a small-scale model, a weak summary of its own conviction . . .

OF THE MORTAL POSSESSING SPEECH

He knows that he dies [. . .] The Universe knows nothing of it.

—Pascal

Like those who may have fallen into a very roomy ditch, a vale of tears with banks of grass and basalt, a cirque with a steeple of stars, with a backdrop of funnel-dark, and doomed without supplies to a slow, shareable, distracted death

The wind blows to the south
Turns to the north
Round and round it goes
Ever returning on its course.
(Ecclesiastes)

(and or not but now for then)

And so we will have passed through a valley, the valley not of some geographical shady side to be climbed, properly speaking, nor because from the walls of the Uterus to those of the nearby individual grave it is instead a fairly muddy decline that the slope of life informs, or enclosed for many like the dens of Guinea with a cult, a god, for every pore of this terrestrial crust, insular territories like the craters of the Great War where those being tortured had to dig in and die, but;

and we will have been the last ones of a cult, I recall the foster children sticking out their tongues licitly for the spoonful of cough medicine and the distribution of azymes, the beautiful Latin of procession, the great barrel of rolling confession, the special boredom of entoptic preaching, the shrill rattle of Improperia, the weekly usurpation of God's name, and always the clan of Blanche de Castille women, even if Buñuel is on TV in the evening, making their way down a flattened Golgotha on their way to Saint-Sulpice, getting wind of morning sin ("for it would be better if my son were dead than a sinner") from the dogs, the garbage cans, the ditches, under the hanging gardens of Zion-Laputa behind the clouds of a Zion forever without Jews, and, beneath their feet, lies hell with its power outages but unstoppable like a nineteenth-century locomotive;

while waiting for the perspective of western theory to make yet another trip around the world (Magellans of the King of Kings, ambassador-writers, detectors of raw materials, reporters of flaming wars, anthropologists . . .), each time more terribly disinterested, to return for a look at us, treated in the end like a clan in its last days, finishing up with the cult of the white wafers in Saint-Sulpice;

perhaps we are, we will have been, the last ones of religion, that quite extraordinary thing; through our childhood we will have belonged to that which will someday appear as primitive and as astonishing as the Fuegans or the Papuans and other contemporary "primitives," belonged to that which amazes us—religion. Is anyone as singular, as ancient, as anthropological, as close to the Bushmen and Bedouins as the *bourgeoises*, with their knees knobbed by their dead, their family sins, and their eternal life . . .

And once superstition was set aside, the stagy sermons covered up, the harassing unbelieving skirmishers were let loose upon the city and upon books, churches, and city halls with a right to pillage, and there failed to appear, for all of that, a clear definition of the phenomenon of living, nothing at all was cleared up, and those human discourses tolerated were still just as few.

*

All words are infirm
How could man say
The eye fulfilled by seeing
And the ear by hearing

Beautiful tautologies go round and round. They compare us to what we know, and the pleasure of knowing ourselves as comparable disguises us. The human who is libidinous through sex, glory, and knowledge transmits the lure, each time re-encoded, of a secret reopened, then covered over again.

Everything is forgotten of past things
And will be forgotten of the things to come
Which will go away with no memory
With those who will be the last

Merde à Dieu screamed the walls of Arthur Rimbaud's Charleville. Which means: thought that speaks is not compatible with the excremental, the hole of pestilence and things related through the body. We had to choose. There couldn't be any of that. And there wasn't any of it for hundreds of millennia. The animal is not a monster, but man is, because the animality that becomes knowledge hates itself. And not "thinking" among other participles (spitting, sweating, crying, sleeping, dying), not even those of the psychic domain (feeling, imagining, wanting), but thinking—that he spits, that he sweats, that he imagines, that he wills . . . that he dies. The aroma of the shithouse rises to his divine nostrils; incontinent, he cuts himself off. Artaud, the impossible-to-put-up-with, thought that thought, turning it over seven thousand times in the tongue hole, he thought that thought and its reversals, thought with and against it.

> My son know this
> writing is endless
> too many studies too many books
>   weary

*

The species is recent. Another mutation is underway. I can feel it. A last one? Everything will be new under the sun.

The condition of modern man is that his condition is stripped bare, exposed as never before, a horrible definition, at an impasse and schized.

*

The public enemy, universal, unconditional—the only "absolute" there had been, there was, there is: death. It is death as ever. Because forever, and always, the species sought to have it, to consider it, to tame it, to pacify it, to order it in some way, to regulate it, to domesticate it; to deal with it, to envisage it, to tame it without defeating it: through sacrifice.

The remedy in the illness, homeopathic habit, dependency, familiarization, being-with-death: sacrifice. Recognition, Mithridaticization, worship: sacrifice. Like a condemned prisoner who refuses the blindfold, refuses the last wish, refuses the drug or the wine. And gives a face for facing up to it, face to face. A function of the sacrifice. Giving life, giving one's life; show death in. *Imagines*, divinize death! Let us affront the dead and death. Let us sacrifice. Death on the inside; in the world, in life, in the house. And the dead one by one, prepared, stored.

That's enough now! Refusal. His modern condition is that his condition has been integrally carved up. No god lies beneath the flayed modern man. . . . This is his definitive condition on his ravaged earth. . . . Us guys, uncultured, unreligious, we know that we are mortals. Ineluctable death is like nothing; death without capitals, without a face, without an article, without personality, without divinity: The impasse of death. He passed. Man no longer passes.

And that is intolerable. It must not pass anymore. That shall not pass.

Since death is the back wall, it must be knocked down, blown to pieces. If man is mortal, then we will change identity. Trotsky, cited by Roland Barthes, said: "Will there not be one day a socialist revolution against the horror of death? [. . .] And if death is bourgeois, we will *stop death*."

Now, against death there had been and there was: resurrection. This was the belief. And today still for thousands, for Islam, there is the traditional struggle against death, put another way, martyrdom. They rush to take on death, in the antique manner: it was a kind of deal; in the holy war the martyr casts himself away, "sacrifices" himself; it is war to the Death, and like salmon making themselves go on forever in a last spasm, "I" pass to the other side; I pass into paradise. I pass.

That doesn't work anymore, even if for years to come, before the desert of unbelief has expanded to sand up the whole earth, or rather to dry up the world, before the last lights of our last crematorium go out, by the thousands the martyrs will continue to explode, giving a face to death, and thereby facing down death.

And many other antique solutions, old instruction manuals, are still in use, chimerical mixtures of the very ancient and the very modern, transpositions of the crypt into the laboratory, a tale to be dreamed by day like the fable of Frankenstein: the cryogenic mummy in a nitrogen bath offered to "Progress" and to EDF [*Electricité de France*], the obscene superstition of the technically assisted wealthy. And quite a few others: Madame the Duchess prepares to clone her dog, her fetus, her lover. Anything but the death that is everything. And we will change our cells, one by one, but this body will no longer be a corpse. And as longevity is elongated we will endlessly push back the end, disappearance will disappear. If it is the individual who persists in his mortality, we will make him fall back into the ranks of the generic, we will abolish his finitude, in a new manner, still unpredictable, for philogenesis is imperishable, and the collective cannot perish. If it is necessary, we will create paradise on earth, a here and now that will resemble advertising, the publicity of happiness, and this is my body, an athletic body, tanned, of bronze, at leisure in the sunshine of the palmy shore, taken in the moment just before orgasm, the coiled androgynous couple will freeze upon its frame. Death will no longer pass on.

*

And I feel, I who will, and I dare to write this, die, I feel the mutation surrounding us, trembling in a thousand signs; metamorphosis is messing with us. Into what will Daphne or Castor and Pollux, the Dicoscuri, be changed, I do not know, but look:

Look at everything that displeases the reluctant old man, everything that is taken up enthusiastically by the teenager, by the fan, by the current slang, by the remote-controllers, the eliders, the technos, the with-it, the videographers, the cloned, the texted. A thousand grandiose or ridiculous twitches and shudders—how he dresses, how he codes, how he installs, how he mutates against his bases and his traces, how he capsulates, how he formulates, how he makes métissage in the city, how he assimilates as info, how he silicones, how he scientologizes, how his genius transgenes.

II

NOTEBOOKS OF DISBELIEF

IN DOUBT

Mallarmé saluted Villiers de l'Isle-Adam "who is dead": This crazy game of writing, it only exists by virtue of a *doubt*—the drop of ink related to the night sublime—some duty to recreate everything, with reminiscences to prove that we are truly here where we ought to be (because, allow me to express this apprehension, *there remains some uncertainty* . . .).

Mallarmé read and meditated Descartes and his *Meditations*; a doubt subsists, he maintains, well aware of Descartes. God, "this nasty plumage," no longer supports his "continuous creation" in being, nor does he extend a hand across the abyss separating knowledge from being. This permanence of uncertainty is perhaps one of the modes of what Stéphane Mallarmé calls in a letter, "the sensation of nothingness," from which it is not a question of fleeing—and that later (but not that much later) will be consigned by Heidegger to "anguish." Doubt subsists, deepening the void, this *void* that obtains for the imagination a schema of representation for "nothingness." An opportunity for me to evoke the other poet, I mean Victor Hugo dreaming of the Fall of the Angel ["*La Chute de Satan*"], and striking this incipit for Satan: "For four thousand years he plunged through the abyss." It suffices for us to change the name of the pro-noun, putting man in the place of Satan, and to add a few years to the count—without spoiling the count of the Alexandrine verse, "For two hundred thousand years *he* plunged through the abyss"; and that's our fall, which goes on . . . ["*Depuis 4,000 ans il tombait dans l'abîme*"/ "*Depuis 200,000 ans* il *tombait dans l'abîme*"]

Doubt is not a step that we can get past, and dubitation, synonymous with meditation, active, is at the heart of this quest for truth, as Malebranche called it, which we call more compactly, "Research."

There are two thrusts to this quest, two strands in this weaving; one of which is doubt and the other of which is this power of pro-posing, this humor of affirmation, I would say to psychologize things a little bit. . . . The step of advancing is each time (or all together) hesitant and martial, and if in this "French" language, then, where the injunction "clear up a doubt" [*ôte-moi d'un doute*] rings out early in our memory, the grammar of "if" confounds the "if" of conventional and of indirect interrogation. The "if it is true that" of the hypothesis, the "if" of what is not real, and the "if" of "I asked her if . . ." are one and the same word—even if the constructions which they order differ.

I said advance; the lexical series of advance should be dissected: "to advance a truth; he advanced up to; to be in advance for something; the advances of research" . . . How do we advance? Linguistically this time rather than psychologically, I willingly repeat that any enunciation brings with it both denunciation and annunciation. "They told you that . . . and now I am telling you that . . ."

Doubt is the exercise of intelligence, the oxygen of the work of truth. The suspension of belief is the beginning of wisdom, and any truth, however provisional, rises like a wave on an ocean of questioning, in the same way that in the field of intersubjectivity, of "diallelical" interlocution of one by another (but is there an other? And we are, each of us, an other for the others), our experience is that everything rests upon confidence . . . which is always *doubtful.*

Everything has been said on the subject of the subject in the four hundred years that Cartesians (and antis) have been *cogitating.* It is impossible, nevertheless, not to re-commence by remembering Descartes: he is the Moses of our nation, as Hölderlin said of Kant, the school teacher of our *logos* (spirit and language): French is Cartesian, or at least that should be our ambition; but we are a long way from it . . .

Doubt, this Evil Genius, is like a god, one devil of a god! Hence an idol. Descartes devotes himself to it as if to a superstition, a belief that invades everything, a fiction that "sticks." This belief will push aside all belief and in this reversal, the thinking-being-subject puts itself into play. The skeptic in the trivial sense and in the philosophical sense should recuse this "all-powerful-stranger." It is as if we could not or could no longer believe in it. Lassitude sometimes murmurs, "I just don't believe it any more!" the addiction to confidence that forever "forced itself." When everything "falls back." . . . The moment of *Hyperbolic Doubt* is strange because it joins believing to this dis-belief. I *believe*—or I don't believe anymore. "It's incredible!" says language at the moment of the impossibility of not being able to bring itself to belief. The not-(being-able)-not-to-believe-in gets enlaced with the not believing.

For a retroactive effect, in the famous "I know that I know not—or I know nothing"[1] of the Platonic *Apology* we hear and understand a kind of Socratic *cogito,* even if this expression seems a bit difficult to accept for a Heideggerian ear. Indeed Socrates's formula is not itself of the same form, circular, or if you will, or iterative, as that of the Cartesian "I cannot doubt that I doubt," the buckle of which does not close up again upon nothing, but rather makes a first truth.

The Second Meditation says: "So, after considering everything very thoroughly, I must finally conclude that the proposition, *I am, I exist,* is necessarily true whenever it is put forward by me or conceived in my mind."

A tightening-up of doubt upon itself, the folding-up of doubt into itself, the *cogito* turns it inside out like a glove as soon as it is empty, and draws from it "every single time," that is, "each time" that the operation is triggered, "in fact": this *factum cogitationis,* first truth, is a truth of fact, or rather it is as if it were anterior to the distinction between truth of fact and truth of right.

In this way, doubt, the devil who shakes up and dissipates all "sensible certainty," in the famous Hegelian expression, proposes the model of a truth of evidence, a species of "simple nature," as clear and distinct as it is possible to be.

God will do the rest we know; to correlate all of the correlates, the *cogitata* with the *cogitationes* of the *cogito*.

Truth of fact; "there is"; that there is something rather than nothing; and that this something is not nothing. The thought of doubt doubting everything and its own being cannot be eliminated; it is presupposed in the moment of doubting; pursued by doubt, it cannot suppress itself; rather then it feels itself to be like something different from all that is dubitable. *Self-fulfilling thinking* [in English in the original], if I may say; the subject closing up on itself vouches for itself. The *cogito* doesn't think. It is the fact of thought. I think that I think that I am, a kind of "indubitable" value as it is all the *same*, being and thought. . . . There is no other *cogitatum* than the fact of thought thinking of nothing else.

Attention is synonymous with defiance: it is circumspection. "My" incessant suspicion, which has become "primary," is there to welcome any utterance, any *doxa*. A kind of "evil genius," attenuated and vigilant, a domestic guardian who never closes an eye, whose incessant asides murmur something like Montaigne's "I don't believe any of it." Antidoxical *doxa*? Skepticism in general, indifferent to its own contradiction, is an allegro movement that surmounts its own refutability like a snowplow crushes everything in its way, what its very advance has piled up before it. A "skepticism" then that suspends adherence, accompanying every intellection like a questioning smile, all the while maintaining an alert deference to meaning, a deference for that which seeks to be said.[2]

How to "lend credit" to the *adunata* [the impossibilities], that is what this worry wonders about. We call the faith that does not analyze the ingredients of an oxymoron blind or simple faith, which cannot abide the impossibility that it poses and does not seek to transpose that impossibility into a self-consistent paradox. It is not rare for great intelligences to profess such *adunata* as naively received truths. This is what surprises.

From another angle: a "truth" is such that only paradoxical utterances can *approach* it, can attempt to "seize" it—with a pair of pliers having opposable jaws neither of which is sufficient on its own, and which it is necessary for us to constantly sharpen up and to refine. I'll make up one example with relation to our modern anguish about the establishment of generally shareable truth, and here, axiomatically, is the formulation of a rationalism of the reasonable: it is reasonable to hold as unreasonable the hope of agreeing (or "dialogy") (or inversely: it is unreasonable to hold for reasonable the hope of agreeing). . . . The paradox as an asyndetical apposition of opposites (in which contradicting truth gets itself contradicted) oxymoric, antinomic, this paradox is such that it is necessary to push the opposing poles ever further back (eg, man is an "omnipotence—a paralyzed omnipotence"; and not merely a weakened power).

"Compromise" or "middle ground," does not consist of dulling the extremes or "bringing them closer together" by attenuating the tension. Common sense—for example, Tvetzan Todorov in his preface to Northrop Frye's *Great Code*—writes, "it is possible to live in complementarity rather than in contradiction."[3] But what if "true" complementarity *is* contradiction or, as I might prefer to put it: what if complementarity plays itself out with and within the contrariety of the contraries? These propositions are not at all mutually exclusive but are *all the more complementary for being contrary*. From that point on, "identifying the problem" is 1) properly striking the formula of the oxymoron and this is not only for the sake of elegance, and 2) diving into (we also say digging into) the complexity of that coupling (which is another copulation than that of the copula "is").

It sometimes happens that Derrida abbreviates this as "the *law* is *double-bind* . . . ," and "deconstruction" is there to analyze in what and how the contrariety *consists*, each time "rigorously." The utterance of paradox is only the formal program of the solution. Deconstruction makes its game explicit and prepares its regulation. Adverse propositions must come to a compromise among themselves.[4]

Doubting favors a life lived out within "just-a-little-bit-of." (I borrow the relation to this little-bit from Proust's formula, "*un peu de temps à l'état pur*" [a little bit of time in the pure state].) Although the massive assurance of certitude gets itself carried away in a logic of all-or-nothing. Extremism is the enemy.

The skeptic "does not *abstain in* doubting." But on the contrary he sees opening up (like an "enormous country where everything demands to speak," I would say, to quote and deform Apollinaire) the salutary regime of the many little-bits. (The eighteenth century's *je ne sais quoi*? Jankelevitch's "almost"?) The "search" tacks against the wind in order to "maintain its course" (the other heading). A "golden mean" (*mésotês*) can be calculated "between" the extremes *for* the extremes. How to adjoin the demon of doubting (the familiar evil genius) on the one hand to the measure of the *mésotês*, and on the other hand to the composition of "good" opposites (different from bad contradictories)?

There are impasses and then there are impasses. The first kind, the "bad" one, is when nothing at all can pass. And the second kind? Digging deeper into the impasse is a way to advance on a "road": making the back wall recede is to open a way. The *poros* is *in* a-poria—which opens up a contrariety that would be substitutable for "bad contradiction." In vernacular language, which is the language of thought, the apodictic is the paradoxical with which we have come to terms.

"NON CREDO IN"

Article by article.

For example: I do not believe that a man descended among the dead, to come out alive. There is no "among the dead." They are not—distinctive recumbent figures—like us, we the living. Or: they are only such, distinctly recumbent, for us, the living.

I do not believe that humans, living human beings, met him, saw him, cared for him, invited him to dinner. That he was a "god." Or: no one is recreated out of nothingness. Like Thomas—and I certainly have the right since Thomas is attested to—I would only believe it if I saw it with my own eyes. . . . There was a time when that was belief.

> What has not happened has never happened
> What has happened has already happened
> But what happens?
> Never a prayer suspended gravity
> Never a will troubled the calm division
> Never a god's body burst again from the stone

That was the poem that I dedicated to Pessoa in "*La Rose des langues de Paris*" [The Language Rose of Paris] (*Jumelages*, 1978).

TO MOTHERS

May I speak frankly with myself?
—What do you regret?
—Having never known my mother.
For I wasn't old enough, and too dim-witted
—being barely over fifty—when I lost her: she died
before the wisdom of my love. Who was she?

And once more the best man of all, the unique being for this world of many, was dead and desolation would never end.

The earth was depopulated, the emptiness of the loved ones
eternal; meaning had perished
the darkened heaven was at three o'clock torn
like a divine curtain
the tombs themselves emptied

But already the point of view of the sun was rising
the neighbour was singing while doing the washing. An only
child was reborn unto them, and the village wanted to
give its Son to the whole world

and that the whole world delight the same day
in the same name and in the same image
and thus the wood of his death grew again

"The death of God," Cardinal Ratzinger said in Paris at Lent (2000), "is hell."

And how! That's it precisely. We are in hell, punished and dying. "We are dead." That is where we must live. It could hardly be worse.

And for God to be dead, he must have been killed! He was, historically: there was a "deicide"; the fact that it is never said anymore changes nothing in the matter. For Christians, the Christ was God. The "Jewish people" obtained from Pilate his execution.

Latin translation: "deicide." One has difficulty seeing how a Christian could call that anything else.

The gods did not die easily, of old age. The question is how we are making them die now. We declare the nonexistence of God. Do we think that we are doing it in a noncriminal fashion, I mean without the *–cide* becoming contagious? Does deicide demand all of the other *–cides*? A relevant quotation of Dostoyevsky affirms this. But I prefer the Kantian one: since God died, nothing is permitted.

In the imagination, "I" turn toward "God." This is "prayer."

Those images that wrap "God" in their care may come down in fact to two or three main imageries.

That of "God the Father": a God-the-Old, millions of centuries now (not so long ago, it was just a few dozen; he ages in his aging), with a beard as big as the Milky Way, God of the Sixtine or of Alfred de Vigny ("Who with a disdainful foot casting [us] into space,/ Returned to his rest" ["*qui d'un pied dédaigneux [nous] roula dans l'espace*"] "Le Désespoir"]).

A predicate of that paternity is power.

A neighboring imagery, closely connected and implied, is that of God *omnipotens*—THE Lord—*Herr*; the Master. *Thou, Lord!* God of the Armies as we translate it in the mass, who are the legions of angels. The God whose capital letter subjugates the lower case of the other gods. Prayers to Him invoke the miraculous-efficacious. He who commands the wind and the waves—among other things. It is he who will give *me* victory.

God the son-brother, "I" am his beloved. He loves me "infinitely." He takes care of me. I hang up an ex-voto in Lourdes. I passed my baccalaureate or got over scarlet fever thanks to him. He punished my neighbor's cat—or caused a thousand enemies to perish—who had prayed him to do nothing of the sort. Or he brought safely home the two American pilots, *God blesses America* [in English in the original], which implies that he loves the Iraqis less. It is strange, if we think about it, but let's not think about it. After all, it is perhaps not the same god? . . . Where are we going?

Voltaire wondered how to bring humanity out of that childhood. Not everyone has the good fortune to be an orphan, sighs Jules Renard. Maturity is not coming tomorrow, in spite of Nietzsche.

*

It is not because there is no God that there is no prayer. Man prays. At any moment, millions of praying mouths whose wishes would cancel one another out. No prayer is granted, it cannot be answered, even if in the clinamen of possibles it happens, it cannot not happen, that chance, as we call it, grants more than a few. And death for an instant is deferred. What is it to pray? The wind rises; perishing is getting set to cast off. Peter is in the skiff, he throws himself into the water, prayer seizes him, keeps his head out of the water for a moment, his lungs imploring before flooding. (It is so difficult on the high seas, *mari magno*, assailed by enormous waves, to turn back toward solid ground, as inaccessible as the heavens, the shore from which the sage seated once more salutes you and prepares your funeral wreath.)

If only! O, the vocative—and the optative! O You whom I would have loved [Baudelaire, "A une passante"]! If only someone could hear me! Does the cloud not have the form of a big ear? My god, save my body along with my soul! The whole being drawn to a point in the hands joined like a delta, a verse, *clamans in deserto* . . . And all of the past mobilized behind it with a glimmer of alert fear! It's impossible that the impossible is no longer possible! Necessity twists insurrection into resignation, turning the terrible into an offering . . .

"The patient breath of the bull" (Marguerite Yourcenar) is one of the "thirty names of God" (Israel Eliraz).[5]

What humans need to call God (it is a name) is shown for example in the snout of the bull. It does not follow that God would be like Anubis or Ganesh, but rather that something is showing itself which is called god in our language, and elsewhere something else. A "theophany."

God. Gott. Gud. Des. Dio. Herr. Θεος. Boha. Gâoko. Dios. Slowo. Ige. Dumnezeu. Bog. Gair. Dieva. Jumal. Söz . . .

Who is God?

The text says of God that he "saw that it was good."

What is that "divine gaze"?

What does it see?

For example, in the street these two women side by side, the black woman and the white woman: there is no racism for the divine gaze; and for good reason; it "created" this; unlike Wilhelm II, it "wanted this."

So it is a matter of acceding to the "divine gaze," which is nothing other than our own. A point of view from which "I" can see that it is good.

Right away it is the right way of looking—without waiting for a judgment to come, extradivine, which might fix it all up, retribution, punishment, etc.

Without passing through "belief in God" and the imagining of a point of his view: without theodicy.

CHRIST

Is it possible that he could have been that strong, two thousand years ago, when we still didn't know very much? Not really.

May I sum up the genius that he had? It was:

–to divinize man ("I am the truth . . .")

–to separate him from the world

–to go toward death; in a sacrifice-redemption.

We owe him the modern meaning of sacrificing-oneself-for; the mother for her children; the priest of Auschwitz for the young Jewish deportee. That meaning of sacrifice that metamorphosizes primitive sacrifice; the "last" sacrifice of which Nietzsche spoke very ill; and about which René Girard claims that it does not make of the Mass a sacrifice.[6]

We may understand that a very pious man, very holy, very just, might take himself for a god; might feel himself being god, inhabited by god—and without madness.

THE INCARNATE

Jesus is the model. We think of HIM as "incarnation." And on the basis of that model, as we consider ourselves and everyone around us, we reckon that incarnation has not really worked out so well. "He" is athletic, perfect, young. A spirit "in the image of God;" a son-body, Son of Man, son of God. But ordinary incarnation: something like the humanity of man gets his legs under him and warms up; tumbles down-here, gets his body all tangled up; and, as if in a fairy-tale, wakes up embarrassed and confused. "What are these calves, this hair?!" The "I" takes advantage of the awkwardness to detach itself: That's not me!

Why continue to seek out a "lack of god"?

We must do without that very lack.

What I miss is you, and you. You, perhaps . . .

Do I miss you, or X? How? Who do I miss?

What I miss is that I do not miss others enough and am not missed enough by them. "We all make for one another such a cruel want." [self-quotation] The lack or inadequacy of others brings us no succor. We don't miss each other enough.

We are the "gods"; for lack of lack.

Nothing will be destroyed, not this fire, nor this place, nor this blue. But "I" will be destroyed. And not the "I," the *cogito*, but *this* I—I/I. The coincidence of this body with this I, with this embodied I; like a bubble bursting.

But there will always be just as many beings and just as much being.

What does monologue say? I am called "I" like you. I am abandoned. You abandoned me. Nothing takes place.

If I go outside for a few minutes, it is to experience this. "I went out under the moon . . ."

Abandonment.

We must leave him. He is in a state of abandonment in the state where he is. We can only leave him.

Since the body is being forgotten and death is being forgotten, like organs in the silence of health, we might think, "I" might think—that I am here (*Da-sein*) for something other than to live my life.

And I might think that existing is seeing, judging, knowing, understanding; non-mortal, exactly, like those gods whom man *believed he saw*, as Rimbaud said ["*Le Bateau ivre*"], for millennia, the ones he proffered before his face at the same time as his language, invisible, very fussy, overlooking the hills and mining the soils, or growing beneath the crust of stones, omnivorous, and each one of them is all the others. Argus and Proteus, consuming living beings in their smoke plumes, irrigating the gargoyles of death.

Once the keeper of an isolated lighthouse, shipwreck survivor with a brief light, imagine him now, a mobile guard with probes and satellites, in an orbital relation with the Universe-enigma, from further off we see him, his back to the zodiacal abyss;

a cyclone here, there the fire of deserts, a column of soot, he like a *sur*lunary god, he receives the sacrifices, watching the cap melt, and the Niño veer on Peru;

amoral videographer sweeping the time zones on a circumterrestrial drift, enunciating fears and axioms, world weather, imprecations and auguries.

The same "decisive question," the future of an illusion, inhabited Nietzsche and Freud: the former discovering that we would have to "pay for the Loss" if we didn't know how to change "the death of gods into a great renunciation and a victory over ourselves"; and the latter asking himself if "we will manage to reconcile men with the necessary sacrifices and to compensate them for it." The gods are hungry said our own Anatole France a little bit later. Yes, thirsty for the blood, one of another. Some gods are still blowing people up before our eyes, with dynamite. For example the buddahs of Kabul with the explosive called Allah. But these are human beings. And all of that comes afterward.

The sacrifice of the gods, then, that is to say the "renunciation" by humans of their gods; and the "compensations" which would be neither interethnic killing nor hallucinatory opiates of compensation (*divertissement*, distraction, Pascal would have said). The twentieth century showed that human beings in the society of nations couldn't manage it. How can it be done? Is humanity about to hit the wall? One might say so.

The bifurcation is that of super-humanizing or ending up as cyberneticized clones. Super-humanizing means becoming "sons of man," "human brothers."

One of the equivalents of *sacrifice* is "demythologization." This is unlike the movements wished for by many, gurus or drugged artists, which would be movements of remythologization, perhaps through a sectarian swarming, perhaps through spectacular technological syncreticisms. The urgency is to demythify. Let's say, as a minimum, in Thomas Mann's way.

Everything is mythical, you only have to read anthropology—except for my belief, except for my god, the believer mutters to himself. Yet long ago there were criteria to separate out the true and the false gods: for example, victory. The god of "Israel" was the strongest, and he proved it regularly. The "version of the losers" had no currency. Those criteria have since disappeared. "Demythifying" requires that I also put my own god through it. If all the gods are idols, then mine is too. If Christianity consumes the end of paganism (René Girard), then Christ is a-theistic.

Demythologizing is translating and betraying the religious. Let us recall Thomas Mann's humorous solution: Joseph the Egyptian is assimilated to Felix Krull, the worldly conman ("the great conman," Melville would have said), and reversibly Felix is assimilated to Joseph: both are characterized as *Hochstapler*).

And let not the religion of literature replace the literature of religion! We want no lethargic ersatz. If profaning religious Revelation was art's destiny, how can we now make an original revelation (Joyce spoke of epiphany) with profanation completed? Or even: how can we make ineffaceable that which has become unbelievable, that is the function of literature—one of the modes of the Hegelian overcoming (*Aufhebung*), coming in "relief" or loss-preservation, that is "metamorphosis." Literature reemploys mythologemes and theologemes (The Great Code, said William Blake and Northrop Frye).

Where are the *precious relics*? In language. The religious is that which remains when we've forgotten everything else. Palin-ody or literature, general translation (and translating's treason) of ancient into modern meaning, that coming into the game in "relief" of the gods or of their loss (active loss: the question is how to lose them), such is the future of "culture," the duty of civilization.

It is certain that it is necessary, in place of a superstitious worship, to give a sense, some meaning, to the "relics," to the traditional locutions of culture, to the writings of our language: what does "eternal," which was one of the names of god, mean for us today? Or "blessed art thou," which is in our language and in its poems? And I'm only speaking about our own religious area, the Greek-Jewish-Christian one. To each inheritor of each revelation, his own specific task. This transfiguration cannot come only through a lexical translation. A human can no longer (eg,) believe that God dictated his Book; no more than that he created bananas and frogs (or the reverse) from Monday to Saturday.

In order that, thanks to this mis- or dis-belief, or generalized disenchantment, humans might surmount themselves (*über-mensch*), there is the complex operation, of very special interest to art, the operation with which what is called literature, including poetry, must cooperate, obviously; poetry whose vocation can no longer be to wander sobbing through the ruins and the "Dream" which has fled . . .

The operation of literary translation requires that we both restore (attain and support) that which was thought (what did *ethos* mean to Heraclitus, or *daïmon*?) and prepare its possibility of sense for us.

And so it goes with the use of BEING, demands Heidegger. If its value as a logical copula eclipses any other (eclipse of being), and it is therefore replaceable by a *sign*, well then, adieu to Being . . .

RELICS

The relics are in language.

Blessed art thou! "*[. . .]is blessed.*"

Strange injunction, a subjunctive optative with a worry in the voice . . . it suggests "is perhaps *not* blessed;" or simply "that's not used anymore." What has become of benediction?

What is *blessing* today if not that intonation, like one that could decipher a half-effaced inscription? A quasi-citation. . . . A bit of prayer's anamnesis . . .

May my child be blessed, mine among all wives, and not ill-fated, but "happy." May she . . .

The afterglow of an out of use subjunctive, current speakers don't even know its grammar . . .

*

Among the relics is pity.

— . . . No, for us, it is not the same thing as piety.

— . . . Yes, I know: "terror and pity;" *pius Eneas*; Michelangelo; and right up to compassion with Jean-Jacques.

I'll leave behind this series, to try to glimpse it from another angle: by relating it to its polar opposite, laughter. Thus: in us, the non-human (of which the inhuman is the catastrophe) takes its position, that of a quasi-divine view. And so it was with Christ whenever he *wept over* something. Over our humanity, and thus his own. Crying over the only-that of the human; *just that.* I do not know if my death will happen to you, but your death comes to me. I think of our death, and I am "invaded by tears." Lazarus! Of course, he is dead, and has been for a few days. He will not be getting up; he is not coming to have dinner with us as if nothing had happened. He lived in flesh and blood. Now the flesh is decomposed. How to resuscitate him? Make him live again with us, in us, Lord!

An abyssal sadness over all of that. Over fragility, infirmity, our terrified mortality, condemned to the worst, devotional.

It is like laughing, for which the human is ridiculous. Not that one aspect would be laughable, but it is the whole ridiculousness of our aspectual character that bowls us over. Take a little distance! Laughter is the laughter of the gods, our laughter when we are as gods, as the devil promised us. (He took him to the top of a high mountain and showed him the earth with a broad gesture: all of this is yours! [Matthew 4:8].)

OF THE HOLY FAMILY

I call family the place where we love each other. Making a family exists in order that there be some loving; some life of others, some good. *Meletê tou agathou* [The milieu of the good]. Grief only affects the family.

The Joconde's smile tells her secret: "I am still alive; they are too." She is like a Madonna—without the bambino. But he isn't far. The holy family has not been dissipated. I am waiting for him, my arms are crossed to receive him, my hands resting on my lap, folded like a homemaker who has finished peeling the vegetables. The boy is next door, playing in the barnyard with John.

Love one another—like in a family. Christianity was the predilection for this great comparison. There is circularity between the model of a "holy family" and the salvific injunction to love one another. The parable is the holy family. Let us love one another as the three of us (or a few more) loved one another for years in Palestine. We might even think that the strange affirmation of virginity (a hypothesis that does not come, no never, from forensic medicine) detaches, in order to insist on it, the moment of post-sexuality: the society where we love each other, the family air; a family party is one of these moments, quite different from the moment of sexuality where man and woman "join themselves," not man and woman in general, but these ones right here, to the exclusion of all others, "alone in the world." They make love, that is to say also that some love will happen. They make its possibility.

More than two in the crèche; for example three—perhaps even four, counting the favorite cousin. Not counting the animals that are led to the house.

And at the same time I follow my shade. Seeing myself and seeing myself seeing (in Valéry's words: one of the one hundred ways of saying the *cogito* with its reflection), I cling to that overhanging view, doubling myself up, following or anticipating that double at the same time as I see others who follow themselves in the street, who pass beneath our windows, like the walker in cape and hat who was conjectured to be "human" by Descartes, or that shade in the Underworld rounded up by Ulysses, I ubiquitize myself, envisaging Homeric phantasies, entering into a dialogue-with-the-dead with these human-brothers-who-are-living-with-me [Villon, "Ballade des pendus"]. I follow my own double and I do not know which of the two is less mortal than the other.

"All of that comes back to us"—it is this very statement to which I would like to subscribe more fully. What it seems that a religious revelation is uncovering for me—for example, that you are an immortal soul that will rejoin its sisters in the country of the dead—and which comes from outside, from some Pythia, prophet or shaman, all of this falls to *me*, that is, *says* what it is to be a speaking mortal.

It is up to me—to appropriate it for myself.

The fables, the "living" parables that we are in our existing, the scenes that we play out for one another, the minor roles that we invent or take on while playing the stipulated roles that cultures preserve and assign, these are the mnemonics and riddles, the sphinxes sending back images in order that we might recognize ourselves in them, these charades of what we are.

Ghosts, doubles, spirits are not other beings but that is nevertheless what I must in a certain way believe them to be, "believing in ghosts" in order to gain access at least through superstitious credulity to the full depth of my humanity. They are the fable, living on the outside, which I must interpret, as both an actor and a textual interpreter; the *guardian angel*, in which I believed as a child, thanks to my parents and the priests, confabulates this doubling up which constitutes me as a thinking mortal. It is my guardian ghost, I am doubled up in order to be. I believed in him as the one who awaits me after death in Dante's book, where instead he figures "my being," a barely recognizable image of the self-portait. The one who accompanies me throughout my life.

There are certainly other *just men* in the city, and in the world. Outis knew three or four. But, as God no longer existed, they weren't enough to have us spared.

However, to contemplate that very thing that has just been written, thought Outis, the narrator, wouldn't it be necessary to count oneself among the just, in any case among the number of those who would recognize their own offspring in the just? Could I judge the just and the unjust if I didn't occupy a site of last judgment? No one is just involuntarily.

The end of metaphysics, they say. In other words, the end of dualism and of all of its duos and dyads and duels: body–mind, passion–reason, etc. Hence, the end of limitation, of self-limitation (that term was used by Solzhenitsyn's translators). The end of stoicism, of "spiritualisms," of asceticisms.

The monism that this end liberates is the monism of the body. And what body? The modern body of eternal youth with prostheses. The unlimitation of the prosthesis: a body that will corporeally devour the world along with the earth, or the earth along with the world. The frenzy of potentialization, of envy, of consumerism. A Leviathan of bodies, with no tyrannical monarch; each ego become a desiring body "without organs," that is to say, without any possible satisfaction of its limited needs, but all by itself the equivalent of all ("worth all," J.-P. Sartre), capable of devouring everything "all by itself:" every single body, infinitized by technique and obeying the law of the authenticity of desire, and no longer that of Ennui, "would swallow the world." (Unless precisely that famous Baudelairean catch phrase of ennui had in fact been one of the first formulations, already murmuring through its "yawn," of Desire.) Look out in the city, into the street, "liberated" bellies and sexes are ordering the ravaging of the earth for their own satisfaction. Enslavement to the absence of Law. Even the "Shariah" will end up there.

How do we think an "end of metaphysics" that does not unleash this incorporated individuated life? What kind of incarnation is there without a body? What would Jean-Luc Nancy's *Corpus* say about this? Does "deconstruction" undo the knot of the dualism, and its couples, without nihilism?

Here on the damp terrace, I glimpse the conspiracy of enjoyment, *jouissance*: light wind, warmth of the palm trees, tumescence of fruit, a spreading "desire" extorting from the earth the vague yet guaranteed promise of desire's "enrichment"—promise of beverages, kisses, images. I read Camus's variation on this theme inscribed upon the Tipasa stele: "*Glory* would be the *right to love* without *measure*."[7] A strange, adolescent motto; almost incomprehensible. The "revolution" cannot be gauged by that measurelessness. The I-enjoy [*le je-jouis*] is not the measure of being—if it is true that its nihilistic tonality resonates more like "*après moi, le déluge*." When the *jouir*, the climax of enjoyment and pleasure, is no longer the *gaudere* [rejoicing] of theology, what is its objectivity then?

*

Here is a tautology: the "law," is that . . . the limit must not come from without but from within, from interiority (and for Saint Augustine, from love: the inside of the inside is less "law" than it is "love:" *ama* and "Commandment"? Love cannot be commanded but it commands.)

The question "for us" (the twenty-first century) would be: What does the voluptuous character of the revolutionary (according to Baudelaire quoted by Pleynet![8]), what does this *I-enjoy* encounter as self-limitation? It is impossible that only the *I-enjoy* of another would constitute de facto a limit to my own. For whom? The just (de jure) cannot proceed from the factual (de facto). There is, there must be, a *factum rationis*. Without which, it is the war of pleasures and the reign of force; and so of violence. I rape you—and you have to have an orgasm (Sade)! But it doesn't work out that way on its own (Fourier's dream, or "utopia" . . .). It doesn't just happen, doesn't happen justly, as it would in a game where everyone wins. And *in fact* we can see this, we never stop getting in each other's way, bothering each other; constraining one another; hurting each other: the "postures" do not "work out," except, perhaps, in the Marquis's novels.

The other cannot remain outside; the principle cannot be exogenous. The definition of liberty from 1789, incontestable in a regime of empirical observation, from a "scientific" point of view (ie, juridical sociology), that is to say as a freedom "halting" at the point where it harms others (but liberty does not stop by itself, that's the whole problem! It must be constrained!), that definition is external. It cannot be simply in encountering an obstacle, namely the pleasure of another, that liberty would receive an injunction to limit itself, to forbid itself something. Prohibition is addressed from within to within: intimation, injunction. Freedom does not get its *thou shalt* on the outside.

METAPHYSICAL MEDITATION

The Nazi is a metaphysician: he separates high from low. In order to foreclose on humanity for some humans, he bestializes them, reduces them to the excremental, vegetative state; they are esophagi, intestines, sexes. Holes. He forbids gazing on the gaze. They must *lower* their eyes. Lowness. And he, the supreme one, in the heights: he has the word, the right, the language, the spirit, the meaning. He divides.

His enemy is the libertine materialist, who unifies, who subverts, as we began to say a few eons ago, that is to say who loops together, in a kind of Ferris wheel, the high and the low. The libertine materialist allows the cut to scar over, not allowing the two sides of the crisis to fall away from one another; intellectualizing the body. Like love.

Love collides, smashing into things; making portmanteau words and glossolalia. But it does not believe that the real will follow nor even that the real should follow. Because reality does not fall directly under the authority of words.

DESCARTES AND SOCRATES

Common sense is anterior to the *cogito*. The first lines of the Cartesian *Discourse* say this: and in it we can hear some sort of ironical Socratic aside, stage-whispering with an agora smile, that every speaker considers himself endowed with common sense and indeed so "well-equipped" with it that no one believes that he is lacking in it, as if this good sense were a quantity.[9] Yet Descartes corrects himself almost as quickly: all of us cannot be wrong; so it is that this capacity, about which each of us seems to be vain, "testifies that the power of judging well [. . .] is naturally equal in all men."

This is the first and the principial, the formidable declaration of "natural equality." And because it cannot be in every matter that I judge well, I can at least judge well about my aptitude to judge well; like any other. I do not know; but I know that I do not know and this step back, this falling-back "on oneself," which uncovers the self thanks to taking some distance, empty and equal, where I can grasp myself (again) by withdrawing, this precedes the *cogito* that will close itself up on its own certitude.

The humble ignorant old woman, the well-known illiterate servant, from Thales to Lenin, questioned at the bottom of her own well, which is her world, about a question that she doesn't know, immediately recognizes its nullity, detaching herself from herself, like Socrates under the influence of the oracle, and so asks herself: she knows that she doesn't know; a removal without "restraint"; the subject is supposed not to know, and in this she is like Socrates, like any other, reckoning herself at her true value or nothing. And so opens up originally the strange modality of the knowledge of something indivisible from the knowledge of self, "all or nothing"—*noeien* and *legein* opened-upon, sure of nothing.[10]

What is properly human, not transferable to a machine, even to an animal-machine? Isn't it just judging oneself, myself, as knowing that I know not? Sentiment and intellection are related to the *cogito*, but different; for the expression *cogito-sum* is a philosophical operation, different from the ordinary consciousness-of-self, and different from this moment of reflection where I am pausing right now, one which is common and constitutive without being the product of any philosophical consciousness. Namely: self-esteem would be the proper expression to distinguish it, if we do not understand by this any moral appreciation, neither praise nor being cut down to size following any axiological scale. It is the moment that equalizes all humans through negation, nothingness is the correlative of knowledge. A considered not-knowing that sets up an empty reception for being.

Enough with the science! cries the non-scientist. No, says Primo Levi: "Research" is the inevitable principle, the ineluctable Sovereign, the destiny of humanity. I am going to cite a modern witness: Primo Levi. First of all I will reiterate the question.

What gap, what indifference, or what adversity separates the imaginative seeing (Dante) of literature, of poetry, which *envisages* the "future phenomenon" (Mallarmé), on the one hand, from the scientific gaze on the other, that *seeing* which determines coldly, that is to say objectively, with a *special detachment* that is rigorous, autonomous, and in principle foreign to emotions and extrinsic limitations (eg, ethical ones)? On the one hand there is human apprehension, on the other, the progress without moratorium of "inhuman" scientific mastery? The question left pending is: what relations do the vision of art and the views of science keep up?

How can we assume the consequences of a double vision which encourages schizophrenia and which has come to the paroxysm of its acuity—for example, today on the stage where the humanist and the experimenter of cloning confront one another, and so forth?

Are we seeing double or have we got the power of double vision? Primo Levi helps us, he who went through an extraordinary mutation, inasmuch as, from scientist he becomes a writer, thanks, if I dare say it, to the infernal experience of which he was the subject, the witness, and the result: an Auschwitz survivor. His learned scientific intelligence became literary; a metamorphosis which is reflected in his speaking mirror (I am making an allusion here to the stories and fables of his *Mirror Maker*)—and which we might call Kafkaesque, if he hadn't told us about his indifference to Kafka.

Here is what he says of the scientist's science:

> It tries to purify [facts] of all emotional ingredients and to free itself from false memories and hallucinations; it avoids wasting time in explaining phenomena whose existence is dubious, but it builds for itself year after year, its own mental and private museum in which, for future memory, are a number of indubitable facts that science does not know how to explain. I have never been a physicist, but I have not forgotten thirty years of militancy in minor chemistry, and my private museum is not mental but material.[11]

Primo Levi crosses the barrier of genres (heterogeneity), bringing over to the side of art (literature) his scientific know-how and way of looking in order to serve the intelligence of his time (ours) in the frightful conditions of the bath into which he was thrown, which gave him the authentic mark of a witness's immersion and which he has related *objectively*.

As a writer he does not leave behind the scientific *êthos* but treats the phenomena of the new referential (Auschwitz), the inhumanity of which demands to be observed coldly, with the exactitude of an experimental protocol. Science and literature pass into one another. The scientist becomes a writer; the writer guards memory; and if he was able "himself" to survive, it is as a scientist, tossed into the experience and the experiment of his mutation. A strange, sharp cold that is not the cold of irony. From what Archimedean point of the spirit does he speak, a point of view that is not that of Sirius, nor of the Huron, nor that of the mystic, but from whence science keeps watch and keeps watch upon itself and judges while explaining? A fixed point, perhaps, but not out of the world; rather, at once of this world, the world of humans, and of the universe within that world, which is "physical." Two referential systems in one for the point of generalized relativity, the system of human habits and that of non-human regularities. Putting them into apposition, decanting them with precaution, comparing them and translating them into one another.

In Primo Levi's book, one may read a kind of fable, which is at the same time an observation; a fable of the tadpole changed into a frog, which I take as a portrait of Levi's own mutation. He is himself the chimera that fascinates him; a chemist or a "naturalist" changed into a writer, in the physical conditions of the infernal laboratory. His *testimony* gathers, matches up, and rigs out childhood stories; literary criticism, fables, memories of the House of the Dead. He "makes his mirror." Imitating this tone, perception and heart, in the service of the phenomenal that is our human sojourn, visible and moral; being capable of that tone would be to become a wise knower: a *sophos*.

In a certain manner *charity*, too, has mutated "exponentially" along with the destructive forces. I can blow up my neighborhood, my city, and the world, by arming my madness with an "absolute weapon" produced by a thousand years of techno-science, "miniaturized" today; antithetically, but from the same causes, "we" can save one hundred thousand famine victims thanks to "scientific progress" and to the "humanitarian" organization of the world. But charity is not "good will" (Kant). Thinking the consciousness of the difference between good and evil from the perspective of art, or, to say it with an example, if I wonder with Apollinaire how to explore and show the "enormous country" of silent goodness, I know that I cannot educate my city, my country, my fellow-speakers of a language to beauty and truth by putting before their ears and their eyes a beautiful work; it is as though the latter had no power of exemplarity that would be proportionate to the task. All the more so because the opinion of the "modern public" believes that it is a matter of doing "just as well" (rivaling the "creative" force of an exceptional artist; *anch' io . . .* ; I will show them that I can "express myself," etc.). Rather than admiring the thing and the things, interested in the finger rather than the moon; interested in the artist's hand rather than in the objectivity of the work, as beautiful as the world, without an author.

Nietzsche said that we had to speak low in order to be heard: he is wrong. The admirable whispering of thought silences nothing, is without effect on the unfolding of events in the world. And Beckett's *Worstwards* ["Worstwards, Ho!" in *Nohow On*], which accompanies this race, at worst does not modify it. The mass spectacles and the great mediatized circus orchestrate violence mimetically, hoping perhaps to paralyze it like Medusa. It is murder that paralyzes us and which recruits us into the tragedy.

"Reason, art, poetry do not help us decipher the place from which they have been banned. In the everyday life of 'over there,' made of a dispatch enhanced by horrors, it was salutary to forget about them, just as it was healthy to learn to forget home and family." (Primo Levi)

Literature and evil—how can we look again at this question in the light of Primo Levi? Shouldn't the ambition of writing a book in the West now be measured by the testimony of Primo Levi, a touchstone that would make the sound of stupidity ring out from so many writings?

The knowledge of evil, essentially distinct from science (B. Muller-Hill)[12] and essential to the survival of "humanity" cries out to be taught. This is the role of literature. Yet literature, except for "great literature," does not do it, and what we take for "literature" today in the culture called mass, given over to cinema and the audiovisual, shows indifference to this problematic, and shows amnesia, distaste or hostility toward it. Speaking of that, and of Liliana Cavani and of one of her films, "beautiful and false at the same time," Primo Levi writes: "This is not virgin territory, it is, quite the contrary, an awkwardly laboured field, trampled upon and turned over. . . . I'm not competent when it comes to the unconscious and to its depths, but I know that a small number of people know about those things and I know that this small number is more prudent [than Liliana Cavani]."

Ordinarily, mild manners prevail; I mean that an acceptable society puts humans, fellow-citizens, into a situation where compassion and empathy must prevail, and must make the norms; society should draw on the best and not the worst, that is the criterion of a civilized society. Prevail over what? Over complicity; complicity or belonging a priori to the indifference of good and evil (or the suspension of ethical judgment). Complicity, this congenital "empirical character" is congenital if each one of us is firstly *complicit* with the group to which he or she belongs, "my crowd," "us guys," and so is like a mafioso through culture. Complicity is the root of racism in today's very generalized sense (anti-old, anti-young, anti-women, etc.); it creates a state that is as far as can be from a state of innocence, the "intelligible character" of which will need to be demonstrated again. Culture, and its "cultural," will have to be called into question again, right to the very root. The strange expression of "naturalization" reveals the *doxa*: culture tries to pass itself off as a nature. There is an urgency to bring a spiritual, intellectual knife-edge to bear on nature and culture, in the very place and time where, confusedly, chaotically, each of them has passed into the other. It is urgent to speak again of a "human nature" severed from any and all culture.

If "ecology" is the *-logy* that worries about the "survival" of humanity, then, as a human "ethology," it should take up and direct ethics and proceed with a radical critique of "The Cultural."

The relation of literature to the good is henceforth to "defend and illustrate" [Du Bellay]. Teaching the literature of masterpieces in order to teach *what* literature teaches: how do we teach that?

THE COMMON NOTHING[13]

Marcel Gauchet has seen it well: the alliance, the alloy—yes we're in concreteness here—of the neo-individual and his clannish community, of something matricial-fusional with something of the minority, the flip side of which is the vernacular revulsion (natural-cultural) of one "ethnicity" for another; the eternal xenophobia, for which the other is non-human. Hereditary vengeance is like a torture in the hells of antiquity. The Revolution (the French one) turns its back on all of this with its resolution of universality. The universal is constructed abstract space, the secular space of separation. The empty space of fraternity, somewhere between the compassion for those who are near and dear and the indifference or the suspicion with regard to those who are distant. The unemotional space of humanity's recognition. The exact opposite of Nazism, it is the decision to include, a decision that is perhaps identical with non-violence. The content of the universal is determined by the revolutionary motto. I enjoy reading the latter as a sequence of implications: liberty (the freedom by which what I do does not harm others) requires equality (Sartre: there is no liberty as long as one—who is another—is subjugated). The case of equality, which is not geometric because by "nature" we are unequal, is only possible among "brothers." The question is: how and through what are we brothers? What does that mean, since we are not all brothers by our biological lineages?

What the Separation of 1905 was separating and what needs to be separated today, namely the combatants, are not the same things: can the term and the concept of separation nevertheless be useful again?[14]

The secular motive of separation implied the installation of a *no-god's-land* [in English in the original] between the intimacy of the private conviction of believers and the places of worship of the "sacred" and divine domain. Can this motif be transposed to the separation of enemies: to that of a truce? Enough, please, time for a truce-of-the-gods! That would be a cry of fatigue. Let us attempt something-among-humans! Now just as any effective separation, "in the real," as common sense has it, will imply an intellectual discernment that first operates on the distinguishing of entities (in the way that thought, having been able to distinguish powers, could manage their separation and manage to project that spacing out from the sites where each could be exercised), what essential distinction demands then to be analyzed now, in order to be "practiced"?

Humans are mortals, enemies, brothers. Enemies of their mortal brothers; brothers of their mortal enemies; mortals for being enemy brothers? . . . Mortality, enmity, fraternity, are those the three decisive traits which must be analyzed, disconnected and composed, perhaps opposed as complementary adverse polarities which thought, following the method sketched out above, seeking axial contrariety ("harmony of opposites"), might paradoxically bring to a paroxysm?

We say of parts that they are *integral*. What then is the *whole*, integral and with integrity, of a human integrality that does not consist of irreducible, hostile particularities, so repugnant among themselves that they cannot enter into composition? In what do they consist? In "nothing." It is in being nothing that I belong to the whole. Not unlike Rousseau, thinking how the heterogeneous particular passions would cancel one another out, "Reason" surging up from such a reciprocal canceling-out, this is the marvelous resultant, that of a common part that is separated out, which then may stand for the sought-after rational whole. But it has no content. What results, the "product" of the operation, is *nothing*.

There is only the nothing-in-common to unite us. We identify ourselves through negation; through privation (effective subtraction, withdrawal, retraction: *abdication*) of any predicate that had been prejudged to be "the same."

Socrates's privative operation seeks the passage (to the other; or toward the other) through negation: knowing that I know nothing. He wants to bring others to this. There. If they were to profess it, they could unite around it.

There: at this point where and from whence I know that I know not; nothing. The only *common* point; the "general point" of our union. That of a being-together, then, in a common-unity, a community [*comme-unité*] where nothing in *particular* would separate us. This is the absolute point from which any one of us can judge himself or herself, just by hollowing ourselves out. Coming to nullity; null and valid [*nul et advenu*]; common sense. . . . The passage from I know nothing to I-am- . . . nothing? It is this extreme point, the eye of the needle, where, if, as null as I may be, I can judge that I am null. I know myself. I know that I know nothing and hence am nothing—nothing but a being in I-am (*sum*).

This is not a moral judgment that evaluates qualities and, with modesty, judges itself and knows itself "a being worth all others" (Sartre).

God distinguished us: the good on the right, the evil on the left. But it is no longer God's Last Judgment that counts. It is the judgment of humanity about humans.

Here's a question: is this the same "metaphysical" point, that of common sense in Descartes, the point expressed as neither-neither-neither by Saint Paul (neither man nor woman nor Jew nor Roman, etc.), the point of nudity with Saint Francis of Assisi; that point from whence speak Sartre or Genet ("anyone at all . . .")?

Is this the point from whence the poem may be read: outside humanity? The point from whence the poet speaks, when, *dividing* humanity in two, "those who believed in heaven/those who did not," (Eluard, "*Les Yeux d'Elsa*") he occupies then a terrestrial u-topian balcony, neither on one side nor on the other, the point *for which* humanity comes apart from itself, a disjoined whole.

THE REPROACH MADE TO KANT

Separating the combatants: does this open up the space of separation which no longer lies *between* "communities"? And indeed, which concept are we talking about—will the universal forever be too abstract?

How can we make more room for it again? To whom is the secular "message" destined, addressed? Who is the *subject* of the spirit of secularity? Is it the "brother"? Human brothers who *with us* are living. . . . *Mon semblable*, said the poet; but how are we *alike*, in and through what are we fellows?

Don't the worry and the destination or goal, both of them "fraternal," cross too quickly and too lightly over the intermediary zone of an "us," the generality of the particularity of a group, certainly out beyond "individual egotism," but falling somewhere short of a generosity that is too quickly invoked? Is there an intermediate order of magnitude between group belonging (the "roots") and the "human race"? Could this be the nation? Is the nation an "us" on another scale than that of the community; a median and mediating identity, to be reconstructed for and by a common reason?

Let us listen to the reproach made to Kant.

The question is this: doesn't the universal or the stripped-down character of my "maxim," which makes it apt for universalization, leap beyond the intermediate levels of generalities (particularities) that are given? Doesn't the Humanity of the Rights of Man overstep too quickly the given, historical humanities?

Not to forget the heterogeneity of the orders of magnitude. In this case, it is the difference of scale between the order of subjective singularity and the order of the Great Numbers. The incommensurability of these "scales" is manifested as follows. On the scale of ego ("solipsistic"), change for the best ("wisdom" through *metanoia*) is 1) brusque and sudden, coming in a single stroke (conversion); 2) nonmaterial: it is this change "in the head" (mental, moral, spiritual, however we want to say it) that counts. On the scale of social being and of humanity, the change is 1) progressive (there is indefinite "progress") and 2) there is only material change (in "living standards"), a change that has an empirical reality. Collective man is *produced* (by material conditions, or, if you prefer, the dialectic of his struggle with material conditions).

Let us return to the difficulty: on the one hand, it is best not to forget the Kantian imperative which is to not break the link between the end and the means, their articulation, in order that "always at the same time" (Kant, Second Critique), the end will be moving in the means and animating them, lending to them their essence as means-of-the-end, or *measures* of the desirable and the wanted.

But, on the other hand, the passage from the singular to the universal is not that from the particular to the general: moral universalization ("practical reason") carries with it an illusion. We take it as true that passing through the first categorical imperative, a step that verifies the conformity *without contradiction* of my maxim to its universalization (the *id est* that is not to cause that with which it is concerned to *disappear*), is moral, as a relation of freedom to the good, *formally* through good will, which ensures that freedom is not pursuing its own interest). If that passage is a moral one, the operation does not cooperate in the construction of a better world for many and for all, nor does it guarantee a step toward that goal. Nothing ensures that what is morally good in the universal would have to be good for *one* multiple (a subset, a "world" in the universe, a nation, an ethnicity), in the other sense of good-for, its material meaning.

The Kantian springboard of universalization implies a leap (*Ratio facit saltus* [reason makes leaps; Leibniz: *natura non facit saltum*]) from the scale of what is good-for-my-conscience to the scale of what is good-for-all. This leap is a transformation, an immediate passage from micro to macro, one that would be plain for all to see. As if human rights, the rights of this human and of any and all humans (these are as *undivided* as the *ousia prote* and the *ousia deutera* in Aristotle [first and second substance]), in their "proclamation" as human rights, could *not* hit an empirical wall (as we speak of the wall of sound): the Wall of large numbers (cf. Canetti's *Mass*), or the Wall consisting of the plurality of human worlds (we say "cultures" today), of "humanities." Reason comes up hard against identity. Using neighboring terminology we can say: the scale that is intermediate between the ego-atom and Humanity, that of a nature defined anthropologically (that is to say in animal terms), is neglected by Kantian reason. The vernacular (or "cultural") (from the familial to the clannish, the ethnic, the national), in other words the sum of lived experience, is bypassed in one stroke. Two men (Shylock and his judge; or two contemporaries of Sartre in the Nothingness which they have in common) can actually meet *within* Humanity, but two "tribes," two peoples on the earth cannot. . . . Unless they are shown that it is the *same* earth; and that is why ecology is the future. Ecology properly understood, that is to say non-utopian, is just the opposite of the return to nature. Ecology is anti-Rousseauian. That of which it speaks is neither good nor evil. It speaks of the exhausted earth, seeking a relation with that earth.

"MINIMA MORALIA"[15]

Yes, Kantian, because of *respect*. (The only moral sentiment, says he: reason makes itself "respected" even by our very "pathological" nature.)

I am going to say two or three things about respect that may not be well calibrated among themselves. It is a value, as our contemporaries like to say, which seems to be the source of other values, and which operates their division; it opens up the originary difference between what is of some worth and what is worth less, or even worth less than nothing. Respect would be the principle of differentiation itself. Like olfaction that immediately distinguishes and separates what is good and bad for it, respect has a good nose, it sniffs things out. Yet respect can be educated, the sense of smell hardly at all. One takes it "absolutely," as though its correlatives were secondary; as though it were not posterior to values that could "force" it; in Kantian terms, not a posteriori but a priori. But how can something that has no experience be "formed"; through what "epigenesis"? Auto-revelation favored by experience? That's easy to say. And the heteronyms of "respectable" are so numerous (except for Kant, obviously), moral law, reason, life, humanity, and so on; the faces that it turns toward being and beings are so diverse (admiration, attachment, all the way up to "tolerance"), that we may ask ourselves if it is always really a matter of respect.

Each time it considers and bows.

I will look to Pascal for help in finding a way out of this. There are three orders of greatness, say the *Pensées*: of material establishment (or the flesh); of mind; of charity. And what is visible in one order of grandeur is not in the other, nor for the other. What "leaps out" at mind doesn't shine forth for the eyes of the flesh nor does it exist (we would say) for holiness. Let us say that respect learns discernment, cutting across all the orders, changing its level and scale (a scale of "value" precisely, not a metrical one); and it can learn how to discover that which is hidden from it in one sphere in yet *another sphere*; through analogies, then. Respect suspects that a greatness of another order may be hiding in what is "unapparent," in its "air of nothing," like Demeter, secret at the hearth of Celeos. *Attention*, said Pascal and Simone Weil.

LOGIC OF DOUBLE NEGATION
OR
OF NONMATHEMATICAL, PARADOXICAL APODICTICITY

Here is an axiom of reasonable reason: it is reasonable to hold as unreasonable the hope of getting along; or: it is unreasonable to hold as reasonable the hope of getting along.

The god-who-might-save-us[16] would be none other than the logical power of paradox. A god speaking in oracles ("revelation"). The character of the oracle is, and has forever been, its "ambivalence" (cf. Plutarch); its intimate ambiguity or intimate contrariety. The latter does not come from a pleasant grammatical equivocalness such as the one that introduces the Latin infinitive proposition that is as reversible as a pancake, depending on whether the syntagmas in the accusative exchange their position and their role as subject or transitive object. It comes instead from a logic of reversibility, of "carnavalesque" balance, of the overturning of meaning, of intrinsic undecidability. Or, let's say, it is time to leave the pleasant level, or even the level of pleasantries, moving from grammatical cleverness to the interpretation of the looping of sense in its two senses, its two ends, or paradoxicality. Paradox and oracle are one and the same power.

An oracle is a word, an axiom that would say at the same time as its utterance how it is that the *manner of saying* constitutes the tenor of wisdom, the salutary character of what is said. "Soteriological" salvation would be nothing other than wisdom—wisdom lying in the "content" of the oracle that is more or less esoteric, that is nothing other than its ability to contain and to carry meaning. Its secret derives from the very form of speaking as oracle, potentially and in the given case, paradoxically. Theory and practice find themselves imbricated, undivided, paradoxical. Practice, or effective wisdom, is to think as the sounding of the oracle urges us to think—namely, "paradoxically."

Contrariety, the internal movement of meaning which consists of saying "one thing and its opposite" in a loop, a negation and the negation of the negation, and then, in its turn, this negation of the negation swings over into the negation of the negation of the negation itself (as when we entertain ourselves by unfolding, aloud, the indefinite paraphrase, rolled up upon itself, in Epimenides' paradox: 1) A Cretan says that all Cretans . . . 2) so he is lying, 3) so it is not true that all Cretans are liars, 4) therefore he may tell the truth by saying that 1), and so on).

In such a contrary, confounding, regime, the circularity of the two poles in the polarity rolls thought back onto itself, like a wheel of fortune at the fair. In such a way that the movement of swinging back and forth and of turning upside down, balanced by the successive alternation of the low becoming the high and the high becoming the low (or the alternation of right and left, if we set the game up on a horizontal plane) ensures the performance of the set and thus its very tenor.

From another angle: no assertoric proposition (simply affirmative or negative, of the kind "it's raining" or "Bolivia has no access to the Ocean" or "Allah is great") is the solution.

To the questions that we call philosophical questions, there is no simple solution; their solution, which is explication, the deployment of their problematic or aporetic, is an oracular answer in a double negation. Put another way, apodicity in vernacular thought, in words of human speech (*logon echôn*)—if thought is the *adoptive* daughter of mother tongues—consists of gaining the form, "it is impossible *that not*:" a double negation to the power of which Mallarmé carried his poem and his poetry, substituting, for example, the "ecstatic impotence to disappear" of the dancer for the report of apparition ("you appeared laughing to me"). The dancer cannot make an appearance, neither a (simple) woman nor a (simple) dancer, but a "metaphor," and so on; nor a white water lily, they cannot not show through, *appear-across* [*transparaître*].

Simple, blind faith believes that there is an emergency exit at the end of the impasse—or hidden somewhere on the shoulders of the dead-end road. But adult thought that measures the diametrical opposition, as we say, or the diameter of oppositeness (*anthropos* parametron *panton*, of old Protagoras [man is the *measure* of all things]), knows, learns to know, about a knowledge of wisdom, learns to know that no abracadabra nor trumpet of Jericho, not even a modern ideological revolutionary injunction, can knock down the walls. We only get out of the cavernous impasse, said Plato, by being untied (by whom, by what, how, that is the question) in order to come out into the light of day of this lowly world. If there were an exit at the end of the dead end we would know about it, for the one hundred thousand years there have been humans who . . . , etc. Therefore it is a matter of holding together, originally, what has already been thought and said. Vernacular demonstration can achieve its apodicticity, but nonmathematically. That is to say, in the logic of the logion (of *logos*), thus in the phrased form of "It cannot happen that not:" a double negation that revolves upon itself, as Camus's Sisyphus knew in his own way. A sphinx-thought born again from its ashes, that is to say, such that two paradoxes (themselves in a double negation) are relayed, each one getting back on its feet thanks to the possibility–impossibility of the other. Double-bind. Apodictical is the paradox; it revolves upon itself, reestablishing itself by going back on everything.

"Reason" is such that its intimate contrariety makes it oscillate. Thought must work at it; spiritual exercises: for example, "the dead end is the way out." It is a matter of developing, unfolding the two sides of such thought 1) the way out is through the summit; 2) the summit has no way out. Or: deepening the impasse (like a tunnel's back wall which I push back by digging), *that* is *opening up a way*; the way gives onto the way. Tao.

A task: to invent "sublime" paradoxes.

III

SIMONE WEIL FROM MEMORY*

*MD note. The first state of these pages was for Alain Finkielkraut in no. 6 of his *Messager européen*. Published in 1992, it is anachronistic, "running late," with relation to the considerable aggravations that may be noted in the first two parts of this volume. Don't bother repeating it? But I want people to read the preparations for the more elaborate palinody that is ripening in it. Why not put it at the front of the book, then, out of concern for chronology? But I want the reader to dive *in media res*, not into memory but into the current effervescence (2002).

LIFE AND DEATH

You have to imagine those young people in their gray smocks, in the gray morning of the rue Saint-Jacques, through the high windows of *Louis-le-Grand*, translating or reciting *The Odyssey* [11.489]: "*mallon k'éparouros ôn. . . .*" Violence against children, opine today's Education Studies. . . . Probably, and it was a violence that prepared the relation we called a relation of culture to the "gentle columns" lying near the river of Arcadia a few years later or the tender recognition of the Panethenaeans in profile in London, and which linked our generation to that of Simone Weil, in the sharing of the sources—Greek, Biblical, Latin . . .

More than a half-century ago, Simone Weil was to die in London without having known the *liberation* for which, at the request of Marcel Schumann, like her a pupil of Alain, and who directed General de Gaulle's press service, she had written the report published under the title of *L'Enracinement* [The Need For Roots]. Camus would found the collection "*L'Espoir*" in 1949 in order to make Simone Weil's thought known, and that is how the *khâgneux* in their *classes préparatoires* and those studying for their *agrégation* examinations in the 1950s came to discover the work and the legend of the Jewish Antigone.

She had a considerable influence on "us"—that is to say on a part of the philosophical generation of the post-war—a considerable influence that neither my own infidelity to her thought, a rigorous and resolute palinody of whose movement I will tell, nor the ill-motivated and semi-competent suspicion of journalistic intellectuals who would like to repeat with her the coup of defamatory rumor they pulled on Péguy (Pétainiste Beauce, etc.), will prevent me from retracing. The journalistic suspicion would be fed, in this case, by her publisher Gustave Thibon's reputation as a happy rightwing laborer, and even by the later, Heideggerian, connotation of rootedness (*Boden, Blut*), or nourished by the nunnish side of Weil (sister of charity, of virginity), an upside-down caricature of her mysticism, fabricated in order to discredit this pure and excessive life work.

That is why I begin here with an anachronistic portrait of Simone Weil, mixing and overlaying the traits seen by our admiration and our assiduity of the 1950s (at that age when we like to push our need for illustrious models to a hyperbolic veneration of the extraordinary) and the reformed and deformed traits seen from within that long aftershock in which I am still writing. I write in respect and recognition of her teaching, turned toward that ante-purgatory of the non-baptized "pre-Christians," wherein she inscribed her desire. Despite her, I believe, I mean despite the entirety of her being, her henological passion ("truth is one"), the monomanias of her integrity, the violent and passionate economy without concession of her engagements, my respect and recognition collect her, draw her together like a figure of contradiction, a torn-apart sign of tension, an unliveable hesitation at a threshold, and, yes, a figure of compromise, that is to say of the simultaneity of a yes and of a no: yes ("Christ took me"), and, no, I will not join the Christian community of the baptized.

Of what would this portrait be made?

The legend of her life—of one who was almost alone against almost all—that we, future academics, threatened by grayness and myopia, need to fictionalize as a reality going beyond the real, the horizon of something unequalable and the lesson for our courage of something not-in-vain—reported her irreducible spirit of discernment of the worst, of judgment, of prophecy and resistance: no to blind pacifism before the nascent monster of Nazism; no to the ideological idolatry of revolution, blind to Bolchevism and to Stalinism; no to the sated blindness of the ownership class, dominating, subjecting—no to the power of money, of error and lies, of conformism and cynicism.

I will only make rapid allusion to the feats of arms and of justice, to the behaviors and engagements of Simone Weil which are well known and available in the published documents that await, every new school year, new waves of young readers (?); to her struggle alongside the Spanish Republicans; to her "establishment" with Renault as an intellectual worker; to her constant preference for the powerless, the damned of the earth, for the insubordination of the subordinate. The sense of Justice, yes in capital letters, that is to say, not merely irreducible to the way that Justice is done, to the way that injustice reigns, but rather a sense of Justice sharpened up again, reaffirmed, redefined everywhere that it is losing. This is to say, Justice as a "discernible" idea, resurrected from the carnage of the balances of power into which it sinks, giving to determining judgment, to vigilant jurisprudence encumbered by so many unsolvable cases, enough to start up a thousand Dreyfus affairs per year (per day?) and to propose reasonable and impossible to apply sentences.

OF PURITY

How—without even being able to recall the multiplicity of the sources where her lucidity was educated—the Greek source burbling in "*The Iliad, Poem of Force*," in Antigone or in the stoic hymns; the biblical source, where the "winners' version" cannot manage to black out the "supernatural," the evangelical source of the Our Father—how to seek to condense in one formula that coincides with her trait, her tracing, her discerning surging-forth, the source of all sources; "from whence" does the elucidating lightning flash come?

There are terms, "vocables" (but what do we call them, that is precisely the question) that are not concepts but that play a decisive role in thought—words, perhaps, then, passwords, big words, whose function resembles that of "proper nouns" in their denotative value, but without the denoted "thing" being perceptively referenceable, words that are not, for all of that, simple *flatus vocis*, conscious "nominalist" convention, nor magic formulas evoking an "entity" for a superstitious mentality ("dormitive virtue," and the like).

In and for Simone Weil, PURE is one of those words. The pages of *The Need for Roots* mention it relentlessly.[1] And discernment is the discernment of purity. Such a vocable probably "refers" to something, but to an experience that is not shareable in the way that a percept, an event, an experience seeking to be precisely communicated and to persuade are shareable . . . through the reiteration of the word.

The experience that is Simone Weil's is that of the purification of the pure; of the separation of the pure and the impure. How to untangle the purely good, the purely beautiful, the purely true from the rest?

The experience of this difference furnishes thought with its goldminer's classifier screen, a critical analytics that must divide out; trenchant, differenciating thought, for which the sentence is the sharpened, acerated blade, it will go anywhere to remake difference—separating the pure from the impure. On the one hand, "the world," on the other, "that which is beyond the heavens." Gravity—grace; force—that which "comes from elsewhere." The *reign* of necessity—the realm which is "not of this world." A *miracle* (a Greek one, eg) is that of the apparition of that Other in this world.

A sequence that is at the same time discontinuous, rare and indestructible, recurrent, attests to the reality of the other order: Sophocles, Jesus, Francis of Assisi, Joan of Arc. . . . It would not be difficult to pick out the names, not very numerous, of these witnesses, who are not all Westerners either, of course. Is it a dualism? Or a "monistic parallelism"? The two realities are homologous in that the two laws are . . . from the same "legality," coming out of the same essence of "Law." One of the consequences of this radically metaphysical parallelism (Platonic)—whose parallels meet and touch from time to time, if I dare say, and the points of historical tangency are named with the name of "saints," in whom the two natures meet—is that the regime of Weilean thought is metaphorical, analogical[2]: the difference of the two regimes in general condemns thought to speak of the transactions, the exchanges, the (dis)similarities between the two realities. Only a materialist monism, if that were possible, could forbid such a circulation, disqualifying vernacular thought too.

ATTENTION

This trait is common to Pascal, Malebranche, and Simone Weil: attention to attention, "prayer of the soul," which is the virtue of virtues. The relationship of Simone Weil and of Pascal is flagrant, multiple, and would merit a detailed examination. Learning to think and to work at thinking well is an injunction common to the two of them. *Writing* has no price for Simone Weil unless its care exercises the virtue of attention: the writer implores us to pay attention. Attention is attention to the other; to pay attention is to come out of the self. *Epochê*, self-limitation, on principle. And the most other is named God in their language. Obedience is the human response to the divine kenosis. And if, quickly anticipating a conclusion, I pass from Simone Weil to Hannah Arendt (as indeed I did encounter them, read them, and love their works, in that order), I remark that what is for one the supreme value, "obedience," is, for the other, a child's and not an adult's virtue.

Discernment among things, judgment in particular cases, these may be educated and refined through attention to language, to phrases. Simone Weil tells somewhere of her admiration for the Curé d'Ars, an illiterate peasant who had to take up sacerdotal Latin and who gave such an effort, with all his soul, to its study that by a "mysterious transfer," he became capable of paying attention to souls and learned how to listen "in confession" to thousands of hearts. But what is such a "transfer"? To believe in such a capacity is to believe that the sphere of the soul is at once thoroughgoingly natural, as a psychic mechanism, a site of necessity (force, movement, "psychic laws" . . .) and therefore undivided from the sphere of "gravity," and, at the same time, entirely other, as spiritual, as "grace," a welcoming of "God," "supernatural and eternal." We might say, in the same way that the profane is . . . profane *and* sacred. Simone Weil hates nothing so much as the "orthodoxy" that separates them (cf. the end of *The Need for Roots*).

Identity of Same and Other? Is this Gnosticism, a species of dualistic monism? It is the strange, feverish, violent movement of Weilian thought, in no way dialectical, which, from one extremity to the other will sometimes separate the two poles, and sometimes bring them undividedly together.

I will return to attention: it is the condition of critique and of the power (the obligation) *to decide*: it is cutting. Educated by and in the study of language, attention to masterpieces of literature and to their matter (language), a vigilance that hones itself within language "against" language, (objectification of stereotypes, of etymologies, thematization through references, quotations, etc.), that attention becomes a diacritical and a discriminatory power, a pure blade of the soul, capable of analyzing, distinguishing and separating the pure and the impure.

OF CONTRARIETY

In the tone of a testamentary axiomatics, the first part of *The Need for Roots* deploys the principles of Simone Weil's political thought—the theory and the articulation of theory with practice: a compendium of ontology, psychology, morality and sociology. It is a flaying alive of her thought that strips bare the logical nervures of her "theory," or the organ of the vision of things. Apodicticity uttered with the tone of assertorical evidence.

I would like to underline a few of its distinctive traits:

It is a matter of laying out, exhaustively, the "needs of the soul": in order to get oriented in this "very secret arcana" (we think of Kant's words about schematism). Heuristics does not take as a "common thread" some logical table of judgment. Its *logicity* rests instead on and within analogy.[3] It will go with the soul as it goes with the body. The unicity of being is double: its dual singularity.

Two predicates characterize essentially the being of *need* and allow for the determination, through analogical induction, of the hidden face, or "soul," of our being: 1) saturable limitation, and 2) contrariety: any need can be satisfied (unlike desire); and *needs* always come in "pairs of opposites" (the architectonics of non-deconstructible dyads).[4]

The general teleological perspective is that of *order* (which one comes first, at the top of the list?): in the end, it is a matter of disposing the conditions of realizability of a human order (social and political) *inspired* by the consideration of the natural order, the beauty of which we admire, the splendor of necessity, expressive as they are of an eternal Providence about which some Greek artists and thinkers (more so than the Bible) were able to speak, "while waiting for God."

The problematic is a Leibnizian one, that of the best of possible worlds: the optimum character of a social order is measured against the (effective, real) compatabilization of (com)possibles, that is to say, of intelligibles, called "needs," coessentials, and what is more, they contradict one another: the structure of the soul is contrariety.

The supernatural is *quasi*-natural. The coefficient of "as if" is not applied to the supernatural. At the bottom of Weilian belief, let us not forget, there is mystical experience, the certitude of "God." I will come back to this later to finish up.

Reason is not at all "dialectical": there is no order of time where the contradictions of Reason are revealed and set straight. The fixed order is that of non-dialectalizable opposites; neither are they mediatizable through a "golden mean." The impossibility of a concrete layout of their nonsynthetic composition is on the "political" program. Eternity is not accommodated.

The self-contradicting of the needs of the soul, which make up the concrete, human "reality," is more abyssal than simple contradiction. What is beautiful and poignant in this thought, in these classical propylaea of *The Need for Roots*, where the columns of Needs are aligned, is the unbending rectitude of this condemned Antigone staring down Death, the sun in her face, before walking backwards into the tomb. Who concedes nothing.

The definitive "contrariety" of our finite "nature" should be understood less as an unfortunate, infirm constitution than as a fecundity, a matrix and an inventivity, a richness, in the way that *crisis*, which passes, in the eyes of the optimist, for merely a nasty phase of things, took on in its original thinking (Hesiod) the meaning of the incessant and constitutive (re)distribution of human dividedness. Contrariety is such that its "paradox" should pass less for an embarrassment than for a springboard and a resource, in the way that a fable that is impossible to resolve will set off investigations and more literature; in that way, a logic proceeds from contrariety, a paradoxical logic, therefore, to which I return later.

AND TODAY

But for now I'm going to linger in our millenary situation: what would the admirable resistor say today, she to whom Alain (this is reported) said: "Simone! *Dim your lights!*" what would she say in this today which the "sickness of death" (Duras) is overtaking, this "crazy world of prisons" (Char), this world today that we would even speak of as drunk on its genocides; when the vernacular (Ilitch) collapses into cultural vulgarity, when the pleasure principle, the motor of the market economy (against the unlimited character of which Solzhenitsyn appealed for a principle of *auto*limitation[5]), individuates, by the hundreds of millions, people who are released from Weilean obligation, essentially delinquents, and unleashed for the terrestrial pillage, and whose subjectivity (at least in its psychological *for-itself* and in its fusional belonging to the "minority" collective, whether clannish or corporate) rises up in terms of rights—a right of priority that consists of accusing of arrogance anyone at all who does not recognize "my" right to arrogance. What would admirable Simone-in-revolt say, ever more foreign to the ultramodern revolting world [*l'im-monde ultramoderne*]?

And if ecology is philosophizable (I think that it is), I imagine Simone Weil interested in ecology, against economy. For the ecological principle (*Prinzip Hoffnung*[6]) appeals for a new separation (*crisis*; critique) of the human and the non-human; of what has become monstrous (the anthropomorph) and of the quasi-natural; for a moratorium of "autolimitation"[7] against the "headlong rush." Ecology declares a theoretical and practical war on "pollution." Now it is anthropomorphicism that pollutes: the human makes waste; its productions, now become excretions, cover up the earth; the humanoid is covering over everything, and its ideological and publicitary imagery, infantile and cretinizing, is that of "Disney."

The fresco of the *Deluge* for a contemporary Sixtine, if these things were conceivable, would attempt to show together the megalopolistic street-peoplization of misery, a band of painful shingles circling the hot earth, eater of its own waste, and all of this world that we call third dying of hunger on the laterite, eye-sockets full of flies turning their gaze toward the cameras of already-deterrestrated satellites, their gaze of incomprehension, and the trivial nihilism of consumers, the luxury conspiracy of grand and not-so-grand hotels where consumer society consumes the banquet of its apartheid, deepening the ditch that separates the victims, remaking the South everywhere, waving its handkerchief toward the shore of the poor which is unmoored, it is the same casting-off, and the immense delinquency, abandon of the abandoned ones, the banditry, ganglanditry, wandering in the generalized suburb, the suicidal massacre of fratricidal minorities and the anthropomorphic narcissism of the Disney sect.

"Purify"? A different sharing? As if a stoic "critique" could separate out once again what depends on us and what does not depend on us; as if man now become humanity were able to respect the non-human, to make some more of the non-human? But the impossibility of distinguishing any longer between the human and the "natural" (or a side that would not depend (too much) on us) creates the confusion of quarrels between ecological reason and scientific reason (if I leave aside the vain accusations made by each against the irrationality of the other); scientists against scientists; ecologists against ecologists.

The nature of the "contradiction" has changed. And we who are no longer reassured by the beautiful constructions of Hegel and Marx, those rational tamings of contradiction, we should set off again, "phenomenologically," in this inquiry, and begin by diagnosing, like doctors, the new maladies of contradiction that are spreading like those unpredictable viruses that explode in epidemics, renewing the great human plagues and disconcerting medicine . . . I am not talking about what the poet Nathaniel Tarn called "the beautiful contradictions" [in English in the original], about which the art of love and the love of art discussed and exchanged, but about broken-down collisions, amalgam-mixes of things repugnant amongst themselves—a recent example of which is Shiite fundamentalism putting a price on the head of Rushdie in the planetary Western, a price *in dollars*! It's the glue that has become powerful, not the synthesis. And if today art and waste have managed to come to grips and come to maneuvering with one another, in a strange kind of collaboration, it is not because a Franciscan love of the humble has come to reign. It is the glue, or technology, which can hold together "anything at all and its opposite," and we could show that the artifactual postmodern violence of the collage agglutinates sects like glue-débris, readymade: sects proliferate and hold together with and through the techniques of collage, to a high degree sectarian, and which discredit the nice, polite syncreticisms of yesteryear. It is no longer the possible which makes the real but the "technically achievable."

The problem is not a "world on its head" (Hegel, Marx) but inverted or specular worlds; worlds which flip around, every one being for itself the "model," and every other simply a reversed or perverted image: it is not a matter of other worlds or of "possible worlds," but of upside-down worlds sharing the world. "It is YOU who do everything backwards!" north–south; Arabs–Jews; blacks–whites; them–us; and so on. And the West has discovered with terror what it was to be a "heretic," to be "satanized," that is to say accused by the Inquisition, in this case put to death by Fundamentalism (the Rushdie affair; the declaration of a holy war by many Islamic terrorists), while a "new world order" is being worked out (at the United Nations), a common optic that would be imposed by the American Empire as being "right side up"—or Right—international Rights or Law redressing all of the "upside-downs" of all the others. In more familiar terms: our world is getting twisted; in being knitted together, and getting twisted, the knots of these internecine wars make for a worldwide *occlusion*: an absolute quarrel.

Is the quarrel "paradoxicalyzable"? Is contrariety in being and truth something we can take on, assuming responsibility, is it viable, can it be put into paradoxes that surmount manicheism—or rather, must they be paradoxes of the form "mortal illness"?

The task of thought is not simply to dismiss "dialectic" so as to endure the intrinsic contrariety of what is true, the direction in which the analysis of the "needs of the soul" engages us. Its task is to dig deeper into the paradoxical "stricture" of the true in all of its forms and to augment paradoxy in order to investigate its modes and types. By way of example, here are a few methodical exercises to train ourselves for paradoxy:

Example: "I scorn us for being scornful." Or: "to be scornful is scornful" . . . the only case of the validity (the value, the justice) of "scorn," is found by the subject in applying it to itself, the *sui*-reference, a non self-destructive pronominality, "non-*noo*degradable." "Scornfulness is scornful," this proposition (which may be similar to Lichtenberg's "knife without a handle"), somewhat vertiginous, does not create mere nonsense. The subject is revealed . . . on the condition of being *nothing*, and stripping away all predicates: the subject has passed over to the side of the *us*, we the contemptible, we who may be scorned. Intolerance for intolerance is not intolerance. An intolerance with no blade, lacking a handle, is not nothing from nothing: it is a sort of wisdom, instead, through privation of any content, the singularity with no particularity at that moment: that of *keeping nothing for oneself*. This turn (a full turn) of language, apparently self-effacing ("paradoxical," in effect) devastates everything, makes the void . . . or the subject. This is the case of stripping-down, of saintliness, and why would such ascesis, or "perfect" humility, require the u-topia of a God? We can do without God in being nothing.

"Spinoza has the pure gaze which allows him to have an overview of himself, and which contemplates the world as it would contemplate a god that he loves." Where did I read that?[8]

The *I* is that being that cannot not "follow the worst," even while "seeing the best," according to Ovid. That is what it is to be an *I*, double, then, "in the first person," insofar as the *I* is divided according to the destiny of the *meliora probare* against the *deteriora sequi*, while speaking to itself about just that, that is to say seeking an overview of its own scission. Crack and recrack, flaw, schize of the *I*: the same one, doubled-up, which never makes a mistake (Pascal) when it "objectively" or "universally" takes a position overlooking all things, all the while attaching itself to the worst as an individual singularity.

A "subject" is capable of that scission, of that duplicity, of that withdrawal [*retrait*] of the self, of that ascesis. But what about *us*? What about the collective subject? That is most difficult—for a clan, an ethnicity, a nation.

Contemplating again, then, at this point, Solzhenitsyn's famous principle of self-limitation, I will say, and let him remind us, that there is a possibility (in principle) for good imitation ("after you"; "oh, I couldn't" . . . or a maxim of courtesy), which sets off good imitation, propagating the right composure of self-control, well before the voracity which wants "the same thing, and serve me first!"—and I will add that this movement is the most difficult one for a community, a set, as if there was nothing between expansion (Thucydides) and collective suicide.

OF THE DOUBLE-BIND

Of course, the poster "NO POSTERS" posted in the window to protect it from postering disfigures the window while "contradicting" itself. Nevertheless, analysis cannot content itself with maliciously remarking upon the "double-constraint," an analysis that would only be semi-competent. For the proscription does not completely close off the window, or the wall, in being the first to contravene its own injunction: so it is at least partially functional.

"Denegation"—one of the exercises of paradoxy—is to be rehabilitated, if we may say so: a resource that offers unconsciousness to consciousness.

One of the means is offered by "preciousness," which sharpens up the extremities of the bow and holds them together ("sym-bolically," then, if we hear the etymology) in the hypertension of oxymoronic formulation: the hyperbole of contrariety memorizes for thought (memory of hyperbole, I would say, then, to take up Mallarmé's formula from the other end ["Hyperbole! of my memory" "*Prose pour des Esseintes*"]) its own hard Heraclitean condition. It is the same for antiphrase or irony or any other manner of drawing from rhetoric the means of the wisdom that rhetoric refines, which are means of holding together, copresent, through and for thought, both the theoretical contrariety of adverse compossibles (here, "the needs") and the "practical" value of making them compatible. The Leibnizean god, hub of the solar wheel, of antithetical maxima that are realized, represents fairly well the reasonable program of an anthropodicea. Only the oxymoron can tell about a single and Same (eg, love) in itself thwarted, frustrated, countered, only the oxymoron can tell of its insupportable tension, the rending, devastating life of relation. Only the paradoxical oxymoron can tell of that for which there is no resolution, no surpassing, no relief; that is to say, only logical truth (thought grasping itself in the word) procures, if not a calming-down, at least a kind of calm desolation: that of someone dying at peace with knowledge.

Self-contradicting, or the "reversal of for and against," formally regulates the passage from theory (which can simultaneously see the opposites) to practice—the sequential linearity of which cannot allow the two to happen "at once." There is no continuity, no simple passage (*poros*) from one to the other. *Ratio facit saltus*. The system of couples of matching opposites does not allow itself to be exhaustively described once and for all, nor hierarchized, nor invented: its set has the contingency of a "human nature" of "needs."

This is a reason not to flee the "political," but instead to attempt to envisage it "paradoxically," in the judgment or the discernment that considers the possibility of the task, and considers the decision that determines an emergency strategy to match up the extremes.

Now if there is not some liaison (affinity and consequence), some link between the political, the juridico-ethical and morality, then no law will be able to *obligate* the citizen, who is the same as the moral subject.

The arbitrariness of exception or privilege (the ferment of *corruption*, well ahead of the temptation of money) dissolves in the acid of furious reactions against the unjustifiable, and destroys this implicit consent that supports any order, which cannot be submitted to unless it is accepted. Only exemplarity can stop corruption in its tracks.

We know that perhaps the only utterance common to the two Simones (Weil and de Beauvoir) will have been, "truth is one, error is multiple." I would willingly reverse this proposition, on behalf of our aporetic times: error is one, truth is multiple.

Error is identitary, realistic, substantialist, literalist, fundamentalist, fanatical. Truth is confounded, frustrated; put another way, wisdom has no content, she "adheres" to nothing, Valéry might have said [only idiots and oysters 'adhere'—remark ascribed to Paul Valéry]. Truth is of pure form: gathering the *homo*logic of the "*-logies*."

Said in another manner, the measure of the United Nations is not given apart from itself. There is proportion, relation, some "affinity of the diverse," an assessment or estimate that gets invented in life, in the "course" of a lifetime, commensurate with a task, with a body of work. The taste for unity works away in the common, the comm-*one* [*comm'un*], which is superstitious of no idol of the one.

The truth of truth? What to do with the redoubled blow of this formula, genitive, transitive, tautological? Climbing up on itself in order to surmount and free itself from what subjugates it to the needing-to-be-right of the will to power; its reiteration has no merit except to suggest that it is through an operation of *bootstrapping*, a process of raising to the second power, a process of regenerate auto-engendering, of self-deepening whereby the formal power of reflection gets marked out and an opening toward the heights gets *opened up*, as we say. This is an operation wherein the "notion" of truth is transformed, delivering itself from all dogmatic, empirical, content. Truth is only one if it is no longer determined in a possible, limited, "exact" truth.

The thought which identifies in "God" the identity of the One (God is One) and of the absolutely Other (the "abstruse" alterity of God), the thought taken in this identity of identity and of non-identity, vibrates from one extreme to the other, from the refusal of all that is ("the world") to the acceptance of what is, taken as a sign, *analogon*, of that which is "beyond the heaven." Belief in the otherness of the provenance of the "supernatural" leads us to think that there would be nothing perfect in this world of imperfection but the perfect refusal of its law (Antigone).

And so a thing, one same thing, let's say—to take an example—voluntary servitude ("obedience," she was saying a moment ago), an enigma for La Boétie, becomes saintliness for Simone Weil. And, certainly, no one resisted this more or was more of a resistor than Simone Weil; subjugation to authority was not the inclination of this young teacher who declared to her "Inspector" that she would consider her "dismissal as the normal and rapid conclusion of her career." But how can something that is thoroughgoingly bad, like voluntary servitude, through what abrupt reversal can this principle, by changing the order in which it is considered, become the best? Another example of such a complete reversal of the Same may be read in the last pages of *The Need for Roots* where the most humble manual labor becomes the supreme value. "Physical work to which we consent. . . . and so on. This should be its spiritual core."[9] This is the last word of the book. Work, the consideration of nature's splendor, death as kenosis, tell us something about God. A short-circuit identifies liberty and necessity. In this short-circuit all of the mediations are consumed, all human "values."

To this may simply be opposed, utterly and definitively, these two observations: it is not so, it is neither like that nor for that that humans live. And there is no other world.

Put another way, it would be better (for our wisdom) to formulate things like this: perfection is in this world, a measure invented progressively, in "spirit" through the analogic of the *logos*, through works.

DIGRESSION ON ANALOGY

Analogy is the climbing movement of the logos, or "transcendence," which must attain—because it *can*—a height (*hypsos* was its name in the old treatise by Longinus), that height from which it delights in an elevation that allows it to turn back upon itself, to consider, to comprehend: a site of *everyone and no one* (Nietzsche), chance, (possibility, if you prefer) for a view that is then depersonalized, delivered of the illusion of its superiority over "others," generic and non-genetic, offered to all as the point of identity (human; shareable). The subject there has become impersonal (Mallarmé). No god preceded it there, nor awaits it, "really" transcendent; even if the subject understands that belief might provide the "energy" to reach that place where transcendence is resolved, without being annihilated, resolved in its "as-if," in its "quasitude." No living without "Eden": the quotation marks—a quasi-nothing which makes all the difference—mark and show what is gained, "the step taken" (Rimbaud), *le pas gagné* in both senses, "the step hard won" and "the hard-won *not*." Irony is the breathable air of this clearing atmosphere.

Against the reductive demagogy of sociology which has the very best of democratic intentions, we must preserve the "ascendant sign" (Breton), the movement of ascension in general, or of overtaking, or of distinction, or of elevation, even of "election;" which is the movement of education, ferrying-over, border-crossing, irreducible to what makes up its ordinary condition (that of the social inequalities of class).

As its name indicates, education takes us away from and conducts us toward. Whom? Where? The place from whence one (= the subject) can, by turning around, looking back with an elevated judgment and a synopsis of knowing, understand the difference between a position which is "low" because we can't see enough from it, and a position that is "high," for example in the Pascalian sense of progress; and I might add: to understand the spatial valence (the enhancive spatialization) of all of this movement puts us within inabrogeable metaphoricity, the literality of which makes it such that its "spirit" is in play: the high of the "sublime," is *as if* it were high; the height is defined by its not-being-able-to-be-said any other way but in the metaphorical way that is constitutive of geographical height that lends to "height" its figuring sense.

The capacity to bring close distant realities (we recall that this operation, *rapprocher* in French, was a classically modern way to define the poetic art) and to distinguish the contiguous or the confused, required that elevated view or vision, which coincides (like the literal and the figurative in any vocable) with (terrestrial) altitude "properly speaking," where it was learned.

On the condition that such height let go of its illusion (has measured critically its metaphorizing tenor that can lend itself to illusion, and without being able to eliminate this risk of error that haunts it), which is an illusion of natural superiority (genetic, racial, hereditary, "calendary"[10]) over the other. But it is not because a chance or a possibility is not effectively grasped (or even graspable) (it is of no importance here "whose fault" that might be) that that of which it is the chance or the possibility ceases to be the aim. The exit is the summit; the definition of the summit is to have no exit.

TRANSCENDENCE

Let's strip the capital letter from Revelation. Revelation is not "external" to reason; it has not got another provenance. At the same time, let us renounce the driving couple Reason-Revelation, which has only produced the prideful infatuation of rationality and the unreasonableness of the rational: the spell of the theologeme par excellence ("God")—in terms of deconstruction: the onto-theological prescription of metaphysics—is *historically* one with the unchained violence of the Power of the Rational (Janicaud).

What is revealed is the self-revelation of thought to oneself in experience. The endogenous and the exogenous are in relation, make relation. The reappropriation of the revealed *as if from outside*, that is the way of wisdom. The future of the mythical illusion of the exogenous is . . . disillusion, which maintains, in full awareness of its very lure, the illusion of transcendence. Don Quixote's "sorties" purging the earth of its enchanters, up until his final disenchantment, have much to teach us still. The nomothete receives the law as if it came from above. I only keep of "revelation" what has the sense of a poetic way of proceeding for thought. As for limits, there is one only: the absolute of nonviolence, the secularized absolute of the profane identity of being and the human, in the trinitarian equation of the terms "equality, liberty, fraternity."

AN ASIDE

Insofar as the One and its henology only make for idolatries (and, I've said it, we Westerners are in the process of experiencing what it is—and therefore what it was for others—to be heretics in the eyes of an earthly inquisition . . .), let us imagine instead this: far from considering that we descend or originate from one and the same book, from the same trunk, the same god, we should instead, turning away from monogeneism that is always inane and violent, we, while dislocating the *we*, should forge the counter-myth of an extreme alterity, of multiple provenances, heterogeneous, irreducible, something like creatures that have come from other worlds and other creators—which then could fraternize here as extra-terrestrials and humans do at the end of science fiction films.

Giving up on the origin we would take measures—for example, teaming up opposites, making precedents simultaneous and declaring the chicken and the egg to be contemporary, *phusis* and *technê*, origin and beginning, in order not to assign the blame categorically in finger pointing—"it's him, *the other*!"; and we would double up every law in a double-bind.

This is the abolition of proselytism. Each "subject" an other, must renounce, for the other, the universalization of his or her truth; each subject must contain him or herself in his or her difference. *Forever you are other*; let us seek no longer to convert one another.

The infiltration of the conviction of the other is forbidden. Let us begin again with the abstract and abyssal difference between our sameness (humanity) and our radical alterity (religious).

REVELATION, CONTINUED . . .

As an artist, I need to ask myself: "What is *revelation* in *my* experience?" Revelation will have served to send me in the direction ("destiny") where in the end I had to overturn it in my disillusionment about that of which it speaks. If there is a "future of an illusion" (Freud), it is as the disillusion that gives in return its sense to illusion. And I'll take advantage of this to quote again a Brazilian artist's profession of faith: "There is no hope, there is an illusion of joy." The "illusion" maintained (with quotation marks) is the disillusion of that from which it results. Such was, perhaps, the Rimbaldian movement of "illumination." It was necessary to learn the meaning of the determinities of non-sense (literally and in all senses) from which it results, to gain in reasonable determinations the disenchantment of reason itself. Moving from the revealed to the reasonable while gathering up as figures the literal letter of Revelations, and the senseless pride of the rational as well. The perfection of immanence brings with it the safeguard of quasi-transcendence; a transcendental mirage of quasi-transcendence.

But a phrase of Nietzsche's tells us the risk of the perfection of disbelief to which it is necessary to come: "If we do not make of the death of the gods a great renunciation and a perpetual victory over ourselves, we will have to pay for that loss." [*Thus Spake Zarathustra*.]

Nonetheless, that perfection, that "willing suspension of belief" (where I'm obviously hijacking Coleridge [*Biographia Literaria*]) does not bring with it in any way the forgetfulness of the great schemes of figuration, of the revelation of existence; of all the figurative content that religious mythologies gather together and keep in memory. Art, that emergency dead-end, if I dare say, this exit without exit, has for its end to make revelation out of profanation. If what has become unbelievable is nonetheless ineffaceable, it becomes a matter of *ineffacing*, actively, positively, in *works*, the un-believable learned by heart, maintained in the profane as-if.

OF RELIGION

Yet this hopeless movement has skipped over the fact of religions. We need to go back: religions in the plural are at war; any war is a war of *religions*, Maître Alain liked to repeat. The gods are thirsty, not only for sacrificial blood, but for the death of the other gods. And the monotheisms (this curious plural of the singular, the neutral utterance of which requires disbelief), each one eschatological and soteriological in the name of the unique revealed truth, make inexpiable war upon one another because none can limit the field of missionary exercise on which it announces its End and its Salvation, and because the *annunciation* of such Good News, which brings with it the *denunciation* of false religions, cannot be reduced to the peaceful enunciation of linguists. The star, the cross, the crescent, the three books are only three from an external point of view—is it "absolute"? It does not seem like the war underway between fundamentalized religions can be called "civilizing." Are there "religions" on the one hand that work through sacrifice (René Girard) and holy war, and, on the other, one religion, *the* religion, which is no longer a religion because it commands "thou shalt not kill"?

The law, the only law, "you will not commit murder," is improbable, astonishing; and it continues to be so, the least obeyed or obeyable of them all: millennia of slaughters, internal or intestine wars; millennia of sacrificial rituals; the murderous province of Tragedy, or the "literary" scene of the comi-tragedy of modern ways, with the banal persistence of "crimes of passion," that mania of humans for seeking to get rid of others as soon as there is a problem, that strange taste or desire for suppressing the other who gets in the way . . . ; and now there is cinema which never stops hallucinating carnage.

And indeed from whence could come, from whence "can fall" such an improbable law, counter-cultural and counter-natural, *counter-gravitational*, Simone Weil might have said? The answer to this question, simple in its provenance, of the origin of counter-gravity or "grace," the irresistible, simple answer to this question is then that of a nonterrestrial origin, a "transcendent" one, since counter-gravity cannot come from some point on the earth; that is why the religion of that law is that of monotheism, for "only *a* God can save us;" only one God alone, who substitutes his adoration for the ancient sacrificial law.

"Thou shalt not kill!" But the spirit of the law, the spirit of its letter, what is *revealable* in that law, the generalized expansion of its literality, literally and in every sense, in the course of the interpretation of tradition, in the course of the ages, of reading and of experience, and of teaching, and of homilies, that spirit is that do-not-kill means not only don't kill, literally, but it is also a lot more than just "do not kill": it means do not kill *in every sense*, all the way up to "do not harm a hair on his head," all the way to the universalization of the maxim, all the way to respect.

Now *it is the letter that kills*. But how to maintain the difference between the spirit and the letter, without which there is no more art, no more literature, no hermeneutic in general, and soon, perhaps, no more vernacular?

On one side, *religions* only resist their confusion and their disappearance by preserving the literality of their orthodoxy, and that is "holy war;" on the other, *the* religion of the spirit (and perhaps the second law, that of Love one another) from the *Ama et quod vis fac*[11]—that is the interpretation of the first one and it extends all the way to "do not touch a hair on the head of the other . . ."), from Reform to reforms, would it only have a "future" (Freud) by maintaining the indispensable illusion of "transcendence?" By that I mean that inasmuch as the wisdom of the *as-if* ("as if we were immortal"), and in general that of the paradoxical regime of our truthful existences, is only slightly accessible and slightly practicable, belief would be worth more, its faith and its practice worth more than the desolation of trivial disenchantment and its cynical "realism." It is even very likely that it is the use of the *as-if* that maintains the use of the *like-or-as* in general, that is to say of poetry in general and of works; and if the ascetic endurance of the *as-if* is too hard, then believing, the believing-in (which, as it happens, constitutes in every way the ether of the whole sphere of "intersubjectivity") at least favors the illusion—even if the latter does not know itself as such—the illusion of that "Eden without which we cannot live" (Mallarmé). It is difficult to hold to the *as-if* in full awareness of causes, of things, without believing . . . transitively.

OF THE END

And which century has been more murderous than our own? The thesis of the "banality of evil" takes up the famous thought, "no one is willingly evil;" it would be the modern, disabused, bleak, fatalistic, sociological version of that thought. The adverse thesis, that of the *radicality of evil*, is to the first as a proper noun, *Auschwitz*, is now forever to the anonymity or synonymity of common nouns.

Perhaps generalized aboulia, which carries with it the incapacity for willing even evil, growing along with the flood of Lethe rolling over the humans making their way as souls unto death, "without noticing it"—that Greek auxiliary where being turned again toward truth (*a-léthéïa*), the twisted conversion of the encaverned ones toward the light, seeking to get away—that aboulia, I'm saying, fattened up on the prostheses of technique, the complexity of which *assists* the modern Insured subject, somnolent in his ignorance and credulously progressive (out of vanity), is perhaps itself being confused little by little with "radical evil." It comes to constitute this evil while the two antagonistic theses, long ago opposed like a Greek hero and a Christian martyr, cast themselves together, mixing together in their fatigue, into the open maw of the "end of history."

I wanted this adieu to Simone Weil to linger in its brevity, just long enough to propose a few motifs, certainly not polemical ones, for the stupor of intellectuals who are so tormented by aggravation—as a kind of program. I have uttered a few propositions that might have provoked Simone Weil's anger but whose gentle resolution is made possible, faithful still, by her lesson of lucidity.

Of the palinody I will say this:

I think I have changed radically in the course of the years; completely, even, and thus have become "myself," single and same (*solus ipse idem*), far from being "another." The reversal that disenchants, which "goes back on its word," which falls away from—if reasonable disillusion is the "future of the illusion"—far from being a flat "contradiction," imputable to lack of consistency or treachery, is that very becoming-what-I-am, in Pindar's expression, picked up by Goethe. And it may not yet be completely forbidden to think that what can be accomplished "ontogenetically" by one might come to many—and that reasonable man might turn against the idols, and even the idol Reason. But the adventures of liberty do not follow a necessary course.

Too late for the gods?—so much the better. Too early for being?—because still in the becoming of what it will have been.

IV

JEWISH HUMANITY

PEACE-WITH

Let us begin again with one simple thing.

Israel is a good. Not only for the Jewish Israelis, but a good thing for everyone, that is to say for the world. It is a matter of asking ourselves how those who suffer from it, or who are outraged by it, those we call Arabs, can convince themselves of this simple thing. Coming home from a visit of a few days in Israel (my fifth visit, I believe, and this time only on the side of our Jewish hosts, that is to say, without having been able to meet "the other side," as was the case for me the previous time, thanks to the French Consulate in Jerusalem, because programming a meeting with the Palestinians was then possible), I was asking myself this question on the plane: how can the Arabs not see something that is clear from the outset to a French intellectual passing through, someone attentive (I was about to say "impartial"). Israel is good, good-for, good for the diversity of the world, the richness of the world, the sense, the meaning, and the peace of the world. That a people (let's be satisfied with that word for now, a word-subject, pro-noun, while neutralizing that term, ie, detaching it completely from the syntagma that correlates it with *choice*) can be so historical, both in its historical sites and just as well at home, in its home, at home as one really feels that it is there, *that* has real meaning and cannot but contribute (in the long term, alas, because we aren't yet there) to peace and to the sense of the world. Peace is peace-with [*paix-avec*], at least in French grammar. Peace with oneself goes in the direction of peace with others, *their* others, in particular, who are "Arabs." So we must, once and for all, accept them all, recognize them all. They are in their place and there is the place. The rest will follow, including the insoluble problem of the undividedness [*indivision*] of Jerusalem which belongs to many; which, in its being, that is to say in its historical being, its having-become-what-it-is, "belongs" to many, to the three religions.

This experience, this sentiment, this quasi-sensation of loving them in their home because one feels them to be so well together in that society, in a nation, in a State—and you will forgive me for grappling with these second thoughts as though I were in need of a good purge—this is not at all just one side of the coin of a thought whose other side, the dissimulated verso, would go something like this: "Let them keep to themselves, then!"—Europe, after having exterminated them, is at last getting rid of them!—no, it is, rather, an intimate satisfaction with regard to a recognized otherness, in a relation which might find its rightness, its justness, when the justice of a cause, Zionism, has won . . .

I am permitting this sentiment to be glimpsed from a perspective that is at once fleeting and insistent, the aspect of a clear conscience in Israel, a furtive and persistent conscience: what remains, in Europe, of a kind of unhappy conscience with respect to any "community," and of the Jewish one in particular, because our history is not communitarian. This is what shocks us when, here and there, we are shown a "ghetto," an old "ghetto" in Rome or in Prague, or anywhere in the imagination of a civil existence, where the ghetto was surrounded, encircled, cornered, controlled by *another* society, one that was in the majority, hegemonic; all of that disappears, and that is what I'm evoking with the expressions, "at home, in their place." Israel is not a ghetto and must never become that; not a reserved quarter, tolerated, a splinter of diaspora in an a-diasporic world, but rather alongside, with, among the nations; on the same plane as others; in equality, finally. . . . The problem of relations may at last be posed—resolved. In equality, as we say; "between us," "Jew" is no longer pronounced with a smile, a worry, a benevolence, an air of wanting to repair; the sign is no longer the sign of exception or of infamy: the sign is no longer yellow on the coat but black upon the head, it is the sign of an identity asserted, of an equality in difference among the peoples of the earth; in the "Society of Nations." They are all Jews, at home, in their place; you human brothers who with us are living. Them. Among themselves and in the midst of all of the *thems*. In reciprocity; the parity that is *not* arithmetical, *not* fifty–fifty. Small peoples are just as great as the others.

The word *Jew* enters into a normality of usage and common law, a word to be neither whispered nor shouted, loaded simply with the weight of normal denotation and connotation, freed from enormous defamatory innuendo, hateful, criminal or jealous, deeply felt, twisted; it is like "Spanish" in Spain or "English" among the English. In their home they are at home, among themselves, with us, at last others.

Jew is no longer the accusative of the internal object of the verbal structure "to be exterminated," as the famous title of Hillberg let it be heard, as if there had never been anything else in all of history, pogrom after pogrom, right up to the solution that was final, the bouquet, the conclusion, the *telos* of that long business of slaughter, the protocol of the assassins of Zion.

That is what is "good for everyone," and hence good for the world.

And the Arab nations, and the "Arab Nation" too (if any such thing exists) must and can feel and endure this too; and if its genius is the genius of hospitality, as its Koranic revelation and its arts profess, it must be the host of the Jewish guest, the guest of the Jewish host who has returned to the places of its history. It can do it, it has the resourcefulness, it is the first host of the Jewish nation, understood in the geographical sense of the nearest neighbor, and insofar as the second welcome, the second circle encircling Israel, already somewhat withdrawn, in second place, is "us," Europe.

*

Despite that, a question and a very recent experience in Arab society (I've just returned from Tunis) lead me again to fear the worst. I would gladly entitle this post-scriptum, in order to remain phlegmatic, *Malaise in the Orient.*

The question is this: for us, north of the Mediterranean, between the Atlantic and the Urals, there are essentially only the Ashkenazis, "Jews of Europe." In Israel and in the tradition there are also the Sephardim and the Yemenites; North Africa and the more distant East. The Nazis didn't go there to exterminate. How do Jews *feel* in the Orient?

My recent experience was that of hearing once again the evocation by the Arabs of their past splendor, that Golden Age, scientific and artistic, the age of their involvement, that's an understatement, in the becoming and the constitution of Europe and the West. Hearing once again their lamentation and their resentment, as if their decoupling from Europe was to be imputed to that European Occident, as if their forgetting and their regression or a-historical stagnation was the fault of the North and the West, I came to the following reflection: isn't the European West like a closed club, snobbish, from which Arabs are excluded and to which they cannot really belong (the fable of Al-Fayed and of England makes this stand out more for us today)? With that, the Jews of Israel, the European Jews of Israel, if I may say, are suspicious, bored and indifferent where they find themselves, like members of a *Club international* who have strayed off into a suburb. They are not "really" interested in those with whom they find themselves, with whom they have to live, in those who surround them and hold them back. They find those people overwhelming and oppressive, like a huge poor family squatting in a rich family's apartment.

(Vignette: when you are invited into this or that academic or literary milieu in Jerusalem, Tel-Aviv, Haifa, etc., if you are looking to meet X, Y, or Z, you will very often be told: "Ah! He is in New York, in Harvard, in UCLA; in Rome, in Berlin, in London, in Paris; for the next couple of months, six months . . .").

"All men will be Jewish," said Hermann Cohen.

*

The Fable of Adam: Was Adam Jewish? I suppose so, for the synagogue, since he is the first man of the Book.

*

Why contribute here to the aforementioned "Jewish question"?

The question of anti-Semitism is radical to the examination of this "little faith," understood as a remainder. Why does the remainder remain? May my hand forget its skill if I forget you, Jerusalem! [Psalm 137].

I was about to say that there is a symmetry of blindness: as if we needed . . . a Dreyfus Affair which would allow us to redo the division of just and unjust in order that anti-Semitism would be clearly odious to all, and the anti-Dreyfusard an absurd counterfeiter whose only function was to clearly locate the rubbish bins of History.

Instead of being reborn from the earth, inextricable and diffuse, like a hydra or unstoppable and virulent, like the chaff in the parable.

But can we accept—"we" pacifistic intellectuals, profaners of History—being suspected of anti-Semitism; as if a third point of view were excluded, "impossible," between the pro-Israeli anti-Semite (anti-Palestinian) and the pro-Palestinian anti-Semite (anti-Israeli).

*

Freud did not manage to define his being-Jewish (not religious, nor, nor . . .). His being-Jewish is in no way determinable. It is equal to nothing. It is present as an absent, as "not existing," as a Greek *mê-on*. That is like Dr. Benveniste's homeopathy: all of its molecules have been diluted, dissolved, and "the entity" is still there.

Always for Freud, that which is (happens; is present; is phenomenon) *is* only for having been lost, forgotten, lost in amnesia, "repressed," then, *and* for having *returned*, reappeared, for having been brought back up to the surface "from" the unconscious. After a phase of disappearance, it is and it returns. From where? And so it is that his own being-Jewish only counts for him, only *is*, for having disappeared, "annihilated."

Hannah Arendt writes: "As for me personally, none of that matters much. I have never felt like a German woman and it was a very long time ago that I stopped feeling like a Jewish woman. I feel like I am, quite simply; namely, the one who comes from elsewhere" (letter to Heidegger, February 1950).

Jacques-Alain Miller makes it known: "Jewish. Yes, Jewish, as Jewish as can be. Jewish with no rite or religion, Jewish with a circumcised heart and a stiff neck, Jew of the diaspora, Jew with no other family but my father, my mother, my brother, a faithful Jew, loathing treason, linked forever by the given word, attached to the book, and knowing how to read since that is the immemorial trait of one's own, a Jew trembling to affront trials as a hero, demonstrating, while waiting, the worst manners in society whenever anyone at all allows himself to play Pontius Pilate before truth. Son of his father, yes, and how! and debating fiercely with the ferocious super-ego that this admired father caused to be born in him."[1]

And Jacques Derrida: "This sentiment [of Judaity] remains obscure with me, abyssal, above all unstable. Contradictory. At once very powerful and labile. As though a depth of memory were authorizing me to forget, perhaps to deny what is most archaic, to distract me from the essential. This active even energetic distraction, even energetic, leads me away, then, from what likely remains most "constitutive" in me [. . .]."[2] And further along: "This incalculable inner multiplicity [. . .] gives me to reflect on both my belonging and my non-belonging to Judaism."[3]

From time to time, in a few autobiographical pages, I evoke "our youth"—there were no more Dreyfus Affairs, and no negationism or revisionism yet, because we didn't even have the name "Shoah" (it was well before Claude Lanzmann's film), nor even yet a clear enough sense of the bounds of the "Holocaust" to know of the "extermination of the Jews of Europe" (Hillberg). It was the preparatory classes for entry to the *Grandes Ecoles*, the post-war *khâgne*, and I often describe one aspect of it by relating how the friends among themselves had no awareness that some were "Jews" and others not. Neither Derrida, as you have just read, nor Nora, nor Tedesco, nor any of the others other looked upon themselves as Jews and upon others as *goyim*. . . . There was no communitarianism.

*

But how can you put together Rosenzweig and Freud, Benjamin and Derrida, Scholem and Lacan-Miller, and so on? One who believed in heaven and one who did not.

Precisely; that is the point; between the atheistic non-Israeli Jew and the Israeli Hassidim there would be something "essentially" common. . . . What? Not nothing. Judaity. Or again: Who was it who used to speak about an "anti-Jewish Jew" on the subject of Edmond Jabès? I've forgotten. But look: unlike the equation +A – A= 0, an anti-Jewish Jew does not equal nothing: Judaity remains.

*

This not-quite-nothing brought out of loss, this unqualifiable being (without religion, without rites, without a family other than its own, enemy of treachery, founding itself on the word rather than on any thing, this attachment to the book and knowing how to read, with a slightly Greek penchant for heroism and enough presumptuousness to believe itself capable of recognizing Pilate), this loss of faith and of practice, loss of the *gens* and of the clan, of vengeance and murder and hope, preserving only the word, the book and the taste for truth, if that is being Jewish, then "me too, I'm Jewish!" and Hermann Cohen is right to cry out: "All of Humanity shall be Jewish." As in 1968, the famous "We are all German Jews" [*Nous sommes tous des Juifs allemands*] rang out. In his fine book, Jean-François Marquet, bringing forward this quotation, speaks of Rosenzweig for whom "the Jewish people is a unique people, people of the One, who nevertheless claim for themselves, *as a singular, no less everything*: the Jewish God, the Jewish world, the Jewish man take on all predicates, even if contradictory—God being both Justice and Love, the world at once totally profane (and so manipulable) and totally ritualized, the Jew both chosen (and therefore special) and called to the universal."[4]

*

What would be, what will a *negative anthropology* have to be—the translation, profanation, and recuperation of negative theology, the movement invented for "God," for taking away God's ontic attributes? For "man," an apophatic anthropology of the abdication of his humanistic prerogatives, in search of the common-nothing, of the unfathomable (*absconditus*) indetermination or the infinity of his finitude, recanting empirical prides, hijacking and diverting the ravaging anti-ecological anthropomorphistic anthropicization of the world and its earth. "There will no longer be man or woman, neither Jew nor Roman [. . .]"

"All of humanity shall be Jewish"? But this abdication of which I am speaking and dreaming and which would prepare the identity/equality of all "humans," this beautiful apophatic movement (a *roll of the dice* [*coup de dé* (Mallarmé)]) abolishing all hazards of chance) leads (too quickly?) in Sartre to the famous last *word* ("a whole man, composed of all men, as good as all of them and no better than any"), to the last man, who is no longer either Jewish or Roman. And so this Judaity runs the risk (is this implied by Rosenzweig's vow?) of opening up, not onto the neutralization of the human through a trans-humance (if I dare), outside of that which is differentiated and moving toward the universal-singular in its beaming void, but instead onto a particularity all the more tenacious and adhesive for being almost nothing, precisely like Kepler's differential (Σ).

Man? (*Homo sum et nihil . . .*)

The name of each is the name of all.

What individuates IS what identifies, in the sense that it singularizes while universalizing, or: it "same-ifies," if I may say (*idem et ipse*) while differenciating. *The same* separates us absolutely. How can we envisage (inhabit) this explosive paradox? It is where *reason comes up hard* against identity (I'm repeating one of my own favorite formulas).

If being-Jewish in the Freudian (or Lacanian-Millerian) movement of stripping-down is being-human, in the experience of discovering our "pure" humanity; if being Jewish is being nothing Jewish, then "we are all . . ." and the like.

But there is a remainder; or: the movement takes place in the affect and under the sign of a particularity that isolates from others (cf. Sharon). One would say that being Jewish is being a man . . . plus something else—which is nothing . . . less than nothing for Hitler. Not nothing, *decisively*, for Sharon.

I might seek to "feel it" in a festive occasion at the home of Jewish friends, "among Jews" . . . with a few goys, they laugh about it in a friendly way. Here are the dances and the food. Is this a celebration of identity as with the Catalans, the Corsicans, the Bretons? Yes and *no*. Communities? From the outside, and if the commentary was seeking its irenic "political correctness," an affair of "The Cultural" and of minorities, well we'll talk about dances, cuisine, beliefs. . . . But for itself (among us, Sharon would say, non-*goyim* . . .) it is that, along with something more, something which isn't nothing—but everything.

I'll start again with Cohen's and Rosenzweig's words. We know well that our contemporaries—all of us in the "daily prayer of the gazettes" (Hegel) in the church, the mosque or the synagogue, and in the corner café or the agora, cannot receive in its literality Cohen's cry, a synagogue wish.

Imagine that were to quote it in a General Assembly of UNESCO where the prism of Nations polymerizes the gray glow of humanity. Taken at the letter, it provokes a hue and cry! No way! Impossible! China, India, Tibet, Japan, Arabia in general . . . Black Africa. . . . Not even possible in the form of a parable! No more than the Ayatollaesque watchword of the universal Islamic Republic. Jews as protagonists of modern and contemporary History, exterminated, and then both killers and killed, are, as a particularity, an integral part of humanity and have the other parts of humanity outside of themselves. The Jews have formed a nation among the nations, Israel, which is no longer understood as "Chosen," as Zion, as Holy Land, except within the circle of coreligionists. Israel, people of God? Rather people of a god, stronger than the others in the West. But weaker elsewhere than the god of Mecca? An intermediary, oriental-occidental, an attached and attaching people-god whom the West has included-excluded and who did not conquer the East.

*

In what way can the *it is not nothing* be something?

I obviously do not believe Sartre: anti-Semitism does not make the Jew, any more than man makes woman. And no more than woman would be the future of man would the Jew be the future of Man. Unless we elaborate this in a non-feminist fashion: it is not *this woman* that we know, today, in her partiality and her combat, homosexual, for example, who is the future of man, nor this man the future of woman nor of humanity, but perhaps a woman transformed, another woman, when, "there will be no more man nor woman . . ." . . . "nor Jew nor Roman": not this "actual" Jew, in his combat, then, but a transformed Jew, as a non-Jew, the future of difference just as much as Roman "man," for example, who was his other in the Pauline proposition, or the Nietzschean one, or . . .

If Sartre is right, the situation is grave: for the Jew must delight in the anti-Semite *if it is anti-Semitism that makes the Jew*! And that is really what we are afraid of, if we see the care which Jews take in detecting the slightest traces of anti-Semitism, that is, those that they allow one another, since being Jewish would protect them from any anti-Semitism.

They are the masters of difference and this is why I am going to propose my remarks upon the *Just*, remarks that I do not think are anti-Semitic. In a moment . . .

*

So if it did occur to some Jews, who had themselves stripped away all of their Judaity, to allow themselves to be treated like Jews (when, for example, the anti-Jewish laws of the Vichy régime led certain Frenchmen to adopt a Jewish family name out of solidarity with the victims, in other words, to reinvent a fraternity of consanguinity which they had precisely erased), that is to say to recognize themselves as Jews (like them), under the gaze of the hatred of others as anti-Semites—the right attitude that any man and in particular any French citizen ought to have taken (isn't this "putting on the new man"?), following the example of the King of Denmark adopting the yellow star—it is then truly hatred, anti-Semitism, which made them again (like) Jews. And they submitted and they submit and they will submit to this hatred while waiting for the end of the anti-Semitic superstition, that is to say, the awakening of reason. This hatred proceeds from a reverse mimetic idolatry of election, being chosen, in other words from a myth of German Aryanity. The work of reason, which always still awaits, is to scrutinize the obscurity of a difference that is reducible to that of "*as*" and "*like*" [*en tant que/ pareil à*] which in French comes down to the homogeneity of the *comme* where this difference cannot be heard.

*

It is because Heidegger could privilege (choose) a Germanity, a *Deutschum*, the *secret* of which was held by Hölderlin ("Until when, Germans, will you be deaf to the Word of the poet . . ." etc.) that he could align himself with (and ally himself with) the Nazis, idolators of Germanity. A misunderstanding that was simultaneously one of good and bad faith; a double equivocity, then, because it favors pretending to be in agreement—a misunderstanding in which one might not hear the difference of these two superstitions, the philosophical one and the mythical one, the thinking appeal to the historial people and the howling (the *heil*ing, if I might be so bold) appeal to the People-Race. The difference of a capital letter might remain poorly understood for a time. A mission of salvation of the Greek West and of ontological humanity that might be confided in the sons of Hölderlin; and on the stage of Nuremberg the purification of the Species might be confided in the Reich and its blonde angels. The Germans of the philosopher did not exist but the Hitlerians existed all too well. The thinker extricated himself from the misunderstanding in his teaching.

Demystification consists of practicing, and so of thinking, difference; difference without election. Understanding and cherishing, through their history, particularities and singularities because, indeed, the Germans are not the Italians nor the French (nor the Greeks!), nor the Chinese English. Without the myth of a salvation, a mission, an elected quality, not even a chosenness reduced to the difference between Us and Them, of an ourselves and of an all-the-others. (Dare I recall that the belief of the paranoid—René Girard recalls it rereading Dostoyevsky's Underground Man—speaks this way: "I am alone, and they are everyone.") Renouncing salvation-by, the salvation by the Aryans, by the Jews, by the Tibetans, and perhaps renouncing salvation altogether, that is the task.

Not even salvation by oneself, of the Germans by the Germans, of the Jews by the Jews, of the Chinese by the Chinese. Perhaps after all we must not "rely only upon our own forces . . ."

*

Race, what is that!?

The idol, that is race. The poison is a nonscientific thought of Race; an idolatry. Thinking according to Race—but we should not say "thinking" because being "racist" is to believe in "race." So: believing according to race is to believe in the *natural* difference between higher and lower races. There is not, on one hand, a concept or a mytheme of Race, and, *in addition*, epithetically, an aleatory predicate of superiority or inferiority. Believing in race is to believe that *nature* is divided into Masters, or Lords, and Slaves, or Inferiors. The nineteenth century will have been the laboratory of these very diverse superstitions (these "ideologies"); from Thierry to Gobineau, among other Frenchmen.

Not that there would be a race of Lords and a race of Slaves; some superior races and some inferior races; but because Race with a capital R would be the natural division of humanity into inferior and superior, those made to serve and those made to dominate. They are of the same race; they make the race; they phenomenalize genre as something racial. Masters and Slaves are Race itself—if we are trying to understand the word RACE, the implacable *ictus* of which dizzies so many billions of times so many millions of brains, as an echo's yell will dig out a cavern.

*

Germanity? Germanitude? *Deutschland*, *Deutschum*? . . . Heidegger's "Until when, Germans," as he meditates upon Hölderlin, "will you remain deaf to your destiny?," etc. The answer: forever. The destiny of the Germans occurred and it was not a renewal of their being. Rather more the opposite; or the counterfeit, the worst inverted realization of grandeur, of chosenness, of promise. And during that time, indeed the time of Heidegger's lessons on the great Hölderlinian Hymns, "Rhine," "Germanie," "Ister," what was happening? The *Lager* and Auschwitz. At the same time, and it was in time, in our time. The most abyssal gap between the thinkable for thought and the effectively accomplished in the human real: the being of the Germans, in the appeal to take up again that being—and, on the other side, the camps. The program of Germanity will have been deployed as an application of *Mein Kampf*, a final solution. The destiny has found its destination. The "German people," German being, have happened. End of the story, end of history, according to Primo Levi: "He recounts again that he tried, one evening, during the return march from the camp in the middle of the Polish mud, to find again a few verses of Hölderlin, the poetic message that in another time, had transported him, and he couldn't manage it: the verses were still there, they resonated in his ear but they didn't speak to him any more."

*

This is how I understand the banality of evil.

Tirelessly, at every instant for years, tens of thousands, hundreds of thousands of Germans, soldiers or public servants, guards, diverse employees, etc., behaved in the way described by so many of Primo Levi's pages ("Right away the kicks and the punches, sometimes on the face, the mess of orders screamed with true or feigned anger," etc.; "To those who do not speak to you or who address you with yelling and cries that to you seem inarticulate, you dare not speak."); they behaved like *no* human being. No normal citizen of a civilized society in "normal times" would allow himself *under any pretext* to be treated in this way by another "human," another "normal citizen." If in the street, the first-comer strikes me with a blow, hints at a brutality, lets himself get carried away, as we say, and lays a hand on me or even makes a threatening gesture, the slightest insult, the slightest cry even, toward "another's person," then that is criminal, a police matter, a matter for complaint and justice. If even the thousandth part of what these thousands and hundreds of thousands of Germans permitted themselves to do to others was to require justice, to plead for justice and sanctions, then millions of criminal acts committed in Germany in the course of twelve years, which went without judgment, had as their effect this: Germany was a population of delinquents, and even of criminals in circulation, the largest society of primal delinquents that ever existed. They were never judged for what they did, never punished for *what they allowed themselves*.

*

The Jews, I asked, are they masters of difference, to the point that they can decide about justice?

Greek-jew? [in English in the original] We know that Israel—the proper name here counting metonymically for "the Jews"—has rewarded with a medal called in French the *médaille des JUSTES* [called in English the "Righteous among the Nations"] those non-Jews who protected and saved Jewish people, "Israelites" as we used to say, from Vichy and from the Germans, most often children whose family names were dissimulated.

If age and courage in those days had put me in a position to receive this honor later, I would have refused it, I would refuse it. Why? Because it is not a matter of *justice*.

If this medal should be given to "friends of Israel," for example, or "human brothers," and so on then I could accept it with gratitude for a recognition of merit. But the just is not defined as someone who saved a Jewish child from death. We learned about the essence of justice, in any case sought after it, turning in a circle around Socrates: "Of the Just and the Unjust" Περι του δικαιου . . . [*peri tou dikaiou*—On Righteousness]

It does not belong to Israel to decree that the just man is one who saves a child of Israel nor to separate the just from the unjust, nor to link justice to the name of a nation.

And so it goes with the teaching of the Shoah, of course! On the condition that it not have as its final object compassion for the exterminated Jews. For what is insane is what the Germans did to us, to all humans. Genocide is a *crime against humanity*. It is probable that the reticences and even the repugnancies, for there are some of those, toward this teaching might derive from this point: that the lesson not end in a Jewish exclusivity in an absolute misfortune that would paralyze exemplarity.

And that is precisely to seek *what is just*, scrupulously feeling one's way along, even nitpicking one's way along in the midst of these distinctions, never melding Justice with any particularity.

Couldn't Israel have called this medal something other than the medal of the "*justes*"? In a just relation to justice but with another name. What we call poetic invention might serve this end. The term *just* is already taken; taken by philosophy, which is Greek, and its Latin translation.

*

The Jewish exception is such, at the limit where we have now arrived, that the pure and simple naming of Jews, a denomination pronounced from the outside by a non-Jew, is as though already possible grounds for the suspicion of anti-Semitism. A strange malaise, almost a misfortune, means that when we simply hear the syntagma "the Jews," suspicious attention oscillates at instantaneous speed from accusation to neutralization: is the *tone* right, which attempts to "neutralize" this use in order to prevent any fear of hearing in it an accusatory denotation like the one which identified Peter in the courtyard of the *praetorium*, constraining him to repeated denial? One might say that no term, no "proper name," not "Zionist," not "Israelite," is beyond suspicion. In my youth, "Israelite" meant neutralizing the risk, the avoidance of "Jew," perhaps because of the pillory attached by Pilate to the "King of the Jews," to denote one confession among others. Then "Israelite" came to be received as an anti-Semitic euphemism. *Israeli* remains, to be understood as a citizenship held also by thousands of Arabs. But who hears it that way?

It is then singular—with a singularity that we'd like to be able to archive as an "out-of-date" moment, one duly noted, beyond which humanity knew how to progress, if something like that were still conceivable—it is singular that you who call yourselves such can gather under the appellation of "Jews" while we, from the outside, cannot designate you that way without being suspected for this, of a first anti-Semitic gesture like the one that excludes you. Where there are only enclosures "for oneself," each one isolates others by the simple fact of designating its own outside, localizing its alterity.

And if we could speak of these simple others who are Jews—this possibility would be a gain—it would be at the price of the communitarianization of our societies on the U.S. model, where "ghettos" are no longer only Jewish but where each particularity gets one of its own, without the stalled melting pot coming along to knock them down.

If what is proper to familiarity, to vulgarity, is to think of oneself as innocent and even inoffensive in the very gesture of taking a gibe at others, or insulting them outright, our neighbors or those close to us, as in the French way, *entre Français*, when we make fun of Belgians, then, in that very way, we would like to be forgiven for such a generalizing insult at the neighborhood café with respect to "the Jews." That would be further covered by the supplementary excuse offered by the equivocal denotative value of a word that aims confusedly at "Israelites, Israelis, Jews and Jewish" in a multivocity of which they take advantage sometimes to suspect the other—goy—a priori of anti-Semitism. But that temptation is base. The first movement is always bad, the slacking off implied by "this is just between us" is always vile; and I'll make this correction:

The fear of vulgar anti-Semitism will help us to gain this more general point: the obligation, internalized once and for all, of not allowing oneself any "first movement" of contempt. On the basis of that obligation we can generalize a respect that would strike with a moral and human prohibition the vulgarity of spontaneous arrogance: this would not be any longer an "opinion" which "believes itself" superior. But how can we hope that vulgarity would no longer be the essence of the *vulgus*? How do we believe in the possibility of the extirpation of opinion, when it is the opposite that wins and that we have come to what may be summarized abyssally by this recently reported fact: as some teenagers were being punished for having insulted their Jewish teacher, they protested: "What about it, then? We've sure got *the right* to be anti-Semitic: we're *in a democracy*!"

*

Being non-Jewish, is that different from being goy? Yes. For them I am a goy, but not for myself. This description is of no interest to me. I don't like it that the milieu of our relation gets determined by a predicate, a differentiation which the Jewish person institutes when we meet.

No more interested than I would be in the sobriquet, the depreciating nickname, the "barbarism," which someone else might stick me with. Frog, for an Englishman, and so forth. Each of us is the under-man of another. But I am interested in seeing that differentiation, that alterity, reduced, lessened between us, goy and Jew; that should be the result of our interminable, exhausting History. Let us compare. If I meet a Sikh in a Sikh's costume, and within the element of the English language that allows us to communicate, a little, I am quite happy that the difference Sikh/non-Sikh should reign and that my side would be marked out by the privative, by privation, because that is what belongs to hospitality, and because we have not lived enough together, have not seen each other often enough. But then shouldn't I say the same thing about goy and Jew? Shouldn't I hear in "goy" an old, finely worked difference, more elaborate than the one I've just evoked, with others who are more other, a difference wrought by "intimacy," through an eroded *pathos*, that of enemy brothers, in hostility and neighborliness, in comprehensive incomprehension, through centuries-old reciprocity; how would we say that? I no longer know.

I feel like saying, "We have all become Marranos," in the sense where the Virgin Mary of the Gospel "kept these things in her heart."

When I meet Lanzmann or Derrida, or Hélène Cixous, my friends, about whom I never "learned" in our youth that they were Jewish, with or without quotation marks, I hope that the ether of our attraction is not haunted by a difference such that it would bend or wrinkle or split apart our humanity, neither secretly nor intentionally. I do not particularly want to hear them theorize about their Judaity unless it is in the way of a Freud or of an Arendt "come from elsewhere." In order to sound out anxiously our common being-nothing, which for them might pass through the return of a different repressed, a second repression . . .

*

I was stupefied as though I were discovering a treason when I learned, listening to a declaration on TV, that a French citizen, Jewish, whose story it is true I knew nothing about, had left "his country" to settle in Israel. I would have been bowled over if some such friend, more or less close, had announced that he was leaving "us" to become an Israeli as though he were rejoining "his own." It is perhaps my emancipation with respect to the religious sphere that explains this incomprehension. My contradiction derives in all of this from the fact that on the one hand I would *turn around* from a future point (but without Benjamin-Klee's Angels' wings) to speak in the future anterior about a stubbornness that will have kept a hold on others, rooted by the feet, like a humanity lagging behind in its idolatries, whereas on the other hand, I hate nothing so much as clean slates, illiterate amnesias, the arrogance of particularities.

I want to be able to detest the Orthodox of Jerusalem as much as the Taliban, the kippa outside of the synagogue as much as the head-scarf in school, without passing for an anti-Semite; want to be able to respect just as much the secular atheist of Tel-Aviv as the agnostic intellectual from Cairo. "Salvation through the Jews"? No. If there is no more "deicide," there is no more Léon Bloy. We have exited the history of salvation. No chosenness. Nothing but wandering and anguish; hospitality and refusal of fundamentalism.

There is a new Master of the Talmud: Adin Steinsaltz! The newspaper (*Le Monde*, August 2, 2001) comes to a boil, witnesses strive to outdo one another, he is "the most extraordinary man that I have ever met . . ." As usual he looks like all the other Masters of Wisdom always have. It is the same "humour"; for example, as Péguy: he knows that he is in God's head, it is the same schema. It is the traditional paradoxical reversal: God in the little things, with an air of nothing. All wisdom is trivial. Even when, O Wise One, you will have reduced the vanities of the ego, the self-service [in English in the original], there will remain the essential dissymmetrical relation, the "I-me"; it is enough that you know that you are dying, and that is your being, to be two, like hydrogen, and two is one too many. I is another [Rimbaud]. Egoicity is forever to be lived, insofar as it is life for every one of us, whether we are full of ourselves or not.

*

Jews, who are you? All of human diversity. From one extremity to another, to what extreme can you not go, like any man today, and indeed ever since "the Gospel": from Pharisean "formalism" and the most narrow ritualistic subjugation (for me, just as worrisome as regular Muslim prostration or the rabid vegetarianism of the Jainite) to the perfect atheism and secularity of this or that one of your intellectuals (and describing the "condition of women" in any society would furnish here the inexhaustible resource of desired examples), with nothing in common between you, except that Freudian nothing that I have evoked. Such a typology opens up and covers the field of human possibilities and isolates nothing essentially different separating us, a different difference of differences, which would make an exceptional exception for Judaic societies. If I neutralize through agnosticism your Judaity, removing your faith through atheism, your religion, your holy history, in brief all of your myths and appose them *equally with all of the others* in the great book and the great anthropological museum, there is nothing left for my friend the Jew that distinguishes him from any other other. There remains no stronger (nor less strong) difference between "us" (you and me; them and us) than that which reigns between a Catalan, a Ukrainian, an Araucan . . . *enemy brothers*.

*

Any particularity is in a minority position with respect to all of the others taken together. Any minority is, then, comparatively weak, its for-itself is threatened, even threatened with extinction, in a state of "self-defense."

Whence the Hobbesian question, but on the scale of peoples or minorities: how to avoid this war of all against all? Yet the Jewish nation—so nameable because it has come out of the diaspora, which was more formidable than Pharaoh, and is installed in earthly Zion—is it not more frail than any other? One would tend to say so, since it has been exterminated and it is still assailed by neighbors and by enemies within who do not recognize its right to existence on its land (on this earth and on the earth) and who fight for its disappearance. Nevertheless, its movement toward the universal, its truth, stagnates, so to speak, in the particularity in which it has got stuck.

All of humanity will be Jewish . . . or all of Judaity will be human? Each particularity wants to take along its properties in the movement of its universalization or to take humanity-along-with-itself in the movement of its own relief (or of a surpassing which preserves). . . . Where do we begin? Singularity (let's say the subject) can probably do this, or tries to bravely, as a conversion or transformation of oneself into a "man," a march toward the "ideal," or however one might say it; this is the movement of Montaigne toward "the entire *form* of the human condition," in the tradition out of which Sartre speaks, "composed of all men." But a collective, a people, a nation, seems to be unable to manage this, nor to finish it. Romanticism against *Aufklärung*; *Dasein* against citizenship ("European," world . . .).

*

Our children of the 1960s, the *soixante-huitards*, had resolved the problem radically, that is to say terminologically: they spoke of the mass and of masses (some continue to do so) in order to be rid of the mortgage of real particularities, of ethnicity, nationalisms, regionalisms and other church-steeples, with a *coup de langue* (a palate revolution?), as if the mass (better still: the masses), human indeed, homogeneous in their indeterminacy, and on that scale not distinct from Humanity (all the more so given that that word has always denoted both the essence and the multitude), magically departicularized (we didn't say the Chinese mass or the Turkish or the Peruvian mass, etc. but the masses) becoming a subject of History even while identifying (incarnating) Humanity: all blended into the mass in an immediately universal truth (an Assumption of the popular People into an immense classless society, *like* the "anonymous" crowd beneath the reviewing stand of the dictator on May Day)? This was indeed one way to resolve the problem.

The problem is that of the passage from particularity (or generality: for what is at stake is the general good, the common good of this society here, or this nation here, but not of "all humans") to universality, through the mediation, possibly, of a "singularity"—if the singular is that which has access to the universal, while the general remains particular. But what singularity? It is to be invented, like that of a "citizen of the world" who would become global in the local through a "globalization" that is other than the economic one. The era proposes a "cultural" globalization, very likely. Cosmopolitanism through cultures? But *the cultural* loses along the way that which we hope it will preserve and carry with it, namely culture in the old, traditional sense. (Elsewhere I have sketched out that problematic.)

The question becomes: what is the singularity (or the quasi-singularity) in the case of a collective being, of a multiple (one used to speak of the soul or the spirit or the genius of a Nation)? And can *the cultural* ensure this function, take up this "singularity"?

*

In other words: the denomination (the humanity of "man," with or without capitals, but it is even better with) does not make a common denominator. The Sartrean formula "who is worth the same as all and is the equal of all" does not furnish a general equivalent, determinable like a currency.[5] Form and content fall back from one another, each to its own side. Montaigne indeed spoke of *form* and the form retains nothing of vernacular habits, of local tastes, of linguistic or culinary traditions, of the regional. . . . Retains *nothing*. . . . Do we have to pass through the nothing? Very likely. I often note this, thanks to poetry, to poetic education. But Béni-Lévy's [*sic*] objection will block the road for all of us: nothingness is impracticable. No to the central void, no to Claude Lefort, he repeats. Man does not live on nothing, etc.

The form of the human condition has something formal to it, without being a simple formality. The Rights of Man are "purely formal." And how! And, Kant will say, following Montaigne, so to speak, that *purely* good will is formal: it is really only through form that I can universalize my (particular) "maxim." All the while, if I may say, the content lags behind, persisting and resisting, not allowing itself to be trans-*formed*. I really want *my language*, *my values*, as we say today, to become universal, but I accept with some difficulty that those of others might be preferable and preferred, "worth more" for this "rising-up," this "final solution" where we would all find ourselves among "Humans," in the plural and with the capital letter. How do we reduce (evacuate) these values all the while making them subsist, in what way, inoffensive and attractive, neutralized and widespread? The only current answer, we would say, is through the market, on the market (and even "into the bargain"); widely available, over the counter: we would dispose freely of the values through "market competition." There would be only one solution: the market where everything worth anything may be found (that is the relief, the rising-up, the *Aufhebung*): all particularities, if not all persuasions, exchangeable, thanks to money (and in dollars rather than gold)?

How would a people shed its untranslatable particularity to enter into universalization? Through an impracticable *separation* that should happen on the inside of each particularity, separating the formal from the material, the legal from the substantial, the public from the private, that is to say, in the end (the end of our history), separating the State from the Church: for the separation bringing secularization and profanation to completeness is secularity [*la laïcité*]. But a people is its god! So? In the meantime, let us wage wars of recognition.

France was doing pretty well until quite recently: she was telling anyone who wanted to listen (and they really wanted to) that she was revolutionary and wanted to bring along with her own revolution the liberation of all others. And they believed it. (Sartre is remembering this when he protests that no one will be free as long as a single human being is oppressed.) Revolutionary and secular France (a hundred years later) decides that her exception is precisely a universalizing one (there is something left of this in the affirmation of the "cultural exception" today); that *her* transformation brings the "Rights of Man" to the universe. For France, it has been done . . . Oof! And how about the others? Whose turn is it next?

The question is posed again: is this what Cohen and Rosenzweig wanted to say? What does Israel (in translation: the Chosen), that we often call "the Jewish State," bring to others?

*

Juridical invention, progression in international knowledge and consciousness of law, may favor a moral regression. In going from the *crime against humanity* (the Nuremberg trials) to the conception of *genocide* (the emergence of which we might date from the years of the Eichmann trial) isn't there some risk of a setback?

The incrimination of "against humanity" indeed signifies that the Nazis by exterminating the Jews of Europe—according to Hillberg's historical title—murderously attacked humanity as a whole, an expression that takes together the multitude and the essence. They "did that" to the Jews, certainly, and in that way, I almost said "above all" (because it's not "into the bargain"; I will use that adverbial structure, "above all," to make myself understood at the risk of shocking) to "we humans." All humans. An irreparable act that no reparation of any kind can efface, even if all of the Jewish families and Zion and the State of Israel, had received compensation, had unimaginably healed, and the scars formed, if I may say. We might even say that reparation, to the extent that there is any, and indeed, depending upon the tribunals, the restitution or despoliation "evaluated" each time, should (or "symbolically" could) refer to, and fall on, a victim of actual substitution representing excluded humanity (what Michel Serres recently called, in an article in *Le Monde*, the "black box," and others the fourth-world, or "naked life" compared to the Muslim in Auschwitz by Giorgio Agamben, all of those who are barred from human society like the *lepers* of yesteryear). The evil has been done. This new formulation of absolute Evil has occurred. Humanity was destroyed, abolished; it failed once and for all; this has occurred, an event more terrible in the eyes of the atheist than when "God himself" was torn apart and sent to the dead. The torture and the programmed dehumanization of the Jews break apart humanity more absolutely than did the crucifixion two thousand years ago. Indeed, for no redemption. It is not a Jewish man calling himself God who is put to death, it is humanity denying itself under the species of one of its multiples, integral to its being-human as Nation, as village, as family, as flesh and blood, as history and culture—an integral part "worth" the whole, there is no other mode. *Homo sum*, thought the Nazi, *et sunt homines quos me alienos esse puto* [I am human, thought the Nazi, and there are humans whom I consider to be other than me]. Anthropocide.

Wouldn't we say that the incrimination of genocide, if it limits the crime, the *–cide*, by circumscribing it to one human "species" rather than to the whole genus, and to an exterminating reciprocity between two *ethnos* (Hutus/Tutsis) banalizes evil and that the possibility of imputing its exemplarity retrospectively would multiply its prototypes at the same time as it unleashes its reproductions (these are the ideological stakes of the proclamation of an Armenian "genocide" by the Turks; it is the "right" or not for an historian to speak of the "genocide" of the Chouans; it is the confused struggle over the absolute "incomparability" of the Shoah)? I was going to say that it labels its own copy, suggesting its own imitations, like the "Rwandan" one.

The perhaps impassable obstacle to fraternity lies in the impossible-to-uproot ethnicity of humans, in the non-superposability of the particularity/

generality pair and of the singularity/universality couple, and if the law of preservation of the *genos* wins out over every other law and takes priority over even the "absolute value" of the person. "There will be no more Jews nor Germans" could be heard and understood in this way: things must not get more communitarized! Ethical inventivity is called to resist ethnicity.

Jewish ethnicity is excepted among the "nations," so to speak by its etymology, since *gentiles* translated the Greek *ta ethnê* (Matthew 10, 5), which itself translates the Hebrew *goim*, non-Jewish "peoples." The Jews are not the Gentiles. But modern history resists this exceptionality and Jewish ethnicity falls back into the ranks inasmuch as the division of pagans and chosen people is no longer transcendental. The God of the monotheists is no longer the Last Judge of History. There is no more Rome, nor Jerusalem. We are all pagans, or all chosen, it's our choice. We are all called and none chosen. Called to "humanity."

From another angle, but from just that point of view where Israel protested its having been put, taking it for anti-Semitic, we could say: why wouldn't its people have "the right" to be, *like everyone*, "dominant and sure of itself," following the example of every nation since there have been nations, as in their time England, Spain, France, Germany, and so on.

Reciprocal contempt, reciprocal disgust and the hatred of nations among themselves constitute the most serious obstacle, still and forever, to any federation in general (that is to say, any subsuming of a group of nations under a more common good, a more general interest; and in the end an integration into the "society of nations" or the subsuming under the concrete universal of a humanity called on to enter into undividedness, sharing the world of the earth). I will take the nearest example from the reluctance of our own nations on the threshold of "Europe." We must emerge from the time of contempt [*le temps du mépris*]. The insoluble heterogeneity of nations among themselves is lived out principally in Babelesque suffering and in the sealed-over quality of idioms, lived out as a we-can't-understand-each-other-at-all, lacking a common language.

It is because "I" am infected with the same evil as you that "I" understand you, that I understand us—understanding the primordial harm, our "second nature," and knowing that we are not, none of us, in any citizenship whatsoever, safe from xenophobia, that detestable and ridiculous first movement—which can be healed, but how?

Translation is the necessary, inevitable future—or nothing. But *into what language?*

It is Nations as such, re-ethnicized in the immense regression to roots, the roots of a re-rooting upon which Simone Weil's program never meditated, that, grabbing individuals and communities by their feet and their weight, are slowing down humanity—at the same time that the cosmonaut in weightlessness, an apolitical citizen of Space and the Satellite, shows off his spacesuit covered with advertising on our utopian screens. All the while, the "humanitarian" deploys tireless energies in the new and immense garbage dumps on the edges of the ethnocidary battlefields, there where thousands of "naked lives" fabricated by warlords get piled atop one another.

What's new since Marx? Exploitation, domination, still; "as though servitude were never to cease." And the class struggle? But into what have the classes been changed? Money abolishes social classes and "distinction"—but not slavery; on the contrary.

APPENDIX A

INTERVIEW WITH MICHEL DEGUY

Stillorgan Park Hotel
Dublin, Ireland
Saturday, December 15, 2012

CE: Ten years already. The objective in this interview, a little different from the frequent oral interviews that we have conducted and made together over the past nearly twenty years, because it is based on a series of preliminary written questions and exchanges, is to resituate *A Man of Little Faith* for new readers; to situate it within its trajectory, for itself and beyond itself. The questions mirror to some extent the main emphases of the Introduction to this translation but open up for you very broadly a space of re-vision and retro-spection, as you sometimes like to say, looking back at the Bayard volume from a distance of ten years and more than a dozen subsequent books (not including the Gallimard anthologies, the *livres d'artistes*, the *grand cahier Bordeaux*, as we call the work of compilation of your late friend Jean-Pierre Moussaron, or the various volumes in translation from Brazil to Germany to . . .). The Man of Little Faith who opened the twenty-first century with a palinody has continued to mingle alarm and exhilaration, poetic reason and lyrical unease in a unique and prolonged witnessing in and to our "aporetical times."

The five main thrusts or five axes, overflowing and overboarding one another, will be the following:

1. The place of palinody in a contemporary literature of wisdom.
2. Motifs of afterward and of exit.
3. The relation of your poetics to deconstruction through the paradoxical operations of the X without X.

4. The "little faith," the new faith and persistent earthly piety.

5. The cultural situation and ecological resistance.

MD: These are vast and difficult matters.

CE: Let's begin with the palinody. *A Man of Little Faith* is a palinody; you set it up that way and it is perhaps the best generic description for the book. The palinody disenchants and it descants. It is a matter of "becoming oneself," in a theme with variations that you borrow from Goethe who took it from Pindar, through a process that mixes conversion and treachery. It is also, it seems to me, a matter of taking stock and summing up, of doing the work of mourning, too, mourning for many things and for many beings, many ways of being. There is something testamentary here, and with that, a taste of beyond the grave. What are the accents of your palinody today?

MD: In an autobiographical tone, I'm somewhat astonished to have been taken by the palinody in my own life. If, let's say, I had died at fifty, it's a theme that I never would have had the time to consider. That is quite extraordinary, but it is, at the same time, in the becoming that you are calling above the becoming-wise of the poet, that the movement of the palinody gets started.

What does it mean, palinody? It is a movement in reverse, but with no return-to, that is no regressive integrism/fundamentalism, it is not a matter of returning to the starting point, so then, it is a return in the form of a loop and which does not return to the point that was left behind, what we call an integrization or a regression, the movement of someone who says to himself, I made a mistake, I'm going to go back. Put another way, it is at once a loop and an ascension. That is why recently I picked up again an old formula of mine that you quoted yesterday, namely "To fall and in falling to fall." I say to myself that at bottom that is also "To fall and in falling to rise . . ." which is even more astonishing. This is a movement of re-turning and of elevating oneself. So then my whole motif of elevation is the question of the trans-. Slight transcendence, transformation, rising above, toward, but it is a transcendence that I call slight transcendence, we might say human transcendence. Put yet another way, it is the movement by which the human, homo, superhumanizes itself. It is precisely he who raises himself up from the ground, which is a paradox, for example in the paradox of Münchausen, the bootstrap paradox. Ultimately it's impossible, how does one raise oneself up?

CE: But both as a human being and as a writer isn't there a risk of being torn apart when one feels caught up in some kind of fall and also pulled toward some sort of ascension? How can anyone manage all of that?

MD: That is indeed the question, the question of the fulcrum point for managing all of that, how can we raise ourselves up? There are a number of ways of thinking about this. Perhaps a little bit like Freud, and that is the transformation that we call sublimation. It is really the same movement, that's very surprising. It is the transformation of the libido, or sexual energy, as you wish, into something else through sublimation. Through what must we pass, from what fulcrum of what lever both above us and not exterior to the human? It is not a god who saves us in that way but an exit from ourselves toward a point of support. In Baudelairean language, it is Elevation. Elevation is really odd. "My spirit you move with agility . . ." ["Mon esprit, tu te meus avec agilité" "Elevation"] There, that's a question, can man pick himself up with his own forces, including among them the strengths that we call Freudian for the transformation of libido. And that is what we might call wisdom. We cannot really say, that's how we need to do things, but that is the question and in which the work of art is caught up.

CE: And so that's it, then, the fulcrum? The work of art?

MD: Yes, yes. Of course and I don't really see many others. Because if we only think in terms of economy, if we only think in terms of desire and satisfaction, there is then no mechanism for a raising up of oneself, that is to say, a raising-above the hominicide, above the risk of a continual abasement of humanity. I think then that it is art which is the point of support for the fulcrum, which is an immense ambition, at heart quite Nietzschean, that of the truth of the work of art. Sometime ago that was called beauty; that was the fulcrum point, one that was visible and fixable as a call to something self-surpassing or self-elevating. It is all of that which is undergoing change and in mutation and the names of which the poem or writing modifies in alloys and pseudonymies, heteronomies, and that's really the affair of writing inasmuch as it is salutary to the beautiful, obviously. There is a major reflection: we believe that it is a way of passing time, entertainment, or rather that it is the means to an end which is safeguarding, salvation, but once again not in the terms of religious salvation. Is all of that possible? It is desirable, it is very likely within the grasp of a certain power, but it is not certain that it will come to pass.

CE: Does your approach remain palinodic? The growing presence, at once hoped-for, sought-after, yet dubitative and at times ironical, in your later work of the *sophos*, is it explicable without the palinody? Would the palinody be the poetic find, the discovery of a thinking at the level of language, we could say the linguistic and philosophical basis for that possible wisdom?

MD: You ask if my way of proceeding remains palinodic. Yes, of course, it is the accentuation, the aggravation, the further deepening of that way of proceeding, with some variations. For me, the palinody is synoymous with, or is in synonymy with, the *sophos*, the becoming-wise. There is an old French expression, "*grandir: croître en âge et en sagesse.*" [to grow: to increase in age and in wisdom]. And what is more, the relation of age and of wisdom is very precise, I believe, and very dangerous, very bizarre because that too makes a cut between generations, or let's say, the cut between youth, getting young, being young, on the one hand and aging on the other which is at the same time a perishing. Of course it is like St John Perse whom we were evoking at the colloquium, "Grand Age, here we are!" [*Chronicle*] which is an entering into wisdom and we must not ever underestimate the fact that this makes for an extremely powerful difference which we might conceive of in terms of energy, the energy that seems to be limitless of growing youth and then of the fullness of youth and then, on the other side, the fading out, the dimming and the easing-off that is perhaps a senescence, anyway, all of the themes in which the aging-growing gets designated as primarily a weakening. So, managing to give wisdom credence, not because the years are accumulating, because precisely, the operation of return-to and of going-further is not made possible simply by an addition of the years.

What is it to age, finally? It's not just having eyes that dry up or reflexes that diminish. That would be absolutely without interest because without the favor of something that would be at one and the same time a transformation of the body and a spiritual occasion, if I dare say, provided that we understand "spirit" in the German sense of "*Geist*" that is, in the sense of judgment and intelligence.

I could also say this in a totally different way, look, by taking up a common term, *intelligence*. Obviously, there are two principal ways to treat and to analyze intelligence. What is intelligence? I'm going to simplify a bit by strongly distinguishing combinatory, calculating intelligence, the speed of associations, everything that is tied to an energy, a bodily youthfulness, the capacity of calculation in general. And, on the other hand, judgment and reason, estimation. Said another way, what is happening right now? All of human intelligence is oriented according to the model of "robotization." Recently, I forged a little aphorism that you might recognize, which takes up again Pascal's old formula in an amusing way: Man is a robot, but a robot that thinks [by contrast with Pascal: *L'homme est un roseau, mais un roseau qui pense*]. Man is a brain, but a thinking brain. The brain itself is thought on the model of the robot, that is to say the comparison of the robot with the brain.

That is something assured. At every moment that is the way the world works. But we cannot forget that intelligence is not just that, that there is another intelligence that is not measurable in terms of combinatory quickness, for example, but that is a power of judging, thinking to judge, judging by comparing. That's one of my formulas, "Thinking is judging,

judging is comparing" and there we are on our way toward the ontology of like [*comme*]. Rapprochements and comparisons are not combinatory intelligence and we have to maintain that. So then, the underlying movement, I would say, no doubt a bit too simply, the growth in age is the relaying, the carrying-further of judgment, of the thought of what we call wisdom.

CE: Already in 1981 in *Donnant Donnant* you were posing the problem of senescence in terms of the fragments of aging, in the poem-meditation "*Fragments du V . . . X*"

MD: It is not the same modulation there. There I am taking up more positively senescence as possible growth. Always the same thing. It is not enough to get older in order to. . . . No. It is a chance and an occasion to grasp the other face of thought. It needs to be thought of in the unity of the signified. A moment ago I distinguished combinatory intelligence and judgment, the power of judging there is comparing, discerning, distinguishing, critical power, all of that is the same power for me. Discerning what is the same from that which is not the same in order to judge, given that it is the same or that if the things have nothing to do with each other, we act differently. That faculty, the other faculty, let's say discriminating, judging, is really a side of what we call our experience, that is, our failures, it develops and that is what I mean by "getting old" but evidently not in the sense of exhaustion.

CE: Do you have the impression that a seeking for wisdom has influenced the forms, the topics or the orientations of your recent books? We see ecology as a wisdom, a reflection on Baudelaire as a kind of meditation on modern wisdom, and more generally a lot of texts that seem to me like poetic chronicles of wisdom, with a formal and or generic stretching that goes with that.

MD: Both the subjects and the form. The intensification of difference and at the same time of the difference within the same, in what I call undividedness, *indivision*. That is what I sometimes call the hendiadys, I pay attention to the hendiadys, that is to the one-in-two and in different fields. The one-in-two is an enormous matter. It might pass for a rhetorical figure. I can take that formula now as a formal law of poetics in the sense of knowing how to make a poem. To make *one* it is necessary for there to be *two*, that is the question of the caesura, of the hemistich, you see even the hendiadynic formula one-in-two comes to interest and to captivate the know-how of the poem itself. Here's a question of poetics: Can a monosyllable present itself isolated on a line? I might write, like plenty of contemporary poets do, a monosyllable like "I" or "You," but there, if we need two to make one, the minimal element in poetic writing must have the double character of an idea which is made with two, so then, at a minimum, two syllables for it to rhyme, for it to make one.

The hendiadys is very important. And with that I observe, this is another of my things, that in taking a figure, an item in the rhetorical dictionary, I will make it serve to say something true about the whole of tropologic and figurative thought. When we get down to it, perhaps one might say that each major term of a dictionary of poetics and rhetoric might, like the part that gives onto the whole, serve to characterize the whole area, the whole set. And saying that, in this example, thought is hendyadinic inasmuch as it is tropological. But we could say the same thing about allegory, the syncope, etc.

CE: That sounds like a variation on your idea of a generalized figure, and that generalized or generalizable figure has no doubt something to do with the forms of the texts themselves. I'm thinking of *Au jugé* [Firing Blind], its chronicles or "columns," and of various other mixtures that are not radically new—the formal or generic inventivity has always been there—but this is perhaps oriented differently now.

MD: Yes, well, that is to say that poetic writing cannot help but be sententious, aphoristic, at bottom what prose of accompaniment, paraphrasing prose of accompaniment has to be.

Not that the writer can't make a poem in prose like Baudelaire, that's something else, but he can present his poem in an amphitheater, comment on it, accompany it. The successful poem must sententiously strike a thoughtful formula, a new formula for thought, briefly. So in reply to your questions about a search for wisdom influencing the forms of the poems, I would say yes and isn't a beautiful poem a sequence of axioms, a sequence of propositions that might be isolated like a piece from Heraclitus?

CE: In your last book, *Ecologiques*, you speak of infallibility with respect to a poem by Baudelaire . . .

MD: Well, that is something recent. And it belongs to what I've been calling for a while the conservation, the preservation of relics. The head of the Catholic Church is considered, since the nineteenth century, considered and thought by theologians as being infallible—under certain conditions, of course. I ask myself the question: what is the infallibility, what is the cannot-be-mistaken of the poem? In a magnificent poem, an admirable poem, one among so many others, by Baudelaire or, since we are in Dublin, this or that poem by Yeats? All of a sudden an isolated verse: each one hears that here a truth is being condensed, both enigmatically and one that hits the mark: infallible. To hit the mark, said Baudelaire "To strike the target of mystical nature" ["The Death of the Artists"]. In the end, perhaps every verse is trying to strike the target then, like an arrow on its course. The archer might be infallible. At bottom, the verses that we love, that we recite, that we will remember, they are the arrows striking the target. Infallibility. The poet is always fallible, it doesn't need to be said, some verses are failures, or the thought of a verse fails, and so on, but then, suddenly: infallibility.

Since that human virtue, human insofar as it has been accorded to a man, the Pope, that possibility means that if I transport that thought of infallibility it gives the result that there can be an infallibility of the poem. A great poem may be infallible. That remains to be commented on at length.

CE: I thought that was a very strikingly phrased insight.

MD: Ah, yes, it is very important. Or: the poem of Baudelaire is infallible.

CE: *A Man of Little Faith* and the books that have followed it, amplify the sentiment or the motif, a major tonality in your works, of ends. *La Fin dans le monde*, a singularly evocative, punning title is an important concentration of that emphasis, that tendency or that evolution in your trajectory. Perhaps, as George Steiner had it, we are in a time of epilogue. But I don't think that would satisfy you as a formula and the title *The End in the World* is a title that is never-ending . . .

MD: Here again, as is often the case, there are some themes that began to come up a long time ago, already. In this case it come from the last page of Baudelaire, when he asks himself, how is the world going to end? Of course Baudelaire knows that it is he who is going to die, but the end of the world is in play. His own dying allows him, following a certain metaphor, his own perishing-dying allows him to envisage, to enter into the question of the end of the world.

The theme, the motif of the end appears with the nineteenth century, it is the apocalyptic theme, but it is a theme that took on in the twentieth century all of its amplification, the end of philosophy, the end of history, the end of metaphysics, the end. What do we mean by that? In the end, there is the end in the world [*la fin dans le monde*]. The world where we live is a world where all the time it is a matter of stories of the end, we are finishing up with x or y . . .

I believe that there are two families of spirits, one for which there has been a mutation that is to say a passage to the without-precedent of our time. That is the question of the caesura, in the language of Lacoue-Labarthe.

I belong to a spiritual family that thinks, which sees (the business of warning indicators [*voyants*] and of clairvoyancy) that in the twentieth century, globalization is that very question of the end *in* the world, of the end of the world in the world. It starts with the war, with the First World War, then, there follows the Second World War, then the extermination of the Jews, genocide, etc. And that it is not simply in the long historical sequence, as we may recall in Canetti's famous book, where we read the succession of infernal massacres. No, there is something happening without precedent. This is not just one war after another, one risk after another, and this theme, if you will, is the basis for ecological worry and anguish.

All of these ends in the world are premonitory, but look out! We cannot conceive of this as just predictions and superstitions of a given sect A: the end of the world is happening next week, as we know [this interview was conducted a week before the highly mediatized end of the Mayan calendar]. The world is never through with its ending and in the never-ending ending something like a possible *real* ending happens; what does that mean? That the human comes to a halt? What does that mean, stops, just like that? We'll develop that in a moment.

It means that it mutates into another; this is the question of mutation. The change is not a change, this change that makes it so that we are always in the grip of computers, what I called a moment ago combinatory intelligence, which makes it such that the slightest human exchange now is regulated by very high technology, which means that calculating intelligence is all the time in mediation between us, it modifies everything and everywhere it makes possible all of the artifacts that we make, all of the economic development that it possibilizes. Is that a mutation, not simply one more change adding to the others, and that mutation is called an end with a question mark? The end, that means becoming-other, really other. For some of us, this is not happening. For some of us, it might be a surhumanization and we will say that distraction, entertainment superman, the Superman of films and comic strips, things for kids, is that the human type that is called to be realized, at once super-muscular with a super-computer in his head, and super-powers? All that is childish, we understand, but because we spend our time showing it, representing it, it expresses a certain desire.

CE: But that's not the second spiritual family.

MD: No, no, not at all. The family of which I am speaking does not think in those terms. It thinks of the possibility of an overcoming of humanity by itself in the terms of auto-transcendence. All of this to say the reuse of the forms of art in the logos, not outside of the language of thought, not outside of thinking as it speaks. That is the whole business, since, that is to say not mathematical understanding. It is the understanding or logical reason that is to say capable of speaking, the logical imagination that is a form of life, that is the job of the work of art. To measure these mutations, to worry about the cultural economy, to worry about what I call the general screenization, that is part of the urgencies.

The real, now, what is it? It is essentially the screen before us. What is happening happens to us through the screen. From whence come all of my questions about the image, and there again we have a dangerous homonymy. The whole question of the radical difference in the appearance of the same; and well, it is the question of what I call homonymy insofar as it casts a veil of ignorance over everything.

We might say, well, who cares, it comes through the screen, what does that change? If I make pictures or not? Measuring first and foremost the power of the change in this relation to the new tools, that is what we must begin by appreciating, not at all as a small modification but as it is transformative for all of humanity. We take it seriously or we don't take it seriously. We can say, "ahhh, but I don't have a computer." No. There is a mutation. I think that there is a modification, a mutation in the intensification.

That touches vernacular languages in their loquacity. The sentence has changed. It happens to poetry too. It is a certain ending in a certain mutation.

CE: What, then, is the other family?

MD: The other family is the family of optimists. I'll take a nice example, which is that of Michel Serres who often articulates the questions that we're stirring up here. So, he says, we're just a bunch of cranky old guys but look, here come the youth and they're going to resolve all of that stuff. That is to say that there is now a praise of youth which is not at all the one that Hannah Arendt articulated when she spoke of the newborn, the newcomers, newness in the world; in this case, too, everything is now getting doubled up in a quasi-homonymy. For example, today, the fundamental term is innovation. There is no economy, no growth, no consumption without innovation. Technical innovation. What difference is there between innovation and newness? Or we might well say that it's the same thing, that the change from newness to innovation is just a change that is happening in the world or we might also be inclined to say, "Watch out!": the essential difference passes between what *was* the new, the novel, the "the virgin the vivid and the beautiful today" ["*Le vierge, le vivace, le bel aujourd'hui,*" an untitled sonnet by Mallarmé] and what we call innovation. Everything rests on innovation. It has to be a slightly crazy economy to think that at any moment, let's take a kind of futile example, one is being told that now you have a razor with three blades, or four or five. Which of course means next time it's five or six or seven. Some people will say, that's of little importance, they all cut, what's the big deal? Some others might say, whoa there, this is the destructive excitation of an entirely constructed desire.

That kind of innovation is the springboard for the economy inasmuch as it is global or becoming global.

All that acceleration of consumerism is what distances and I would even say thwarts eco-logical thought, that is to say the thought that is attached to human habitation and the human dwelling. So, then, it is not just a small difference, there is a fundamental difference. It happens to cleave the ecological family in two; there are those who say, we'll come out of this alright, we can settle innovation down and then there is the other perspective that is more radical. I am always for the radicality of the question, a radicality that is difficult to perceive because the whole network of homonymies or small differences covers over the essential difference. It's what I have just recalled about innovation and what Hannah Arendt had to say about the newcomers; Arendt who said, and this is magnificent, at any moment the newborn arrives, the newborn of humanity, at that moment the power of re-creation is there. That newness is not what we mean by innovation today. At bottom, innovation is exhausting. In the end it is innovation that exhausts the earth.

Invention, perfection of techniques, technological progress; but finally that is at the same time the exhaustion of earthly resources by innovation. It would be necessary for a major economist to take an overview of what we call global growth, production, the number of patents, the reorientation of economies: we still call that an ever higher performance of the economy. So, there is an ever better performance; ecology was simply a brake on that, on the forever better performing, a brake in the name of a sustainable development. We could ask ourselves the following question: Is *development* sustainable?

CE: Could it be thought of as sustainable?

MD: Or there might be a conversion to be made that would have some connections to what I'm calling the palinody. Because it is not simply a brake on development that is called for, each time that we consider, for example, the survival of species, it is a reorientation that is not a going-back either. To invent a reorientation that would not be simply a return, that is very difficult. Among other things, because an important segment of nations and peoples is taken up in a movement of fundamentalism, of integrism. What is that? It is going back. But the return is impossible. The power of the movement of regression, of integrization, of fundamentalism, of returning to the integral is a formidable power in the present world. And so, there too, conflicts are being prepared, in the *going-back-to*. Struggles against fundamentalism in general and of course that passes in large part through the religious.

CE: One can readily identify a few major threads in your thinking of ends and of afterwords; one of them is undoubtedly that of *after the Revolution*.

MD: That is very important. One of the modes of difference that at any moment is being transformed into conflict is the distinction between revolution and reform. Here we are venturing onto a terrain that we'll call political. What difference is there between revolution and reform? Ultimately, the revolutionary theme and momentum are still there but what actually happen is reforms. I believe that the revolutionary hope, a way of passing, of utterly changing relationships, for example between dominant and dominated, that the theme of the Revolution and the hope that it might be brought about politically through violence, all of that belongs to the past. (But of course there are still innumerable revolutionaries all over the place.) The question is that of Reform and we can observe that the parties in power in Europe are the Social-Democrats. That means: what reform can we manage? Is reforming ourselves possible? That is the grand Lutherian term, and we would probably have to take together the political understanding of the term and the religious, Lutherian, one. Religion was able to reform itself in the sixteenth century. In Reform I cannot not hear that. That's wonderful.

CE: So, then, what does it mean to be a reformer? To opt for Reform?

MD: It means that we must also, taking up the grand and magnificent motifs of the Revolution, treat them as *Relics*, to use my term from *A Man of Little Faith*. That is to say, liberty, equality, fraternity. What's more, that sequence is itself really interesting. We would need to examine why everything begins with liberty, then we pass to equality and it is fraternity that comes along third. Is there some kind of order of implication, of consequence in these three words that are linked up and which could make a sentence? So, the difference between revolution and reform that I am evoking may be summed up this way: that between liberty and liberation. Liberty and emancipation. So we're not at all abandoning the motif of emancipation, of freeing-oneself, but freeing oneself from *what* is our question? And it is the revolutionary radicality of liberty that must be interpreted as a relic and that Socialism or Social-Democracy needs to work out. The problem is that it doesn't please anybody. The revolutionary attached to the Revolution says to himself, "no, no, no, that's not what I wanted." And for the worried conservative, if he's not too keen on reforms, they're not very useful either.

For me, the middle way is a way that must be looked at very closely. I would say it, using political language, in the following way: The center, holding oneself at the center, the invention of the center, is not at all to be found through a formula like "neither-this-nor-that," it is not by a reduction through the amputation of the extremities that we come to hold a center, but it is through something like a "both-this-*and*-that." Put another way, the formula of the Reformists is not 'neither-nor' but 'and-and.' The center being all the better assured if the scale that balances the two extremities is more open and more vast. Put yet another way, thinking in terms of contrariety, naming what is contradicted, thwarted, paralyzed, in such a way that the two poles of the contrariety wouldn't be bad opposites but would require the operation of a "*both this and that*" which would ensure a center.

The way out through the center is to be invented with "and-and" and not with "neither-nor."

CE: So your movement is really a double one, not a compromise but a reciprocal intensification and a search for the middle way through the exacerbation of contradictions.

MD: Yes, the middle way through oppositeness, contrariety. Then, applying that to each thing, as we just sketched out for liberty. For example, let's take equality now. What is happening in the name of equality, if we think of the Third World, or of the growing inequality in the West, is always surprising. I'm going to make a precise allusion to a number of the journal *Critique,* which I read last week on the question of the difference of humanity as man/woman, as sexuality. An issue that argues overall that for there to be equality in the world, it is necessary to suppress that difference which used to be considered natural, which indeed was nature, the male–female difference. Of course these aren't the same thing, masculine–feminine, male–female, but the basic polarity ensuring the natural continuation of the human species is put into question, attacked. Probably heading for disappearance in the name of equality. But what is that equality? It's not simply a kind of dumb equality in terms of financial criteria, and so on. Suppressing generic human duality in the name of equality, that is to say, a being-the-same, a man/woman equality/identity. There is an extraordinary essay in that issue that sums up with respect to Judith Butler et al. and the post-gender movement how to get woman out of nature (but that also means woman/man, man/woman), how to extract, then, the natural duo by means of technique from nature, in such a way that the difference which passed for natural gets effaced. So, one of the great questions of today for philosophers, that is to say for us, is where has nature got to? What is nature?

We remember that Rousseau enchanted Europe in the eighteenth century by saying, here is nature, behold nature! Natural education, natural religion, natural law, everything is natural, it is the return to nature or rather the invention of nature. Man in the state of nature, consciousness of nature, God in the natural path, etc. But, let's be careful, it is as if already in the eighteenth century there was a disappearance of Nature, because when Rousseau comes along and he says, behold what nature is, all of Europe says to itself, that's fantastic! We've found nature, in its slightest details, like breastfeeding mothers, like the natural education of the human species, and that is the *Emile*, the natural contract, and that is extraordinary. A kind of inflammation, then, of nature in the eighteenth and nineteenth centuries, the Romantics are born of that and then, wow, suddenly, *Nature has happened*, as Hölderlin said, nature *disappears*.

My question is what must equality be, how do we think the equality that is being sought, one of the aspects of which, one of the modes, is perhaps what we call parity. . . . Equality is being sought in different ways. How to think equality?

CE: And how can we think it while making the connection you seek to the relics?

MD: Equality may be confused today with what we call identity, in the sense of the same, the same, the same. As Elisabeth Badinter put it, *L'un est l'autre* [*One is* [is/and est/et] *the other*] between one is the other, or even, one is masculine and feminine, and this is my theme, one is *like* the other [l'un(e) est *comme* l'autre]. What difference ought we to maintain thanks to the ontology of the *comme*? What difference is to be maintained, that is to say what refusal of identitary identity can there be? So there is a thought of identity in the text to which I'm referring from *Critique*, equality comes up all the time, but it is man–woman equality, equality itself is never thought. So difference has become impossible to put up with and the question becomes "how can we get out of this through technique?" Because delivering the woman from her productive body, from her status as pregnant woman and mother in the first months and years has become urgent. The mother must nurse the baby, the father cannot, that is a basic fact. And there is everything that this difference brought along with it in the division of labor, the traditional differences in careers, and so forth, it is from all of that that it is a matter of escaping, it is an exit from nature, or from what was nature. In the name of equality, and again I wonder, what is the thought of that equality? It is not the equality that the Revolutionaries proclaimed. So equality can change, perhaps it is getting all mixed up with identity, that is the expulsion from the ontology of alikeness, an expulsion from difference, or in terms of poetics: the expulsion from rapprochement which maintained difference. All of this is under way.

With that, all of our questioning might perhaps simply be put under the title "where do things stand with nature, where has nature gone, is there any more nature?" Does the nature–culture difference have a place anymore, is it now irrelevant, out of place? So, and I'll finish up with this thought, that is why I think that the reform to be recycled, if I can put it that way, is to *reliquate* [*reliquer*] the revolutionary themes, while keeping them: liberty, equality, fraternity.

CE: What is the status of fraternity in the après-Revolution? There seems to be some hesitation in your work with respect to fraternity that would be linked to a certain failure of the Revolution and to a certain deconstruction or failure of Christianity.

MD: Men are not brothers. We think fraternity on the mode of the family, even the extended family, cousins, the brothers of Christ, that means cousins, first cousins. In fact, that means asking through what is man *like* a brother, can men be *as* brothers? But I might forget that *like*/as and if I do, then this thought of fraternity gives us clanism, familialism, families in the most infernal political sense, insults, offences, revenge, violence before the State, etc. All of that should lead us to think through fraternity. And then, the Christian theme, all of us brothers, be brothers among yourselves, but be like brothers because you'll never be brothers in the sense of "born of the same mother," belonging to the same tribe. So, it is detribalization and when you get right down to it, I believe that it is exactly there that art intervenes. The thought that I am calling poetic thought is a thought that is capable of advancing, of proposing and of making itself understood, capable of having itself understood by other human beings for this type of change in human relations.

CE: I believe that a displacement from fraternity toward the neighboring terms of Friendship and Hospitality can be noted over the past ten years. It was already prepared in *A Man of Little Faith* (eg, "mon semblable, ma soeur") but it grows more intense when you deepen your reflection on fraternity through adoption, as well as in your writings on the late Derrida, on "Derrida" friendship and elsewhere. "This nomination [friendship] comes to take the place of fraternity, perhaps even of love, for the possibilty of being-together" is a quotation that we find in *Réouverture après travaux* and in your essay, "'Derrida' Friendship." Am I right to find this distancing significant? Where do things stand with fraternity today?

MD: This may be very pertinent in the sense where it would be necessary to consider together the Fraternity–Friendship–Hospitality triangle, certainly those three terms with, between them, a relation of proximity within difference. I do not think that I have moved away from fraternity toward friendship, because I never stop passing from friendship to fraternity, and all of that happens under the sign of hospitality, if it's not actually moving toward hospitality under the sign of the two others.

CE: Without renouncing fraternity, without a doubt, it seems to me that your triangulation never ceases trying to enrich its fraternity by seeking its less thematized modes, its less visible ones, as for example in the formula that I quoted from *A Man of Little Faith* where you displace Baudelaire's "mon semblable, mon frère" toward "mon semblable, ma soeur."

MD: Christopher, let's say that for me today, fraternity means sorority, fraternity is not any longer used in some ancestral machismo but always brother–sister, sister–brother, brother–brother, all of that is the same thing, it's the business of being of the same blood.

CE: I know that for you this doesn't come principally from any feminist preoccupation but the modulation is there nonetheless.

MD: That means getting ourselves out of fraternity expressed in realistic, naturalistic terms. That is all the more difficult because there are real brothers. So, with that displacement, it becomes a matter of a kind of generalization of nonliteral fraternity and that passes through friendship. What is a friend? A friend is someone to whom one says, ahhh, you are my brother; you are like my brother. That is the extension of natural fraternity, an extension that passes through friendship, and given that, we have to put into that extension the major effort of Derridean thought that always takes the form of impossibility. It is extraordinary.

The thought of hospitality is posed in two strictly contrary propositions: a. hospitality is without conditions, every other is wholly other and every host and guest is wholly other [*tout autre est tout autre et tout* hôte *est tout* autre].

CE: That's an "untranslatable" homonymy.

MD: Yes, and those are the really big formulations. It means that hospitality as it is thought, imagined, imaged in the Greek fashion, we might as well say in the polythestic way, in the mode of the divinity, of the other, is the thought, the image, the imagination of the god who arrives. It is reversible, too; maybe there is no other definition of God, of the god: it is precisely the one who arrives. Athena on the beach or Poseidon. I put it into a poem once, perhaps you recall, Demeter at Celeos's hearth, Demeter who comes as an old woman and whom they welcome to their home and who then saves their child, well, who gives immortality to the son of Celeos; since she's a goddess, she can dip him in the coals, Celeos sees this and is astonished. But she wanted to transform him.

Unconditional hospitality still reigns in innumerable regions, and preferentially so in the Islamic area, the Bedouin area, for example, the desert nomad zone. The other who comes, the hosts don't ask him "who are you"? "Where do you come from"? The question of identity is not even posed. They don't say "where are you from, what are you up to, show me your papers." No. You are-here. You are the god.

And then, point b, it is impossible to treat the other on the scale of the multitude, of the multiple, because the other who arrives, the individual who arrives, he is the god, but if 200,000 Africans arrive on the beach, it's quite another matter. That means humanity in another form. It doesn't arrive like the god. It arrives as a multitude. That humanity cannot be welcomed in the same way, it is not a question of welcoming it, and, sometimes, it is war that befalls it. That is just the mode in which men behave toward one another, violently, with bellicosity, tribe against tribe.

So, with respect to Derrida's hospitality, he knows all too well that unconditional hospitality is just not on, at least not in economic and social relations. Yet he maintains the requirement of unconditionality in the conditions where it is not possible. So, can we, *how* can we think it? And at the same time, thinking it means foreseeing the real modification of fraternity in such a way that it would not just be a *flatus voci* to say that all men are brothers. I recall in my Catholic youth that the parish bulletin from St. Sulpice in Paris was called *Tous Frères*, all of us brothers. Yes, of course, come on in guys, come right in, welcome! And then when we get back out on the street we start to beat up on each other. Then we get out the weapons and begin to kill.

Where do we stand with respect to that? We can't just repeat "All are Brothers!" that seems obvious. Yet, perhaps, through works of art (including the poem, music and pictorial representation) we do. . . . Modern painting is haunted by the Extermination, and so there are German painters, among others, who mostly show the ravages, who show hostility, who show death and ruin everywhere. Who is thinking and trying to give a meaning and significance to fraternity today, one that is compossible and compatible with our today?

Who is changing the relations? Poet-thinkers, thinkers, artists.

CE: We've just spoken about a range of ends that are questioned in your recent books. There's a structure that you often use to analyze them and to make them productive, to exit them without exiting, to conserve them while leaving behind, as you sometimes say, and that is precisely the negation of content and the affirmation of a remainder or a remnant, of *a-little*. You speak of such X without X structures in "Of Contemporaneity, A Talk for Jacques Derrida" very explicitly with respect to deconstruction. It is also no doubt in that vein that Jean-Luc Nancy reads your religious diptych in the light of "demythified prayer."

I'd like to evoke this quotation from *Reopening after renovations*:

> Believing? Yes
> But believing without beliefs,
> That is the formula
> (RapT, p. 152)

This believing without beliefs, is it the "little faith"? How do you analyze what's left after an X without X operation?

And, in the same volume, you make the connection between poetry and this believing without an object of belief: "Poetry is the "cult of images," an iconophilia without credulity or superstition—a believing without beliefs" (204). Can you elaborate on this a little?

MD: Indeed, that is a formula which I use quite often, "believing without belief" and I use it to talk about poetry as a "cult of images" [Baudelaire].

The expression "believing without belief" is of interest for the "little faith" that concerns us here and it also stands for the poem or poetry itself.

Let's think of it this way: the title that I gave to my latest collection in the Gallimard *Poésie* collection replies to this question, at any rate it has a kind of consonance with this question. I entitled it *Comme si, comme ça*,[1] [As if, like that]. You know that I like to take old, found expressions and modify them. The established, consecrated, lexicalized expression is "*comme ci, comme ça*" [so-so, not bad, alright]. It's a formula of approximation, a little bit uncertain and hesitant, while in my title it is *comme si* with an s not a c, *als ob* in German, *as if* in English. The as-if marks out a decredulized belief; in summary, I wanted to make a kind of concentrated *art poétique* as though all of the poetic art could be contained in the "*comme* si, *comme ça*." It's also my manner of glossing on Coleridge's expression, a willing suspension of disbelief.

CE: Which becomes in your work "a willing suspension of belief."

MD: That's it, yes. This has to do with everything in poetry that is superstition, animism, etc. I'm thinking right now of a verse by Lamartine, "*Objets inanimés, avez-vous donc une âme?*" ["Inanimate objects, have you then a soul?"; "Milly ou la terre natale," *Harmonies poétiques et religieuses*]. In the end, animism addressed everything that is, every being, tree, stone, it doesn't really matter, by treating it as a spirit, that is to say, harboring an ancestor, being itself a form of ancestor, in a system of belief, in a religious relation. That tree is a living thing, a spirit that has psychological and other qualities. That is animism.

Lamartine's verse is one way of saying, I don't believe that, but the question might still be worth asking. After all, I am directed toward inanimate objects as though they had a soul. I'm trying to remember the last verse of a "*chimère*" by Nerval. Here it is, in the same vein: "*Un pur esprit s'accroît sous l'écorce des pierres.*" [A pure spirit increases beneath the bark of stones.] That is a magnificent verse!

The granite is there or maybe the dolmen if we are in Carnac or Stonehenge, and it is *as if*. Nerval doesn't say it that way, he is more affirmative, but it is the same question, the same suspension.

Is the relation to what is—held by the imagination as a possible figure—is it a kind of transformation and at the same time a conservation, a preservation by means of the as-if? I am going to behave *as if*, *as though* x, that is to say that I believe without believing. This is a believing without beliefs that I would always like to develop. In other words, we can't do without that figuration, as I call it, and at the same time we know that it is not held within a faith that affirms that the tree, the being, is a spirit. On the other side of the as-if there is *like that*. It's as if . . . as if what? It is *as if* it were *like that*. So the *like-that* is the relation, for example, of the tree with the neighboring house, rapprochement.

Like that in the poem which describes—because the poem does describe—there is a certain thing and its relations, taking the part of things, *le parti pris des choses*, as the other guy would say [Francis Ponge], in their arrangement, their layout. And so our relation to what is, the there-is [*le il y a*], as Rimbaud's or Hölderlin's poems tell of it, what is, what there is is *like that*. That is the schema of poetry. It is an iconophilia without credulity, it is the whole affair of imagination.

Recently I wrote a text for Jacqueline Risset that is a variation on all of that. In the *Divine Comedy* we don't look at it as a report from a human being who would in fact have passed among the dead, gone beyond, visited Purgatory and Paradise, who came back and said, "yeah, it's really cool up there in Paradise, it's full of light, there are roses everywhere, etc." Anybody knows that when we speak of the other world, we speak of it thanks to our experience of this world; I say that I am in Paradise, but I'm speaking to you here, there are fountains, roses; where did I find all of that? In our earthly experience. The earth functions as a comparant so we can speak about the Kingdom. And then there is an overturning that I also call "making revelation out of profanation" and that's when you relate to the earth as if you were relating to Heaven or Purgatory.

Earth is purgatory, inferno *and* paradise according to the model of what the poet imagined in that paradise, inferno, and purgatory were, following the model of Earth. And so there is that kind of a loop, a two-way ticket, one that figuration maintains. That is what I call attachment. There is no possibility of attaching oneself to this earthly sojourn if it is not thought on that model. It is not a bad constraint, in the end, to be attached to the earth. And what I am saying in examining what is happening at this moment, in social terms, is that we are in the process of seeing this modified.

I have been using a new formula lately; it is an extraterrestrial formula. For a long while I would take the Lyotardian word "deterrestration" in the sense of the Heideggerian "devastation," now I'm starting to vary it. What is happening right now? We are in the process of extra-terrestrializing ourselves, we are becoming extraterrestrials. Said another way, deterrestration doesn't just mean that a few of us will get into the space vessel and possibly leave the solar system someday, or in any case go walking on Mars. It is not that simple. It is because we are imagining the extraterrestrials that we are becoming them.

But we are becoming extraterrestrials without noticing it, which is a Platonic formula, and yet at bottom the poem or art in general exist to notice, to take note. Talking about or making films constantly about extraterrestrials, we are by the same token making, fabulating, our relation to the earth, which dissimulates itself, which is getting attenuated. And the theme of attachment is how to remain attached to the earth without the belief that there is another world besides the earth. It is necessary that the other world be of this world.

CE: What is the relation between this extraterrestration and the exit from the logos?

MD: In my own way of turning this over, reversing it palinodically in order to maintain its inverted truths, I have made a few attempts. I am trying to understand, we need to understand, that these overturnings are often an attempt, a try, an essay. So, along the lines of the Johannine gospel, which proclaims, "The Word was made flesh," I will advance, "The Flesh was made word." The belief was that the logos was there at the beginning of the world, before the world, and that the logos took on flesh, was incarnated. We have to think, I believe, that flesh, the human body, and all of human life, is ceaselessly becoming word, put another way that what we call the word, the logos, is a becoming of the body. The flesh is made word.

Imagine the whole process of hominization. We know that there was life outside of logicity before. How was it that after an earth without humans, that is to say, without logos, made of brontosauri, dinosaurs, what do I know, there followed the long hominization, *homo* whatsit, *homo sapiens*, and as I say now, for today, *homo sapiens sapiens sapiens*, or *homo super sapiens*, and so on. And all along the course of that long, interminable hominization, the flesh was in becoming, with the palaeo-anthropologists that means the disappearance of this or that type of humanity and another branch that comes into the picture; that becoming-flesh is at the same time the invention of language, of the difference among languages. We will probably never know scientifically how phoneticization happened, how the human voice set about and managed to invent language. There was surely never a unique language, even at the beginning, but everywhere little beginnings of human loquacity, and it is that whole movement that I bundle up in the expression "And the Flesh was made word."

How is that continued? How to continue that process of sublimation, of transformation? We might say that what threatens is the exit from the logos. The exiting from languages, the wrecking of every language, I mean the ongoing mathematical formulation of everything. Everything that is happening right now under our noses.

There are some French people who say poem/matheme, in other words, the same thing. But the matheme is formulary language, mathematical calculation. Which means that when scientists get together in a colloquium they can understand one another. Each one has his or her so-called natural language, but they understand each other without speaking each other's languages because they go up to the board and write out mathematical formulas and that's all they need, they can do without the rest. Poetry is not like that.

The exit from the logos is happening in all kinds of contexts, it is coming to pass at every moment. Let's take the really simple example of the tearing-down of language. The flourishing of acronyms, abbreviations that is happening in all languages is an exit from verbalization in lexemes, in words. What the heck is all of that UN, NATO, IQ, etc.? They're all abbreviations; they are no longer words. There are millions of examples of this kind of exit from the logos which is occurring, including in scientific research and, coming soon, there is the fact of an esperanto, which I call despairanto, that is to say a transformation of English itself, of Globish, into a language that might replace the infernal Babelian diversity of languages. In simple terms, that's what I mean by the exit from the logos.

In what does it consist? In what way is it a mutation? What does it threaten, in terms of extraterrestration, that is to say, in terms of the detachment from what I am calling attachment to being or to the world; supposing that we can still believe in the world? It is that belief, that attachment which is said, which is told and sought for in poems, in prose. When you get right down to it, it is what I mean by ecology that is a resistance to that tearing-down and to that detachment.

What is strange is that humanity doesn't seem to be taking it very seriously.

CE: Or not noticing it. Noticing it, one must take it seriously.

MD: But some actually seem more delighted than concerned. In other words, the exit from the logos is also synonymous with the economy. For economic transactions, vernacular language is actually more of a drag; it puts a brake on things.

CE: Perhaps what we sometimes call today World Literature, a certain mode of global fiction dominated by anglophone writers, corresponds to that?

MD: Well, Goethe certainly spoke of *Weltliteratur*. What is it that we mean now by world literature? In the end, perhaps literature is not even relevant anymore. What would really be in the game? Music, shows, films from the United States that are showing on all the screens in the world. As for literature, the great bulk of humanity doesn't care at all; the question today is imagery, the screen and not literature. Music has become something like world music with a few sounds that might just be recognizable as being vaguely English.

CE: Or in Korean, like the unavoidable hit song right now, "Gangnam Style."

MD: You actually get that it's by a Korean? It's really in Korean?

CE: Yes, well . . . how would I know, really? There's something like an Asian language in this hit song that is totally in the mode of global pop music.

MD: [laughing] I'm going to take all of this up in what appear to be minor details. For example, dysorthography, the abandonment of good spelling, is a sign of something. In France, ten years ago or so, the famous incident of "*Omar m'a tuer*"[*sic*] with the spelling mistake was a sign. Which all leads to the fact that in the schools today teaching spelling is less important than it was. There was a spelling mistake on all of the walls in the whole country for ten years! What does spelling mean? It is discernment in language. In the traditional system, spelling is not at all a detail that we might or might not choose to neglect, not at all. It is what allows us to distinguish the thought. I'll take a playful example, it's a comic strip from years ago, where the slightly ridiculous hero, a second-class soldier, has left on his chair a message where he wanted to say that he went to eat and he leaves the following note: "*j'ai été mangé*" [instead of *j'ai été manger*]. Of course, if you don't make the orthographic difference properly, one doesn't know if the sapper has been anthropophaged by someone or if he has in fact been to eat. In fact, the *er/é* difference is a fundamental difference of thought. If it disappears, what follows? We are plunged in that.

The statistics are terrifying. Not only is it not getting better, children don't know how to spell but they never did, they have always had problems. Now even the teenagers and young adults don't give a damn, they all say it's not a big deal. But, unfortunately, yes, it is serious.

What I call ecology pays attention to all of that. It is not without consequences. We need to notice.

NOTES

1. Michel Deguy, *Comme si, comme ça* (Paris: Gallimard *coll. poésie* 2012).

APPENDIX B

TWO ESSAYS ON MICHEL DEGUY BY JEAN-LUC NANCY

DEGUY THE NEW YEAR![1]

"Deguy the new year!" it came to me *like that*. I mean to say: the title came to me right away, from the very moment that I was asked for a title, suddenly and without any waiting, without reflecting on what I might say or might want to say beneath that title. Too fast, too fast of course: and that's already like Deguy. We are, one like the other, people in a hurry, precipitated. Afterward, I asked myself where it had come from, that title, just like that—knowing already that with Deguy it would be a matter of "like" and of "likening," as he says, in all genres, but not knowing how.

(All I know is that on New Year's Day this year [1996], having already given my title, I had a suitcase stolen where a first draft for today could be found. I had to change, to begin again from elsewhere.)

But I do not know why I love mistletoe [*le gui*] and the custom of mistletoe at New Year's. I like cutting it in the countryside for the night of the new year. I like this strange plant, hard and brittle, planted in stars, with its clear outline, its little white balls like sticky pearls. What is mistletoe like? It is as though it is at home on the tree which it parasites, it is like a springtime in the heart of winter, its name, *gui*, smacks or cracks like a sharp cry. And with that, stories of Druids, Norma, or Asterix, the whole legend that will never have taken the form of an *epos*, but only an *as if* of an *epos*, and finally, that of a Latin *satura*: mixture of genres, ratatouille, one genre like the other.

So then, Deguy like all of that. Deguy as always new in the dead of winter. Deguy like a poetry that always itself remains *like* some poetry, as if there were poetry, as though there could still be some poetry, poetry that remains and that is thereby renewed, as before, as such, yet incomparable, displaced, deported, today not like yesterday, today threnody and prose, yesterday a great rhetorician, a poet always of circumstance but never established in that state, he has been saying it himself: the status of poetry and the status of the poet are all finished, and as though entrusted to a new circumstance.

*

I said "Deguy the new year!" with that sense of being carried away, that drive which drives me forward, amused and curious, with each book of Deguy's, always elsewhere and new—new [*neuf*] but not novel [*nouveau*], not another, for like everyone else, he repeats a small number of propositions (for he "makes propositions," he says so, he says it, he says that poetry makes propositions)—repeating then what he has to repeat, like anyone else, and very simply, for he is very simple when you get right down to it, but each time new, each time as though anew. Others deepen their long grooves, keeping to a tense tone, a *recto tono*. Deguy plants his tufts of mistletoe all over the place, parasite in all genres, just a bit scattershot, jumping from here to there, changing his manners, changing his turns of phrase from one page to another, or even within the same phrase. Changing his fashions and his modes, turning himself, immobile, toward all turns because, says he, "there is no proposition which is not turned in some way"[2] and, as he says too, as he chants out with precision:

> Every three hours a poem
> Becomes new then tarnishes
> Beneath its reading then grows anew in silence[3]

*

(But as does happen, as often happens to me, after having joyously sent off that title, worry hit me. Worry, itself redoubled later by the fact of having to speak after so many well-informed speeches, in all the senses of informed, of course, around Michel Deguy, here. Everything will have been said, and I will no doubt repeat a little bit of everything.)

*

Speaking of poetry and speaking of a poet—and it may even be of an absent poet, insofar as he is not "poet" but is "seeking to be"—speaking of a sought-after poet: there can be nothing more risky, perhaps nothing less possible. For in the very end, but this should be said right away even if it is a banality, and because it is one, in the very end it is up to the poet to find the poet. No discourse is sufficient for that and reflection knows in advance that it comes up short. He has written that, "Reflection finds itself outdone; there is a remainder in the production or in the dramaturgy of the thinkable, something left over which constrains it to a supplementary metaphoricity, one unappeased, one seeking out a new figuration, an allegory that might be better suited to bringing back into a language of language [*en langage de langue*] speech in its struggle with that which is not itself."[4]

Reflection is outdone, falls short. Philosophy is outdone, outdone with respect to poetry and left owing something to poetry. It is the philosopher in Deguy who is seeking to be a poet—in Deguy as with everyone, that is the common condition. But it is the poet who says that he is not a poet, that he is a "stateless poet," which is also, once again, the common condition. Philosophy and poetry are outdone by one another, fall short of one another—left owing, in supplement, in metaphor, in allegory, in heteronomy, in a parasitism, and in sharing, one like the other. But this is not the effect of the insufficient constitution of the one or of the other. It comes from the fact that they are, together and separately, one like the other and precisely through this *like*, which holds them out to one another while dis-joining them, the mode of existence—the necessarily double mode of existence—of the falling-short of words. The word falls short because it "is in a struggle with what is not itself." But neither is that the effect of an insufficient constitution—like philosophers dreaming of a "well-made language" or like poets, thinkers of silence. This is due to the fact that speech or word *is* the mode of existence of the being that struggles with what is not itself. There is not speech *and* something else, being, world, meaning or truth. There is the being that is outdone by itself, coming up short—the being in a lack and in an excess of its own identity and unicity of being. The speaking being, then, which is not at all man, but being itself and as such. Being that is always more and less than being, being to which it occurs to be, to not be, to be beyond its being, the being existing life death.

As he says, "non-being is euphemism"[5]: a way of saying things well that softens and soothes and will not avow the deafening smash, the stupor of disappearance and the hard knowledge that says: "I know that I do not bring her back to the surface alive."[6] Monique, poetry must be understood in what he calls this "shred of Orphic allusion," at the very opening of the threnody. Not Monique *and* poetry but one *as* the other. Not the one that captures the other, prettying up the other or making the other into something touching. Not the intimate as it is exploited but the intimate that is exposed because there must be a laying-bare, and that is precisely necessary so as not to poeticize. Philippe [Lacoue-Labarthe] would say, I think would say for once in Michel's fashion: intimation of the intimate. Not a poetic trafficking in death, not a morbid traffic of poetry. But one like the other because the same is brought up not living from the past that is past, from the infinite past, infinitely finite, the infinite past with which the bringing to the surface comes to grips. *Euphemism*, he recalls somewhere else, "was invented by the Greek language to *allow death to pass in silence*."[7] Giving death back to its silence while saying it, which also means: letting death speak in the midst of our too-human silence, speaking with its very ancient and very new voice. Allowing death to pass: not crossing through it nor maintaining oneself there, but passing with it, in it, at the level of its eloquent silence, if that is possible.

*

Deguy writes: "in the experience of the *it* which so ordinarily *makes* it rain or makes it shine, and in the experience of a making which is not of our doing, so close to the '*there is*,' I have no control, the sun rises, the world arises . . ."[8] Being, that is always new, and speech comes to grips with that newness. Always new, that is to say that it has always been new, that its newness is more ancient than anything. Always new returning always, always the new year—the recall of the unforgettable: that the *there is* might arise and go off, that it passes. The *threnody*, then, with the new year. And so he has counted all of Monique's birthdays, one by one, simple finite enumeration of the infinite passing, making nothing heard but the passing in the infinitive, calculating the incalculable "*to pass*."

An enumeration like the unhearing metre, like the schematic prosody of the poem's engendering at the very level of the disposition of speech on the edge of what is not speech, struggling with what is not itself. Speech: the mode of existence of what is thus struggling with the absolute passing of absolute newness—which means finally: the mode of existence quite simply, the very modality of the existing (of the ek-sisting), an absolute mode consequently, mode, measure, conformity of being to what is even more remote than non-being, conformity to that which shields itself from that euphemism, from that which could only call forth a blasphemy (a malediction of existence), if—

–if speech, precisely, were not in a struggle with just that. The word, speech, struggling with that which it is not, that is first of all the word coming to grips with what in itself is not it, with a blasphemy that is always near, nearby, insistent, a word, a speaking that would damn being and itself along with it.

Speech struggling with its blasphemy: we see from whence philosophy and poetry proceed together, one lacking the other. But not in order to substitute benediction for malediction, nor to sublimate the moan or the cry. Ridding oneself of blasphemy is ridding oneself also of its opposite: it is ridding oneself of a grip, of a desire to grasp "what is not itself," ridding oneself of a will to grasp "what is not speech, not word" that is to say a grip on the passing, a grasp on the infinitive *to pass*. Being-in-struggle-with is just precisely not-having-a-grip-on. Deguy writes: "There is no pornography of agony. Horror is not sublime either, for the sublime is still linked to the beautiful."[9] There is no pornography at all: no embellishing writing of the nude, if the nude, the being stripped bare, is that with which existing comes to grips, but in that struggle as though with *nothing*, nothing on which it might have purchase, because it is nothing—infinitive passing, the most new, the most ancient.

Consequently, if the poem "makes the very much elsewhere come,"[10] that does not mean that it causes it to return from its very distant region. The recall of the unforgettable is just as well a recall of the immemorial: of that of which there is no memory. Death recalls (us for) that of which there is no memory. And so it is with speech. The poem brings close the very much elsewhere as an elsewhere, while keeping it elsewhere. That is also what "I do not bring her back to the surface alive" means. I come back with the very much elsewhere, I do not come back *from* it, don't get over it, I do not carry it back with me, I do not seize and search it. Now malediction and benediction are the same way of seizing the very much elsewhere. Deguy wants to keep speech out of the way of one and of the other, and to hold it, in that way, to its *diction* alone.

*

It is in that way too that Deguy is a poet "after Auschwitz." He writes that the camps reveal the modern twist in Greek euphemism. Extermination could only be said while allowing itself to go unsaid, passing unnoticed underneath the discourse of the "final solution" and while naming the crematorium, "the international *information* centre," as Deguy notes[11] in order to underline the euthanistic euphemism that cannot leave death to death, to its elsewhere, which conceals it while saying-*well* the unremitting *male*-diction of the killing field. [*bien-dire/maudire*]

After Auschwitz, one can no more speak-ill in malediction than one can speak-well in benediction. This is perhaps the meaning of the Adornian double injunction about poetry after Auschwitz. And such is the sense of a poetry "of afterwards" which is made as such, that knows this and says it. It has the sense of leaving resolutely aside both benediction and malediction, the one obscene and the other derisory. It has the sense of leaving behind itself declamation or the poetic pose in general. Adorno's sentence pronounces nothing about Auschwitz, perhaps, that we cannot know in some other way. But it pronounces something about the poetry of "before," about blessing poeticization or imprecatory poeticization. (It pronounces then something about what poetry "poeticized," well before Auschwitz, something about what at one and the same time exalted poetry, set it outside of itself and put it into crisis . . .)

Responding expressly to Adorno, a German poet of today writes:

> We believe that poems
> have only now once again
> become possible, namely insofar
> as only in the poem is allowed the saying
> of what otherwise
> mocks all description.[12]

Something has withdrawn from saying, euphemia and blasphemy, incantation and imprecation. Something has withdrawn which assured saying beyond itself, which leaves it denuded in its struggle with that which is not itself. Something that made Orpheus able to bring back Eurydice—or able at least to believe it. What has withdrawn is poetry insofar as it could be the announcement of the words of the gods, a voice plunged deep into death, into birth, into creation, into love and into destiny. A speech that tamed and enchanted that which was not itself.

Or at least we used to believe that, at least we wanted to believe it, and we made that representation of poetry, that overdetermined and overessentialized, surrealistic and overdone representation of poetry: the thought of a transcendence over words through words. Then began the hatred of poetry. Then Zarathustra was able to say that the net cast amongst the poets never brought up anything other than "the head of ancient gods." Then it was a question of insulting beauty [Rimbaud].

Then began something about prose, namely, something of untranscendable word and speech. After Hegelian prose, that is to say, to the prosaicness of a gray world, deprived of the colors of life, regretting and hoping for poetry—poetry, or pure thought—to that prosaicness there succeeded prose as the refusal of poetry. The prose of a world which is no longer gray, neither gray nor coloured, that is no longer the question—but a world where the word is openly struggling with that which is not word. Then poetry doesn't even have to damn itself itself—not any more than it would have to bless itself. It deposes, it deposes its turns, it advances straight ahead, *prorsa*, straight ahead toward nowhere, like the everyman, the as-oneness of mortals [*le commun des mortels*].[13] Straight from the very much elsewhere to the very much elsewhere.

Or rather, instead, it is poetry itself that returns one more time from the most distant, from the most ancient, like the most ancient, the very much elsewhere, *elsewhere right here*. Prose or the new year of poetry renounced, not brought back up alive.

Deguy goes slowly over this history of poetry "to be put back into prose,"[14] as he titles one poem. (He ruminates without pause on the history of poetry, we would never have enough time to show that.) He goes at it slowly, softly, taking little stabs, without violence, with no fracas, rather more with play, with syncopated wordiness. Rhythm stirs in the shadows. He says: "All is somber and yet dance, dense, dance and cadence."[15] He wants "an art of poetry that might disconcert poems."[16] Not ruin, not refusal, nor bloodless sublimation of poetry. But the poem's countenance falling, losing its assurance, its pose, and its transcendental mastery. Deguy parasites and dis-assures the poem—that is to say the work and the substance, the thing itself of the poem, the hymn or the *epos*, the formed and closed song. He chooses instead the poet. The poet is not the subject of the poem. The poet is not substance but displacement, he is not subject, but he is to come, the to-come of the "it" that there is. [*l'à-venir du "il" qu'il y a*]

For a long time poet and not yet, never . . .[17]—

poet, the one returned from what is most ancient, which is making no return, but which comes again, ancient as new, the former new. Deguy can say then: "What you are seeking, that is near, is here—and is not that."[18]

His poem is not organized following any organicity of the work. But it surpasses itself, it is the passage and the passing of the poet, its passing-being which sows little pebbles, little calculations of passage, upon the passageway itself. "Everything begins again on each page, everything ends on every page."[19] Going elsewhere, always having things to do elsewhere, agitated, because it has much to do: not to produce some poetry but to render services. Deguy's poem must be "a poem which would not be heard from very much, useful like Martha, translatable, reducible, exportable, which might set off in columns with other supports."[20]

Thus it is that he responds to the great question, to the question that will have preceded and prepared the possibility that poetry might disappear: why poets in times of distress? Henceforth, the question is enunciated: why poets in times of poetry's distress? He responds simply with patient utility, discreet and fleeting, about the patient usefulness of "that which does not make itself heard very much."

(At least he makes himself believe this. He has some difficulty. He still finds it necessary to launch imprecations against the modern world: again as a reflex of poetry threatened in its sacred works, even while we are no longer there, and even when he himself is seeking something else. He seeks to hold speech back from speaking too much, to care for it, giving it bounds, tucking it in as it overflows.)

That, this reserved word, retained, withheld speech—always held back by the distant from whence it comes back and to which it returns—it is that which struggles with what is not itself. Struggling in order to cause to return or to allow to return what is lacking in distress. What is missing is the "very much elsewhere." The "very much elsewhere," that is presence, and it is the silence that goes with it. Deguy says: "presence, that must be made," "silence, we must make it."[21] There we have our job, the poetic making; the service of aid that we must attempt to provide. Caring for presence in passage. Not at all shielding it from passage, but passing along with it, discreetly, almost furtively. A furtive eternity—that is what we are lacking, that is within our reach. Passing beneath a silence of words, speaking beneath the passage of a silence. Immortals elsewhere, very much elsewhere, right here.

*

The presence that must be made, the silence that goes along with it, this is not the immutable present of the gods. It is the fleetingness of being, that is to say, its eternity. And the "making" of the poet is not a "producing," it is a proposition. What the poet proposes is nothing other than "that like what it is."[22] This like-what is just that, here or there, in the instant that passes. The thing itself. Deguy speaks of a "proposition of recognition."[23] Recognizing the thing itself in passing. In passage, recognizing the thing itself. Even in passage, recognizing the thing. This may be named "circumstance."[24] He says that "any poem is of circumstance" (situationist, in point of fact). We must make the presence and the silence of circumstance, they must be proposed. *Pro*posing them because neither presence nor silence are ever posed. Nor supposed, nor, what is more, deposed. But only proposed in passage. To be taken or left, very quickly, at the speed of poetic light. A speed limit, which calculation approaches and decides arbitrarily, in order to fix the limit, the passage to the limit.

We must have recognized in the passage the presence and the silence of "that *like what* it is." Recognition must be proposed in circumstance, in the circumstance of the "that like what it is"—or *of* "that like what it is"—that is to say of the presence and of the silence of the thing or of the being. Proposing them like/as what they are, and consequently, proposing them without withdrawing them from their reserve, their distance, their passage. The thing or the being: what is happening, at bottom, that which passes at bottom, the event of the bottom. He says: "That which you are seeking, it is nearby, is there—and is not that. The treasure is in the field; it is the labor of prose, language holds things at a distance while acceding to them."[25]

But leaving the thing, the being, in order to propose it, to its presence and to its silence, that is no less to give or to take the turn of a particular proposition and one that is of circumstance. For there is not the thing *in itself*. In itself the thing is *some* thing and the being is some taking place. He says: "there is no proposition that is not turned in some fashion."[26] "That like what it is" demands a turn that is every time singular. Deguy is a poet, a prose writer, a proponent of the turn and of the turn of phrase, of the trope which turns presence, like a turn of the turner at the lathe, or like having the knack of drawing.

And that's what makes his trade, his skill, his work and his job of work, that about which he says, "it is the craftsman's life, of making without true knowledge, of life in poems."[27] Without true knowledge, but with know-how, the knack, *Handgriff*, that which the philosopher despairs of catching, like the sleight of hand or the helping hand of a schematism, of the tracing-out of the archi-outline of things, of their sensible identity, the trait of their presence.[28]

For of course *ut pictura*, as he likes to repeat it, the turn of the proposition, the turn capable of offering how it is that the situation stands with "that like what it is," that is the outline of presence. Circumstance—that which stands-round-about—is the exact contour of being, each time in its turn. Such is the imperious necessity of its work. "It is necessary—says he—that I draw her life with exactitude, what was her courage, devotion, endurance and the discouragement, the resolution, the limitation, the permanent dread and the laughter, the defeat and the horror."[29] Already, he does not need to make things more precise: each of these words which by itself only says things vaguely and in general, gives another sound because it is placed beneath the injunction of exactitude, precision, accuracy. It gives the rather dull sound, almost silent, of a unique circumstance, the contour of someone, of a female someone, a person whose face does not appear ("If I accommodate the rememoration of her face that is growing petrified in my head, the tears flood up, rhumus of the soul, the soul is streaming between body and memory").[30] That is because exactitude is not precision, in no way is it precision. Precision approaches, searching within the closest proximity to presence, which it therefore supposes to be approachable, and therefore fixed in some manner. But exactitude is not to be found in proximity that always leaves to "even closer" and even to "as close as possible" the indetermination of the "close enough" [*à peu près*]. Exactitude is exigence—that is its *etymon*—exigency "ex-acted" ["*exagie*"], accomplished, at its term, with no remainder: the strict observance of the thing, of its presence, without the slightest separation. The thing is not approached nor brought closer in rapprochement: it remains in its elsewhere, in the distance of its being, in its passage. It is only, strictly, exactly retraced upon itself:

As it happens in drawings by Rubens, by Watteau—says Deguy—
That the perfect line picks up again so
That several drawings of the same thing
Draw that thing in double impression[31]

Double impression [*surimpression*], or even more—another word to say the same thing of sameness—coincidence. He asks: "What does he favour for the things that are waiting for nothing in the silence of grayness?" and he responds "coincidence."

The thing *itself*, then, *falling* away from itself *with* itself and as though on itself. The thing itself which is itself the "thing itself" of the philosopher, or even the philosopher's "thing in itself:" the very matter of the being-in-itself of something in general of something-and-not-nothing, but the thing itself seized in passage in its very sameness, in accordance with presence and silence, in accordance with the presence elsewhere and the resonant silence of its being-same, being the same as itself. As he says:

The same right
Up against same
In addition[32]

—the thing, then, or the someone, the person of whom it must be said:

She took back her words shrouded within herself[33]

And it is indeed she whom he will not bring back to the surface alive: she herself. Not only will he not bring her back, but he, himself, he will not come back to the surface either. He will not recover from not bringing her back alive either. He remains down there, at her level, the thing, that person. He stays down at that level, fallen down upon her with her.

But it is thus that with her he recovers also his words, he gets back all the words, he returns them to the coincidence of the thing. All of the words of this language about which he repeats on any topic that he loves it or that he is devoted to it,[34] this language that he can't get over, which remains right with the thing where it withdraws.

A long time ago already he had written: "Heading toward the word "fountain" it is (to) the fountain *thing* that he attends; he does not drink of its water: it flows, grief and sense, in memory . . ."[35]

The thing itself as the co-inciding retrait of the word in the exactitude of its drawing. There where another poet says there "where no thing can be, there where the word defaults," he says rather: the thing is in the default of the word, but this defect is the very exactitude of the word. What is unheard of about the thing is there heard and understood, with its own timbre. So it is that "a phrase shakes up language, as a brass instrument jars the musical realm, it is each time the invention of the viola for the audible or of the triangle or of the oboe."[36]

*

From the unheard (of) to the audible [*de l'inouï à l'audible*] from the elsewhere to the here, hiatus is not abolished:

Staunch hiatus in any trial
The incessant aggravation of which might
Gradually be repaired near and far only by the poem's thunderstorm
Aggravating here and there its incessant reparation[37]

Hiatus: the opening up of coincidence, the retracement of exactitude, the gaping of the same. Repairing it and aggravating it, together and one through the other, the one like the other, that is what is called being exact, making a trade of exactitude. (In Horace, it sometimes occurs that *hiatus* means "speech, word.")

The audible exactitude of the unheard, that is timbre. Poetry is like an emancipation of the timbre of word within word itself. "Just as at the moment of entering into a musical state, Valéry preferred the preparations of the orchestra warming-up, trying to find the "A" in all timbres and tones, so it is with us, readers or writers . . ."[38]

Timbre for itself, brought free of any justness of tuning and of the composition of the song—the song at the bottom of the song, the deep song—timbre opened up in itself to its own background noise, the thing itself at bottom struck or rubbed upon itself, vibrating from only its tension there right up against itself, stridence and cadence of coincidence.

(One might also say that prose is the poetry of timbre, the asymptosis of an autonomized timbre, almost without modulation, or instead: the modulation, the mode, the measure and the turn of which would be the striking, the beat or the immanent echo of timbre itself, the resonance of the *same*. As if one were saying: poem, a piece for the rustling of paper alone, or for throat clearing.)

That is how, for him, music might be "elsewhere," "in an *unheard* (*of*) space, I mean non-allegorical, non-reflecting, non-recognizable; in other terms: not even enigmatic, rather: without solution, if the enigma and the solution are together."[39] That which is not allegorical is *tautegorical* (said Schelling): that says the same right in close to itself, and by itself. Deguy wants the same to resonate from out of itself, as such and without resemblance, without it *all coming down to the same*. He wants to hear that, he who can never recover from it.

But he says just as quickly, he underlines that "it *would seem* that there may be some non-semblance [. . .], something at bottom unknown and new."

The non-resemblant can itself only seem to be such. The thing itself exhibits its evidence and its certitude through the exactitude of its "like itself" in the impeccable "superimpression of itself" or the coincidence—and this "as such" can only be presented as *as* (if it were) identical to itself. There is a vertiginous collision in the coincidence of the "as as" [*comme comme*]. That does not mean that the thing itself and *as such* is not. Certainly, it is—and it is *as it is such*. But being as it is, it is immediately *resemblant* to itself. It goes without delay, and yet not without hiatus, from the same to all the same [*du même au pareil*]. From the depth of its retreat it is already within recognition. At the peak of its exception it is within resemblance. Apposed to itself it is in an "apposition that the *comme* keeps under surveillance"[40] and it is thus that it can be the object of a proposition.

If the proposition is always a proposition of recognition, it is always made by like or as [*comme*]. And if the proposition is always turned in some way, the common way of its turns is the like-or-as. Deguy's poetics is a poetics of the *comme*: it is the common assumption of a rhetoric, of a logic and of a dialectics of the like-or-as, just as his philosophy has the *as* as its transcendental. He is as though crazy about as, crazy about like. Because the latter, no sooner has it been introduced, scarcely has it been slid into the intimate interstice of the hiatus of sameness, than it sets off powerful waves of proximity, all of those family stories:

There is some like in being
A family air an air of nothing[41]

The resemblance of self to self, the *as* of *as such*, the adjoining of same to same, that is to say, just as well, its setting apart, hardly is this opened up even just a crack than it opens up onto all resemblances. If the one is like itself, as the one that it is, then it is also already like the other—like the other of the one as its very own other. Deguy loves this vertigo. As soon as we have opened the series of resemblances, they show themselves little by little more different from one another in the resemblance of some to others and the *like-or-as* is unfurled, gets spread out right up to resemblance, general difference, the liberty-equality-fraternity of *as-oneness*, of this *comm(one) ism?* ["*comme-unisme*"] the rule of "us" of which it makes, of an "us" who says "we are neither Jews nor Germans but like them "feature for feature," through a comm-unary trait which is not visible in the visible"[42]—and the same disparity, disproportion, unfolding, and demultiplication that populates presence with its innumerable semblance and resemblance.

He addresses himself to the thing:

Your comparant celebrates you, brings you down to size
Your beauty prepared, with—compared. For what
Would you exchange yourself, am I to arrange your trade
And the metamorphosis I look to measure
every thing with you[43]

Any thing can be the measure of any thing. Every thing can be the common measure of the incommensurable commensurability of all, and of the indifferent difference of the whole, of its proportioned disproportion. *Like* makes for measure: the common measure of being, that is what causes presence be like another presence, and the being as such to be nothing other than its own analogy (old Aristotle made new beneath the semblance of the poet). From which, too, comes a singular ontological lightness, a smiling graveness, a childlike application to playing as not playing.

*

The "how it is" (Beckett's "*comment c'est,*" which Deguy re-cites and makes as though his own)[44]—the how [*comment*] communicating necessarily with the comparison [*comme*] of "it is like that" [*c'est comme ça*].[45] Therefore, the poet is the one who finds the words to propose the multiplied turn of being's *like*.

In order to propose it, it is necessary to transpose. "Blind man, they used to say of the poet, because for him to transpose was to find."[46]

He transposes, he transports, he assembles things, he assembles, says he, "a *thing* character, a qualification which in advance runs through a certain number of "things" [. . .] or: the world being born under an aspect of its common sense . . . A character that would be ontic and transcendental."[47] Deguy thinks like an empiricist or like an analysand in psychoanalysis: he associates. From that moment he authorizes himself, as a poet (but it is thus that he authorizes himself absolutely as a poet, even if that poet were the one he still keeps seeking to be), he allows himself all of the "metaphorical transactions," beginning with the transaction between resemblance and assembly, he traffics in the tropic transport, in all of the possible turns of phrase, from the pun to the metaphor and from the more-or-less to the proposopoeia, with the prolixity and the insolent laxism of anxiety.

What cannot be said
(he says)
Must be written[48]

To write is to allow oneself all of the turns and all of the turns of phrase of the proposition, it is to write one thing *as* another, in spite of and along with *disproportion* (despite and with the "sadness of Disproportion itself,"[49] the "revealed sadness" in the death of she who "aligned, bringing strictly together the two sides of imposed things"[50]), writing for example:

The (damned) poem word-said [*Le poème mot-dit*][51]

and how this poem, in consequence, like that unique poem common to all of the poetry of this poet who seeks himself as poet, like that poem the name of which satirizes all of the poetic sacralities, writing out all of those "metaphorical transactions between this and that thing—he says—that one will find, naturally drawn together and resemblant,"[52] writing then for the reading which will operate, all in all, the similitude of what writing will have put side by side, the reading which thereby makes a second nature, a new space of proximity, the very proximity of the distant, the words like their things and the things themselves like another thing, and always, to finish up and to begin, *Worte wie Blumen*, as he recites from Hölderlin,[53] words like flowers. —but he immediately adds: "the like-or-as of poetry, that is not metaphor, it is something else": the *comme* of poetry is not *like* the *like* of comparison (a question then, in passing here: which like is like the others and which one is different? why are there in French as many *commes*, homonyms or synonyms, or synonyms through homonymy, as Deguy desires, unless it were the reverse, or perhaps both at once), the like-or-as of poetry is not that of comparison which metaphor condenses (in the poem from *Ouï dire* he refused to give comparison the right to name the tropic regime in general).[54] The *comme* of poetry gives us the *like* of *as such* and not the *like* of what is similar or same [*pareil*].

(And so, and in a more than exemplary manner, it will be necessary to say that poetry *like* prose—as Lacoue-Labarthe, another philosopher, says, underlining the *comme*[55]—it is indeed the *as such* of poetry, poetry's essence, the Idea or poetic exigency *itself*: the exigent essence of poetry is there as prose, *in prose*. Prose is not the same, it is much less and much more, it is the insistence and the resistance of poetry itself. On those grounds, prose is still, it is absolutely still a proposition of poetry and on poetry, a manner of saying, or rather of making poetry as such. One manner *against* another, but *like or as* another, also, likewise. Against, everything against: with (comm-, *cum*) in the mode of (*quomodo*, *comme*).

The like-or-as as Deguy wants it is the alike as *as* or the alike which is the same as the as [le pareil pareil au en tant que]. It is as if Hölderlin had written, as he ought to have done, *Worte als Blumen*, *Worte wie Blumen als Blumen*, *Worte wie als Blumen*.

This is *the alike* as it allows the *as (such)* of what it resembles to be seen. *Worte wie Blumen* makes us see words as flowers, that is to say that *as* they are *like* words they *are* in their being flowers. But how are flowers? For Hölderlin, they surge up, they bloom. For Mallarmé, the flower rises, absent. For Silesius, it grows without reason. For Novalis, it speaks, and the poet becomes flower. For Derrida, a friend of Deguy's, there is always a dried flower lost in a book.

The flower is the *damned word-said* par excellence, sticky poetry (Bataille) or inadmissible poetry (Roche), but this is because it raises up the incomparable *comme* which compares nothing—the how-it-is of being which resembles nothing—which we might also say when speaking, as he does, of the "meaning that a life has which has no more meaning—in other words [. . .] meaning."[56] In Derrida's terms, one would say: "there is no difference *as such*," and that's it, that is the dried flower in every book, and the inappropriability of a unique and literal *proper meaning* as such. But Deguy responds: there is an as such of the as such, and it is the as-alike, the alikeness of the nonpareil (as they used to say in the *Grand Siècle*): the unalike flash of the alike, which arouses another blooming, that of desire.

That which resembles nothing, and above all not itself, defers endlessly from itself and is transported from word to word, reassembles desire for its image without resemblance and without illusion. The object of desire is always that which resembles desire, like the blooming of a flower. He says: "I call image that which makes appear as woman a naked woman, nudity gathering together the beautiful and the desire; that which resembles is desirable."[57] Making a naked woman appear as woman, that is putting her into superimposition with herself, that is recognizing her or presenting her as such, or being exposed to her as such, it is making her being (the woman) coincide with her appearing (the naked woman): so it is then to make the being be, nothing less. The image is the being as such, there you have what this definition says (which is not by chance, at the same time, a snapshot allusion, immense, to a whole swath of the history of painting, of photography and of cinema.) The image—and consequently, one might suspect this, all of poetry—is the *as such* of the being, it is that "as such" itself extracted from its concept and from its discourse, that "as such" *as* gesture, monstration, deixis, *presentation of* being. And this very presentation as desire. The monstration of the being is desire for being, desire for the *as such* of being, because that which is desirable is never being alone (naked), being alone, but the monstration wherein it comes to be offered *as such*. Here is what Deguy says.

He says, then he writes:

Palms rolling the pastry of buttocks
Or left hand bracing right breast
And thumb excising you gently . . .
Thighs' horizon spreads open the mauve nymphs
Without image appears the vulva
And then like a face it is [. . .][58]

Coincidence as coitus in a superimpression of its own image like an oculary flower—not an oracular one. For nothing is revealed about the uninscribable, nothing is revealed and all is written, written as the "natural rapprochement" of the uninscriptible, of disproportion "itself," and of its own image. The image is the desirable exactitude of being, and desire is that which gets regulated on the basis of that exactitude.

*

But the image or the figure which the like-or-as makes in that way like a collision and a comparition [*comparution*], an appearance for the purpose of testifying, like the summons of the very much elsewhere to come while remaining elsewhere, that figure makes neither a *trompe l'oeil* nor a *trompe l'âme* [tricking of the soul], as he says.[59]

The flower, or the woman, is also she whom he cannot bring back up alive. Once he wrote of the orange blossom, the one that Nicolas [Deguy's son] carried at the wedding. He wrote:

the hortensias prefer the house
(For her I describe life with exactitude).[60]

And now he writes

Here is the garden of the marble mason[61]

The tombstone, it is the flower, the tombstone like a flower, like a naked woman. The word said like a flower like a stone, and it is upon the stone that nothing, he says, must be inscribed as a *trompe-l'âme*.

And that is why

I will leave the tombstone with only the inscription of the name[62]

The flower that reflowers in this new year is not a flower, it is a bunch of mistletoe [*gui*], like it, dry and brittle and like it, a parasite of its own "like/as." Yet he was able to say even of this that it was like a resurrection: he has always behaved as if he could comm-une in the religion that was Monique's and which is with her in the tomb. He said, indeed:

I believe something like an air of resurrection
is at work with death and it's up to the poem [. . .]
to say of poetry that whatever you bind
in its name shall be bound on earth[63]

The poem resuscitates the world as world, up to and including death as death (the incommensurable commotion of the *comme*) and no world-beyond, no other world.

All of resurrection is in the tombstone, as the name is on the marble: the poem comes there *like* the name, and as if it were accomplishing thereby the very being of the poem and its desire. He cannot bring her back to the surface alive, but her name.

He also says, further on:

Going back up toward the actress ringed by night Vega
Like Yvette Guilbert or the lashes of a Degas[64]

He also says elsewhere, "*Ut musica, Ut pictura, Ut poesis*"[65]: the one like the other, their triple "like" in common, this is remounting the night within the night, but each time isolatedly and with no relation to one another except the gap of the *ut* (in the same way as, similarly to). Among the arts, there is no unity of their assumption, there is only this *ut*, like the tonic of their accord, and thus like their spacing, their difference. And poetry is never like painting and like music except insofar as it is neither the one nor the other: but poetry like poetry, poetry as poetry.

In the same way, the name, the elementary prose of the name is neither the face nor the voice. It is the spreading gap inscribed, the putting off to one side of the one as of the other. It is there, alone and new like never before. The new year happens in the middle of the winter, like the winter solstice. The very much elsewhere is much further than any heaven or any other world. "But—he adds—since we can live only as if we weren't going to die, the thoughts that wear the veil of incurable sadness add nothing to truth."[66]

Immortality as if we were not to die: all of the *commes* refer to this *as if*, to this *als ob* which seems to be borrowed from a Kantian regulation. But this regulation does not consist of simulating what is not and of fomenting a poetic lie about immortality. It consists in regulating oneself absolutely according to that for which there is no object. Our immortality is nothing objectifiable and hence it is nothing, absolutely, but it is absolute as such, as ours and nothing other. Immortality as death. We are already in it and "resurrection" is not a paradisiac fantasmagoria: it is the asyndeton, death/eternity.

Put another way, what is at work with death and that the poem binds on earth, this is nothing that would come beyond: truth has nothing to add to itself, no supplementary negativity to join to sense. The truth of sense is found only in sense as such: that sense which is said, and, as it is said, through all of the *likes* or *ases* of all of the turns of writing, by all of those *commes* that only come down to the same by ceasing their infinite deferral among themselves, in the absolute disproportion of resemblance and rapprochement.

To the law of disproportion among all the turns that make something like sense, there is nothing to be written, nothing but a proper name, the property of which is to have no meaning. Poetry is the "closed-up one"[67] (he is quoting Hölderlin again), it is she, too, in the tombstone. Not under it, as though something or someone subsisted, but within it, compactified, in peace.

He writes: "reading me, stranger . . ."—he reminds us that we will always have remained strangers to all of the meaning to which he will have seemed to invite us—". . . you do not hear the euphemia of this prose—which seeks itself out in truths, which distinguishes between the ways in which meaning goes about things."[68] This prose is the euphemia of damaged and closed-up poetry, of that poetry which remains very much elsewhere and which does not come back up alive. Between all of the propositions with their turnings, there is then some difference, but there is no supplementary turn for difference. What is being sought, making difference, is the poet. He seeks himself, impossible to find, and even impossible to seek. He seeks himself as poet and he finds himself *as though* poet: ahead of himself, further off than self, with neither object nor subject, on his own traces alone, already effaced, struggling with what is not him nor is it the word or speech. He writes straight ahead before himself, going nowhere else but to the common elsewhere of all common sense, inscribing upon the tombstone the asyndeton of the name and the dates, like a poem, a poem name-said, a poem non-said [*comme un poème nom-dit*].

June 1995

From *Le Poète que je cherche à être* 164–181.

NOTES

1. Nancy's opening reflections turn on an unsaid connection underlying his title, the nature of which he elucidates in short order. In Michel Deguy's family name one might perceive the homonymy "*gui*/guy." *Le gui* in French is mistletoe, which Nancy associates here with the festive season, with the New Year, with its celebrations and its enthusiasms. In "How to Name" Jacques Derrida makes the same connection in passing, with reference to turnings, to Heidegger: "I do not believe, any more than in the case of Heidegger, that there are two Deguys; there is one Deguy, there is only one of those and there are more Deguys than we can imagine—he is always new, it is always New Year's Day" (PQCE, 197). The erudite, acerbic French erotic poet Jude Stéfan, writing a text of homage to Deguy for the same E.N.S. colloquium, also had a similar, musically attentive intuition, in his case associating the 'guy' of Deguy with the Germanic paleonym *Wido*. One of Stéfan's forty fragments from his "Lexicon of Friendship" gives this:

29) Patronym
Deguy=Son of Guy
Guy=germanic *Wido* (wid=bois, forêt/wood, forest)
therefore: Deguy like *Dubois*, but more elegant:
Deguy/Dubois = Poet/Evryone [Tt le monde]
PQCE: 15.

2. JLN note. Interview with Deguy in *Le Croc'ant*, (Lyon) no. 15 (printemps-été 1994) 73. [This is a very difficult source to locate. Many of the same themes and expressions including some verbatim quotations may be found in the more readily accessible "Entretien" with Stéphane Bacquey in the journal, *Prétexte* (Carnet no. 9 Hors-Série 1998) 12–26. What is particularly useful in this interview is the contrast that Deguy develops between his theory of presence and that of Yves Bonnefoy, very likely the most well-known living French poet and who has been closely associated with a poetic thought and meditation of presence for several decades.]

3. JLN note. *Poèmes I* (Paris: Gallimard coll. Poésie 1973) 51.

4. JLN note. *Aux heures d'affluence* (Paris: Seuil 1993) 55. Hereafter cited as AHA.

5. JLN note. A *ce qui n'en finit pas* (Paris: Seuil coll. La bibliothèque du siècle 1995) 122 (in this book with no page numbers, I have numbered the right-hand pages in sequence in order to keep myself located). Hereafter cited as ACFP.

6. JLN note. Ibid., 1.

7. JLN note. AHA 128.

8. JLN note. Ibid. 53.

9. JLN note. ACFP 80.

10. JLN note. Interview in *Le Croc'ant, op. cit.*, 75.

11. JLN note. AHA 128.

12. JLN note. Hans Sahl in *Lyrik nach Auschwitz? Adorno und die Dichter* (Stuttgart: Reklam 1995) 144.

13. Nancy is playing here with one of Deguy's serious neologizing puns: *le commun des mortels* is an idiomatic expression that suggests the everyman, the average Joe, etc., but it becomes in Deguy's attentive hearing *le comme-un des mortels*, a perfect homonymy, suggesting in its dilated, hyphenated written form the likeness or the *as-oneness* of mortals.

14. JLN note. GIS 20/REC 19.

15. JLN note. Ibid., 69.

16. JLN note. Ibid., 63.

17. JLN note. *Poèmes* 27.

18. JLN note. ACFP 106.

19. JLN note. Ibid., 17.

20. JLN note. GIS 47/REC 59.

21. JLN note. Interview in *Le Croc'ant op. cit.*, 75.

22. JLN note. Ibid., 77.

23. JLN note. Ibid.

24. JLN note. Ibid.

25. JLN note. ACFP 106.

26. JLN note. Interview, *Le Croc'ant, op. cit.*, 73.

27. JLN note. (lost reference . . . there was bound to be one and M.D. himself cannot find it: That's the craftsman's life . . .)

28. JLN note. Of the transcendental schematism, he says that it is the "wailing wall of philosophers" (in a paper given in Strasbourg in June 1995). This seems to hint that the poet traces out some graffiti there.

29. JLN note. ACFP 22.

30. JLN note. Ibid.

31. JLN note. GIS 35. [I give Wilson Baldridge's translation from *Recumbents* 41. Note his choice of "double impression" for Deguy's *surimpression*; I choose another option, superimposition, in other instances for translating the same word in Nancy. In some of the quotations from *Gisants* that follow, I simply reproduce Baldridge's effective and idiomatic versions. For others, to align better with Nancy's interpretations or my own, I offer my variations. In those cases, I give a page reference to *Recumbents* to allow for comparison, which is after all what is at stake here.]

32. JLN note. ACFP 46.

33. JLN note. Ibid., 67.

34. JLN note. *Brevets* (Seyssel: Champ Vallon 1986) 22, for example.

35. JLN note. Ibid., 67.

36. JLN note. *Poèmes* 110.

37. JLN note Idem., 127.

38. JLN note. AF, 110.

39. JLN note. GIS

40. JLN note. Po 71.

41. JLN note. AF 62.

42. JLN note. *Au sujet de Shoah*, 47.

43. JLN note. GIS 132. [I have given my own version of this fragment rather than the published version from *Recumbents*. I have chosen here as elsewhere to "naturalize" the French word, *comparant*, which one does find occasionally in English texts on poetics. "Comparator" or "compared thing," etc. just do not bring the same punch for identifying the terms of (a given) comparison. I feel it needs to be put into play for the full power of Deguy's reflection on the *comme* to come through.]

44. JLN note. BR 153.

45. See Deguy's play with his recent title *Comme si, comme ça* in the "Interview" (appendix) for a recent example of his appropriation and reorientation of Beckett's *Comment c'est*.

46. JLN note. GIS 30. cf. REC 33.

47. JLN note. Idem., 106. cf. REC 149.

48. JLN note. GIS 131. cf. REC, 183.

49. JLN note. ACFP 128.

50. JLN note. Idem.,4.

51. JLN note. AF 115.

52. JLN note. GIS 106. cf. REC 149.

53. JLN note. Interview in *Le Croc'ant op. cit.*, 84.

54. JLN note. POEMES 61.

55. JLN note. Philippe Lacoue-Labarthe, *La politique des poètes*, collectif, (Paris: Albin Michel, 1992) 63.

56. JLN note. ACFP 14.

57. JLN note. GIS 96. cf. REC 135.

58. JLN note. Ibid. REC, 135.

59. JLN note. ACFP 126.

60. JLN note. Ibid. 11.

61. JLN note. Ibid., 127.

62. JLN note. Ibid., 126.

63. JLN note. GIS 39. REC 47.

64. JLN note. ACFP 88.

65. JLN note. GIS 98. REC 136.

66. JLN note. ACFP 31.

67. JLN note. ACFP 77.

68. JLN note. ACFP 118.

TO ACCOMPANY MICHEL DEGUY

Jean-Luc Nancy

I was not able to participate in the 2006 Cerisy Colloquium around Michel Deguy: I had just been struck—as we rightly say—by a double grief and a very close one. It was impossible for me to work, for I had wanted to offer Michel a word about grief, or a word of grief, had wished that for a long time. To aggrieve myself, to enter into mourning with him. To carry grief with him. Perhaps I had wanted that ever since the publication of his great threnody. Very surely, in any case, ever since the day when I heard his vehement lament, unforgettable, with which he announced to me the death of his grandson. Between the two, he had me read the words he wrote after the burial of Jacques, our common friend with whom I had discussed this undiscussable: whether there can be any consolation or if only desolation befalls us. . . . Thus it was that a kind of funeral procession drew us in.

A very rare, very exceptional bearer of grief, and bearing more than just mourning—bearing its infinite pain—not that of its supposed "work," is the one among us who writes: *and death is to be all alone*. Saying in that way that the deceased is alone and that the one who is left behind is alone. In one way or the other, it is only because of that that we are alone: the death of the other or our own. Are then incessantly foresaken. Essentially so. United by forsakenness.

Perhaps right there where all appearances of links other than those of love are undone—society, culture or world—there where the general regime of living beings gets metamorphosized, it is there that death becomes pregnant. But this *there*, it is here, it is with us, where we live, it is us. The world is slipping its hinges. Life is no longer in solidarity with itself and *love stronger than death* is experienced numb, irradiated.

The summer of Cerisy having passed, in the fall when the year sets about its departure, I set myself to the work of mourning—I mean of grieving, not the work of separating-out and reabsorbing sadness. I received just then *Le sens de la visite* [The Direction of the Visit], Michel's new book. I read in it: "Sadness is assured; it is philosophical" and he continues: "Skin is more or less sensitive. Mine is poetic." I will have to elucidate his ellipse, there. If the poetic is not evenly philosophical, it won't be all sadness either? I promise myself to come back to this.

SO AS NOT TO CONSOLE THE INCONSOLABLE

That is the first promise to make and to keep. Not wanting to dry the tears, letting them go about their work, which is of cleaning and of clarity, their work which is to cloud the view and to clear up the simple thinking of absence.

A very young man recently remarked, near me, on the difference between funerals where all are already consoled and those where only the inconsolable appear. But only these latter ones are truly carrying out the rite, which the others imitate. The rite makes us enter into the rhythm, that of life/death, that of coming/leaving. It doesn't efface the departure, it marries it, it takes on its cadence.

I am renewing in this way that so-recent and already so-old dialogue with J.D., him telling me that there is no consolation, me replying to him that the very phrase, saying it, writing it, and having it published, already carries consolation. Against all expectations and all intentions, irresistibly in a nevertheless extreme fragility, in the desolating precarity, in its turn, of the lightness of words.

Lightness? Vanity? Yes and *vanitas vanitatum*. Putting the word face to face with death: a wind, another death, a confirmation of a death. Yet the hollowness of words has the power to resonate with the infinite and insatiable absence of those who are no more.

At times, it is true, the hollow words, the punctured words, denounce themselves, not merely as vain, but as abusive, usurping, and pitiful. Reason for tears, cries, and shudders.

At times however the same words can offer their hollowness to that same echo itself, to that strange resonance from without wherein they *inexist*, those whom we call our "dearly departed."

And that is why, ever since forever: threnodies and songs of grief, elegies upon tombs, the languageless telling of music, its complaints devoid of words, and the epitaphs whose hard stone counts more than the inscription, the commemorations punctuated by silences. This renewed deepening of the word returns to open up our mouth, to keep open, gaping open, the space of resonance.

What seems at first to ward off absence opens it up and stirs it up. Even once the sadness has dried, grief does not finish. Even without pain, even in joy if it is possible, the cleanness of the cut has not faded, since they are no longer there, nor anywhere.

WHAT THEN DOES PHILOSOPHY SAY?

It has never said that we shouldn't cry for the dead, even if it has said that we must not deplore death. Indeed it says that death is nothing, nothing but the effect of resonance of that infinite cut through which we are separated from the finite.

(The finite: the sense of words, the effects of meaning, the assignments and assignations of truth, the imputations of justice, the determinations of knowing, the prospectives and the retrospectives.)

Being separated from the finite constitutes the property of the finite itself: touching its limit, it does not cross it, but changes itself into itself, an impeccable contour.

That is true, exact. That is just, impeccable. Every figure loops back upon itself, closing itself and sinking deeper into its recess.

But that, we cry, makes no sense. This is vanity. Nonetheless such vanity molds us. Each one of us, every man, every woman, takes on our living with that recess around them, as horizon. With that *memento mori* that has opened up our memory along with our birth and that we forget every morning but that every night revives. Such vanity makes us and makes us live despite itself, it fashions us, kneads and forms us, *knowing not the day nor the hour*—but knowing that any hour is right for making the contour worthy of eternity.

We know that we die but we know that what is vain for the world opens the outside as the fullness of a world. Hollow cavity of infinite resonance wherein we tarry, eternize: we become the Idea of ourselves, not the ideal nor the representation, but the true Form, immortal and perfect in this sense, that it per-fects its figure and its experience. Accomplishing it, fulfilling it, transfiguring it far from any figuration.

Philosophy says very simply that death is the *nothingness* of that finishing. Nothingness because it is nothing more than the end of the finite, the finiteness of the finite, adding nothing to it, not extending it outside of itself, but all the while finishing it, withdrawing it from the bad infinity of perpetuation, of pursuit, of accumulation, and inscribing it as a burst of infinity in an act, immanent to the end of the finite, immanent to that dark transcendence.

In some way, philosophy therefore says nothing: but it says it, and this utterance is worth something on its own, absolutely—not reparative, not consoling. It stands in for the strength of a speaking in charge of taking charge of this: that there is no last word. It substitutes a chagrined tone for a last word, a tone of gray, Hegel takes pains to say.

BUT WE CRY

But we cry. We cry for the dead, our dead, our dearly departed. In crying for them we keep them. We keep their prizedness, their dearness, their endearment. They are our tears, through which the world clouds over and loses its form. Thus we lose them once again. The loss is interminable. It gets aggravated even more when we do not cry any more, when we no longer make the departed one relive in any manner whatsoever. Disappearance disappears as such: there is nothing left, if we want to go looking for it, nothing but the memory of what was and is no more.

Memory is the seal of loss. Loss consummated: that moment when we are not expecting it, we're no longer vigilant for an arrival or a call, a response, all that wasn't yet memory, everything that was always and forever still desperately *he*, *she*.

At the moment of the finite, of the end of the finite through which it accomplishes its finitude, the infinite is opened up. The infinite is opened up and seizes hold of it. But this is at once the infiniteness of the inscription of the finite and the infiniteness of its loss.

At once which is not a passage. *At one and the same time* that is *at once*: side by side, together and without relation, without exchange, without sharing, irreconcilable intimates. At once the infinite as an infinite end, as an incommensurable vertiginous and cosmic exaltation of presence, and the infinite as privation of the end, withdrawal, lack, injustice, ingratitude.

There is no gratitude for the fact that they have lived right up to their death, there is only bitterness for that death. No gratitude for that life that they lived, except when it has born witness through the advanced age it attained to having exhausted its possibilities. We do not cry the same tears when death, in fact, has already fulfilled most of its function. But, in the absence of advanced age, life can appear to have been lived for nothing. And for what else then is it ever lived, if we really ask about life what is its meaning or value, and not about all of the types of works that the living being can accomplish? It is always life for life's sake, for its own motion or drive, the beating of which at every instant keeps it on the edge of itself. Life rubs shoulders with death while oblivious to it, life forgets death right away, it lives on that forgetting, and it is that which ends up changing the absent presence into memory.

But we still cry, we cry without tears and without end for those who left too early, without it being in any way permitted for us to define the measure of that "too" in "*too* early," which all the same we discern only too well.

THERE'S NO NEED TO WORRY ABOUT SENSE

If we know, despite all that we allow to be said, that this one or that one was too young to die, even while the growing count of medicalized old ages may be no less heavily charged with questions, it is because we know something about the justice of living beings. We know that there is a truth with no measure or accounting, a justice of life that preserves itself, that perseveres for nothing else but itself and whose perseverance comprehends nevertheless the end—includes, strangely, an end that is not fixed but that is certain and the certainty of which cannot prevent injustice.

We demand justice and our tears are also tears of anger. Our demand is well founded for indeed life is for nothing else but its perseverance. Of itself, by itself, perseverance is just—that incredible, that stupefying stubbornness of the living who live with so much tenacity, with an endurance worthy—so we think—of a better lot, who live the unliveability of misery, of violence, of cruelty, of pitilessness and also always from beginning to end the injustice of all of those deaths they must traverse, all of those "dear ones" who disappear and whose prized value was to not-disappear and to accompany stubbornness.

We say: "he or she loved life"—but who does not love it provided that its perseverance does not turn against itself and provided that still living does not become what we dread and that we come to be unable to tolerate it?

Michel Deguy writes in *The Direction of the Visit*:

> If the bearers of life could tonight put down their burden, *onus grave*, as so often they dream of doing (overburdened, less and less interested in anything, as though they had fallen into a deep, eternal hole) there might be two billion suicides. What would we say of the man fallen to the bottom of a vast dried-up cistern with slick and high sides right up to the sky, a temple without any resource beneath the vain auguries of clouds?[1]

Overburdened they are, the bearers of life, and this cistern has gone dry from the deaths of the dear ones, the very dear ones, the ones too cherished to be lost. And yet it is not possible that anyone could be *too* dear, *since* they are cherished—the cherishing, the tender care of the loved one, the *caritas* that sets a price beyond price, which makes the priceless price, the price outside of value, inestimable and estimated absolutely, of the loved ones toward whom there is a dilection, a predilection; a privilege then and an exorbitant preference. The dear, here, is priceless, outside of price, without measure or equivalence, without currency, even without value, infinitely prized.

(Less the pathetic, pathic, and violent side of love than its other face, affectionate and peaceful; less, consequently, the desire for the other's dying than that of holding the other tenderly right up to his or her death and easing it for him, for her: the reason for wanting to be there, the reason for being present, for hastening to the bedside, near to the dear head, but so often it is impossible, we are too far away, it is too late, death did its work too fast or too slowly—it will go that far to undo our attention, our care.)

Love is the reason for the tears, but it is also, precisely, identically, the reason without reason of having held to that other life up against our own, for having held to life because it was living with her, with him, with these few ones who are the companions, the company, the accompaniment without reason of the duration of the days, of that pursuit with no other aim but pursuing and accompanying. Essentially, life accompanies life. As we know, the companion shares the bread, that bread on which we must feed to live. Company is the sharing of the life that is nourished in being shared and which goes nowhere else.

COMPANIONS OF MISERY

as the old laments sing . . . companions of company, simply: the care for life is made up of this care among us, the dear ones, the cherished ones whose cherishing consists of being exempted from any care for sense, meaning. And sense only appears as denied, devastated by the death of the dear companions. But nothing has been devastated, nothing but the company of the living which is the only meaning of life.

How not to cry and yet why cry—inasmuch as along with death there also enters into life—has always already entered—the very simple revelation of that insouciance, that exemption from sense that also makes for the taste for life?

What accompanies us the most faithfully is nothing other than this taste, this very humble, very harshly-seasoned taste of the exemption from sense: that we neither must conclude nor make significant, simply pass on. With that, there is nothing left to do: no assembly, no command, no prescribed conduct. No philosophy, no religion. But that puts us in company.

Deguy:

> The big word is ACCOMPANIMENT. Poetry accompanies and it is accompanied? Everything is "of company" as music "accompanies" life, and life accompanies music. The *sense* is with life.

Of course we are suspicious, for today the "accompaniment" of the dying is a definite task, there are norms, it has got its instruments, the naming of which indicates only too well its limit: we accompany, for a stretch of the road, and then the company is broken. But that poetry, that music, that sense that makes company for life, how can we not recognize in it so much more than that little stretch of road? For it is death itself, it is immortal death that keeps company with us.

But the lot of that accompaniment, the fate of that *with*, is precisely that it is not a face-to-face. It is not made of recognition or of any kind of seeing-through. It is made of a closeness to which vision and object-presentation remain foreign. We cannot recognize the poetry or the music of our dead, of our dying ones: that is forbidden to us, we must cry—and in crying remain in their company.

THE SALT OF TEARS

is part of the salt of life; the salt of death that burns our wounds and our pains salts our food as well, in such a way that it is bitter at the same time as it makes us live and persevere.

Why can't the bearers of life that Deguy names set down their burden?

Because with this burden they are also carrying their dear companions a little further. They are still perpetuating a little bit, not their "memory," as we say, for that, memory, is immobile and congeals, fixes on the loss. But they lead the company itself further, for some while, in the accompaniment through which we nourish one another, the beneficial necessity of being-with, that is to say *apud hoc*, close to, within proximity.

The proximity of the *with* is nothing that gets added on afterward to given singular beings: they are, on the contrary, given in the with, *with the with*. They are given living as distinct bodies, the contours of which, the skins, are not envelopes but on the contrary surfaces of contact, light strokes, approaches. Death takes away the body and with it proximity. It does not carry off the soul that remains the ungraspable, the untouchable, the inapproachable that was also there in proximity. The soul turns around, toward that body that abandons it, and is changed into a statue of salt.

HE IS NO LONGER THERE

At its very closest, the other remained distanced by the distance of its soul. Its body made this distance visible, it gave to it something that could be touched, allowed it to catch a whiff of the very delicious approach, the fragrant passage. The salt of tears and their pungency allow us to scent the void of the air, there where there was less void, without there having been, for all that, full continuity.

Less than empty and less than full, the just cadence and the spacing of bodies—passages, close touches, happy and unhappy bumps, transmitted tremors, vibrations of words, odor of skins, sweats, familiarity of faces and of silhouettes that there was no longer any need to recognize, which were knowing itself: the immediate knowledge, immanence of the *with*, of the set, of less than that sometimes, just something of the *just-there*.

She, he, *were there*: all is said. She, he, *is no longer there*. This *there* is not that of the simple place, it is not simply local even if it does designate too the opening of a place: the one that he or she should always have occupied; should still occupy. The *da* of their *Dasein*, not a situation but a coming, an entry onstage, a formation of space, a world configuration. She, he, *were the there*: making a guidepost and a cardinal point, engendering from their body an unprecedented cartography, an orientation, some itineraries. She, he, were here, down here, there, here, somewhere in the map and in the cosmography.

It was not a fixed position, it was the ever-moving coming-forth of a *praesentia*, of a being in advance, ahead or alongside of oneself, who was coming close to me, close to us, who was approaching and moving away, coloring the landscape and making the dwelling, the street, our own presence resonate differently. *Here* was *their* here, like a fundamental note of which she, he, alone had the exact frequency.

That was *somewhere*, *some where*, and we cry for that, cry that there is no more *where*, even only, as it was most often, perfectly ordinary. There is no longer a place or a part where we might partake in its coming, in its departure. And death is not a departure, no one goes off, it is without destination—but there, right there where an instant ago *there was*, suddenly *there had been* and therefore there is no more. Death passes from the imperfect to the perfect, it is done, accomplished, finished. For there is nothing to be understood. That it be finished, this allows for no domestification, no acclimatization to our world: it is the outside-of-world that bursts in.

And beneath that bursting-in, that devastation, even the more distant become close, even the indifferent become dear, although not cherished. Suddenly all are more there, in the gaping place. It is too easy to mock funeral eulogies: it is not only because we always say good things about the dead, it is because death gives them worth, does justice to them without reserve. It is alone in recognizing their right, recognizing each one integrally, without calculation.

ANASTASIS

"Resurrection," says religion—almost all of our religions. And that signifies return-to-life, revivesence, the recovery of integrity but in glory and beatitude. Eternal life intact and prodigious. It is miracle wherein loss is abolished.

Even in religion, however, no one has seen someone resurrected, and chief among them, the one who, for Christianity, opens up and takes on the resurrection of all; he only allows that mystery to be attested by faith. He does not truly give it to be experienced.

Stripped of miracle, magic, belief, stripped of other worlds and the dead surging out of the sepulchre, there remains this, which is perhaps no longer Christian, nor Jewish, nor Muslim, but which comes from further off, from greater depths, which probably belongs to all of them—in the migration of souls, in nirvanas or even in the infernal shades: "resurrection" is another measure of life. It is the setting upright of that which, for the time of a lifetime, stretches forth a shade walking upon a ground. Standing up, anastasis: setting upright, rising, elevation, erection, surging up.

But the anastasis does not follow, like a second life. There is no second life; the first is the only and the last one. Anastasis precedes; it is already given, accorded to the living. This is why the only article which should sum up—should have summed up?—the Christian confession is that of the faith in the given resurrection. Love, which flows from it—the *caritas*—denominates the relation among all of the resurrected: the dilection of all in such a way that each by each picked up, risen, elevated to the true dimension, which is upright—that is to say turned toward heaven, toward the outside of the world. That is how all enter the world and all leave it.

For it is a matter of nothing else: of not being of this world. In this world, drawing away from this world, not to reject it but to open it in such a way that the earth might not be simply ungrateful for the lives that it takes back and buries deep in itself.

But we cry, because this elevation redeems nothing. The horizontal ground absorbs any life that stretches itself out upon it. It is not a matter of redemption: it is a matter, on the contrary, of that which cannot be redeemed at any price, exceeding any price and any estimation. Nothing to be redeemed, or to be redeemed for, purchased. No salvation, said the friend whose tomb in Ris-Orangis Michel salutes. No salvation but a "*salut*!," an address, a "take care, carry on" and a "carry me" . . .

(the same, citing Celan: that is all for the world/I must carry you).

. . . the world gone off, disappeared, what needs to be carried—the man or woman who must be carried—it is each one, each one raised out of the world, *each one as he or she is a rising into this outside*, or perhaps even as he or she is *a rising of this outside in the very middle of the world in flight.*

Deguy finishes up:

> That which is not of this world
> is of this world[2]

That's just it, that is what it's all about, it is about that, that unforgiveable volte-face where death takes a face from its *there*. That in the world there might be room, a place for what has no place, there is being-there for what is not there, and the world is made only of the obscure signals that its absent ones exchange.

That, that absence there, that absence present there, this salt of the earth that burns our eyes, the eyes of we who will not understand, we who are not destined to understand but to take and to cherish with tears those who have neither contour nor skin but the somber and ineffaceable flash of *having been there*, this is what is not a survivor, not a revenant, not a phantom, not a shade, that is what is not of here and that, in that precisely, *is here*, outside of space and time, it is of this *outside-with* that neither philosophy nor religion speak, even while nothing else concerns them. No word says it, but a chant is being addressed. Without rest, a threnody, a *cantus firmus*, a *cante jondo* rises up, in music or in words—poetry, yes, if you will, but first of all, call and lament, first of all the tone which makes heard *here* the resonance of *there*, of that outside.

They make us sing, our dearly departed, they make us hum the *lamentate* in which our tears say nothing but the *saying nothing*, nothing but a speaking that is a crying and a crying that is a *sob*, if the sob is nothing other than the shaken-up voice, sob tripping up in the throat and giving up on speaking, the crying like this renunciation, and this giving-up as a consent to desolation, to its stammering.

This is what philosophy and religion are not capable of. It is at the edge of this that they remain held back: it is the sob. Philosophical sadness is morose, the *Leçons des ténèbres* are majestic: on one side and the other we hold ourselves exempt from the sob, from that hiccup or hocket [*hoquet*] that was once a musical term for the antiphon of two voices.

Like—*comme*, as with, in the same way as, as much as—two voices alternating while responding from here to the outside and from nowhere to *here*, two voices, one of which is saying nothing. But we do not always know which one, in truth.

WITHOUT YOU

Here, to finish, I will allow to be heard what someone close, someone very close, wrote upon the death of a sister whose life accompanied her own for fifty years. Allowing us to hear nothing but a voice, one among so many others who cry, nothing but one in response to that of Michel and to another and to much more than one song.

Without You

to my sister Annik

We do have to keep watch near the dead face
a cigarette
looking at the sea
never again

we forever alone without you
what is there
is no longer there for you
the cigarette burns from your death the sea of your absence
  rushes back

I will take in my hands your dead face
rather the funerarium than the tomb
rather the hospital room
morphine ketamine hypnovel
and not your closed eyes
nor sealed up in your mouth those words which you alone said

And so unto death faces united
this is about you
about the passion of you of our caring hands which held
your shoulder and stroked your stomach
about you
dead stretch
a rose in your hands
frail
in the veil of Islamabad enshrouded
our faces upon your face
Adieu face in May
already we are burying your death
already the memory of you and the awaiting of dreams
in dreams you would say it is like before
o how I would like to carry you again day after day
like the angel on that night
who received your words
"all is dark"

My god—the end already

Hélène

From *L'Allégresse pensive* 203–216

NOTES

1. Deguy, SV 176.
2. Nancy refers to Deguy's poem "Ris-Orangis" in *Desolatio*, 85.

NOTES

1. Deguy refers to two noteworthy conversions. Don Miguel Manara Vicentelo de Leca, a seventeenth-century Spanish nobleman sometimes called the "real" Don Juan, carried out acts of atonement for his sins, pursuing both an active program of conversion of the remaining Moors on the Iberian peninsula and works of charity leading to the foundation of the Hospital de la Santa Caridad in Seville. Armand Jean Le Bouthillier de Rancé was a notoriously worldly seventeenth-century French monk at the Abbaye de la Trappe who converted from a life of pleasures and became a driving force in the establishment of the strict codes of the Trappist order. In 1844, François René de Chateaubriand produced *Vie de l'abbé de Rancé*, a quasi-hagiographical biography of Rancé, as his own act of spiritual amendment of life. Michel Deguy had the reading of this work in mind when he was composing his threnody for his late wife Monique in 1994: "and if I quote *Vie de Rancé*, it is because the memory of that hallucinated reading haunts me while I lead these pages toward a sort of book" (CSCC, 304). This intertext is another important connection between the Threnody and the Palinody.

2. As indicated in the translator's notes (infra), I provide immediate translations in English where Deguy has modified a quotation in an ancient language. I also give the author's name. Unmodified quotes are sometimes dealt with in notes and sometimes with parenthetical translation, as are a range of the most important allusions in this very allusive book.

3. Deguy has indeed often quoted or alluded to this remark attributed to Mallarmé. In response to a journalist friend's indignation at hearing Villiers de l'Isle Adam called a "failure," Mallarmé replied, "But Mauclair, we are all failures . . . what else could we be since we measure ourselves by the infinite?" (Henri Mordor, *Vie de Mallarmé* Paris: Gallimard 1941 665). The Mallarmé of *A Man of Little Faith* is clearly this poet of modern failure and regret (see *infra* 16 for the last words of Mallarmé, found in a note on his desk). Michel Deguy's Mallarmé is also the problematic Mallarmé of "central purity," of the temptation for aesthetic adequacy and of an improbable renewal through poetry of everyday language (17); he is the Mallarmé of the untitled sonnet, "The virgin, vivid, and beautiful today . . . ," so evocative for Deguy's own conception of earthly piety (22, 155); Mallarmé here is also the crucial poetic precedent for a more acute thinking of double negation, outside or short of any dialectical aspirations (83); Mallarmé's famous remark, "We cannot do without Eden," is referenced (114, 120) as part of Deguy's overall attempt to reinvent relics, including what he calls "theologemes and mythemes" like Eden and prelapsarian dwelling.

For Deguy on Mallarmé in English, see: "The Dancer: Mallarmé" tr. C. Elson, in *The Dalhousie Review* 77 no. 3 Autumn 1997, 335–338; and "The Energy of Despair," tr. C. Elson in *Mallarmé in the Twentieth Century* ed. Robert Greer Cohn (Madison/London: Fairleigh Dickinson University Press/Associated University Presses 1998) 19–30.

Mallarmé and Baudelaire must be thought of as two more or less equally inspirational poetic sources for Michel Deguy, with Baudelaire occupying a somewhat more central place. Deguy's *La Pietà Baudelaire* gives us some recapitulative moments where the two figures are explicitly aligned. Responding to recent work by Yves Bonnefoy on Baudelaire (in the Antoine Compagnon seminar [see n. 4 below] and in Bonnefoy's book, *Sous le signe de Baudelaire* [Paris: Gallimard coll. *Bibliothèque des Idées* 2011]), Deguy notes that he will separate Mallarmé to a lesser degree from Baudelaire than does Bonnefoy, all the while maintaining a "decisive difference": "Is Mallarmé less modern for us than Baudelaire? But why would he be? Because of the agnostic piety maintained by Baudelaire in the transports of nihilism to which he submits and which we bring to completion, having needed him as a mediator" (PB, 30).

See also, Christopher Elson, "A Poetics of Summing-Up and Making-Away-With: Michel Deguy and Stéphane Mallarmé" in *L'Esprit Créateur* 40 no. 3 Autumn 2000, 86–96.

4. The poem referred to here, "Duellum," is one of Deguy's touchstone texts from Baudelaire's *Les Fleurs du Mal*. Its general connection to both the thematic of aging and Deguy's poetics of paradoxy and contrariety is made clear in the following lines. Rather than referring to one of the many translations extant, those wishing to follow up on Deguy's Baudelairean references may wish to consult a website providing an wide array of versions of the *Fleurs du Mal* at http://fleursdumal.org/poem/204 (retrieved February 8, 2013).

The Baudelaire of *A Man of Little Faith* is the Baudelaire of *duellum*, the thwarted dualities that Deguy seeks to reconceive in contemporary terms, but is also the Baudelaire of *recueillement*, self-reflective, meditative, contemplative, or prayerful introspection. Deguy's frequent explicit quotations and his many more or less discreet allusions include references to the raw carnality and doomed corporeal frailty of the human in "*Une Charogne*" (quoted on p. 15); "*Le Voyage*," the last of the *flowers* and its heady "plunge into the unknown" (34); a reference to "A *une passante*" as a founding text of passing and passage (notions at the core of Deguy's poetic (post) phenomenology and taken up extensively in Nancy's reading of Deguy *infra*) (176); "ennui" and its yawning devoration of the world in "*Au Lecteur*" (40); numerous echoes and rephrasings of Baudelaire's address to the hypocritical reader as "*mon semblable, mon frère*," a poetic thinking that Deguy renews relative to his reconsideration of fraternity through a deeper account of semblance, resemblance, and an ontology of like. Unpacking the more subtle interpenetration of Deguy's modes and vocabulary with those of Baudelaire would be an extensive undertaking; to offer just one example: a title like "*Confiteor*" (17), which refers clearly enough to a prayer in the Catholic Mass, cannot not also be a reference to "*Le* Confiteor *de l'Artiste*," the title of the third poem in Baudelaire's *Petits poëmes en prose* (*Le Spleen de Paris*).

Deguy's compactly intense 2012 volume, *La pietà Baudelaire* (Editions Belin coll. "L'extrême contemporain") emerged from the writer's participation in Antoine Compagnon's seminar at the Collège de France (the presentations of all guest speakers of the seminar may be accessed at http://www.college-de-france.fr/site/antoine-compagnon/# | m=seminar | q=/site/antoine-compagnon/seminar-2011-2012.htm | [retrieved March 28, 2013]). *La pietà Baudelaire* provides readers with Deguy's current perspective on a "Baudelaire for us" (PB, 19, 27 and *passim*) and is, importantly from the perspective of *A Man of Little Faith*, centrally focused on the two motifs of "piety" and "mystical nature" (PB, 23 n. 13). Readers wishing to consider earlier moments of Deguy's reading of Baudelaire may refer to texts found in *Choses de la poésie et affaire culturelle*, *op. cit.*, and *L'Impair* [Odd Metre] (Tours: Farrago 2001), as well as the brief, Baudelaire-inspired meditation on Paris, *Spleen de Paris* (Paris: Galilée 2001).

For more Deguy on Baudelaire in English translation, see "To Spear it on the Mark, of Mystical Nature" (tr. Wilson Baldridge) in *Baudelaire and the Poetics of Modernity* ed. Patricia A. Ward (Nashville: Vanderbilt University Press: 2000) 187–198.

A thorough and useful critical perspective on Deguy's reading of Baudelaire may be found in Yves Charnet's "*La Profondeur et l'Infini: L'Imagination baudelairienne selon Michel Deguy*" in *Baudelaire: Nouveaux Chantiers* eds. Y. Charnet et J. Delabroy (Villeneuve d'Ascq: Presses universitaires du Septentrion 1995).

I. PALINODY

1. Pascal is a constant reference for the man of little faith and some of the key motifs of Pascalian thought are taken up ceaselessly by Deguy in an agnostic or a-theological recasting of them. (Note that when Deguy refers here or in other works to the number of one of Pascal's thoughts, he generally favors the order of the Brunschweig [Hachette] edition. See *Pascal's Pensées* tr., ed., Martin Turnell [London: Harvill Press 1962] for a concordance of the principal editorial orderings of the *Pensées*, 425–235. The two quotations below are Turnell's translations.) The references in *A Man of Little Faith* reveal the overall, long-term emphases of Deguy's reading and include: here, the end of the section on The Wager in the *Pensées*, "If the argument appeals to you and appears well founded, you must know that it was composed by a man *who went down on his knees, before* [my emphasis] and after it, to pray . . ." (B343); the reference to the relativity of perspective in the ninth *pensée*, "He is usually right from one point of view" (12); the crucial distinction, constantly revisited by Deguy, between *habile* and *demi-habile*, sometimes translated as the clever and the half-clever (28; B327, 335, 337), as part of his ratcheting up of the intrinsic contrarieties of truth; reflections that draw on Pascal's conceptions of human grandeur and misery, the human being, the thinking reed, knowing of his dying and death while the universe that crushes him does not (50/B347) or the three orders of greatness, the flesh, the intellect, and charity (92/ B793); the Pascalian theme of "distraction" with its links to the euthanizing character of our contemporary cultural culture (73; B 138, 167,171, etc.); Pascalian extreme attention, usually linked in Deguy also to Malebranche and/or Simone Weil (92, 103).

2. The references to Longinus and to the Greek *hupsos* direct us to the first-century Hellenistic text, *Peri Hupsous* [On the High/Of the Sublime], which inaugurates the Western tradition of sublimity. Deguy's extensive reading of the mysterious Longinus, or Pseudo-Longinus, constitutes his distinctive contribution to the renewal of French thought of the sublime in the 1980s, a decisive reconsideration by a philosophical generation that he both perceived in its emergence and helped orchestrate through his collection with the Editions Belin and the journal *Po&Sie*. Deguy was the editor of *Du Sublime* in 1988 (Editions Belin; contributions by J-F Courtine, M. Deguy, E. Escoubas, Ph. Lacoue-Labarthe, J-F Lyotard, L. Marin, J-L Nancy, and J. Rogozinski), excellently translated and presented by Jeffrey Librett as *Of the Sublime: Presence in Question* (Albany: SUNY Press coll. Intersections: Philosophy and Critical Theory 1993). Deguy's essay there, "The Discourse of Exaltation [*Megalogorein*]" was not his last word on the sublime. His essay, "*L'écriture sidérante*" on the 'speculative rhetorician' Pascal Quignard, returns to a Longinian sublime in the context of a reading of that singular contemporary author (RP, 187–207). The link between the sublime and sublimation, having to do with the becoming-*sophos*, is perceptible in *A Man of Little Faith* with its programmatic declaration, "A task: sublime paradoxes" (*infra* 89) and also in *Réouverture après travaux* (81–86 and *passim*). In *Ecologiques*, Deguy links sublime sublimation to a contemporary reconception of the soul. See also, "Dublin Interview" *infra*. For a consideration of these matters up until 2000, see Christopher Elson, "*Deguy, Quignard, Lévi-Strauss et l'écriture du désastre*" in *Contemporary French Poetics* eds. M. Bishop and C. Elson (Amsterdam: Rodopi 2000).

3. Deguy's work frequently rereads his past volumes, quoting, referring to older texts, renewing them, offering accompaniment to them. The strategy of relaying poems, beginning a new volume with a text that first appeared in the previous one, for example, from *Donnant Donnant* to *Gisants*, or beginning with a "Summary of the Propositions of the Preceding Books" (AHA, 9–13), is also part of this retracing, incitative relation to what he regards as an uncertain readership. The texts referred to in this sequence include: "*Lecture de Sappho—La Comparaison*" in A,147–150; "*Nu*" in GIS 96–99/REC 134–139; and "*Aphrodiqu'onoclastie*" in AF 23–27.

4. Deguy refers to one of his most admired poems, "*Qui Quoi*" [Who What], which opens *Tombeau de du Bellay* [Du Bellay's Tomb] (Paris: Gallimard 1973) 9. Clayton Eshleman's translation in *Given Giving* begins, "For a long time you have not existed/Face occasionally celebrated and sufficient" and the poem's speaker indeed sets himself, the indolent, negligent, alienated one, at the stern: "This me who refuses to be one of us carried away/From the stern (this jig-sawed balcony over the salt)" (Berkeley and Los Angeles: University of California Press: 1984) 147.

5. The reference here to Martin Heidegger's "Letter on Humanism" engages Deguy's thought of negative anthropology, deeply related to the *little faith*, and points to a reimagining of the human in and for the conditions of distress of our times. *A Man of Little Faith* draws on the Heideggerian heritage discussed more extensively in our Introduction (see "To Conserve while Leaving Behind" *infra* 9–12; and nn. 29 and 30). From the dereliction of the latecomers (106) to the world-opening character of the work of art (116), from the status of the Heideggerian *Lichtung* or clearing in a time of forgetfulness of Being (44) to the copula of Being in relation

to the figurativity of existence, Deguy constantly questions Heidegger, acknowledging his inspiration, taking the Heideggerian questions into his own poetic language and rephrasing and reformulating them for today. The Deguyan translation of "Only a god can save us," for example, might well be "this anthropomorphosis that might fail" (AF, 114).

6. MD note. Impossible in the *corrida* where it appears that banning the putting-to-death deprives the whole business of its seriousness, truth, sense . . .

7. Deguy is the author of *La Machine matrimoniale ou Marivaux* (Paris: Gallimard 1982) and his reading of that theatrical corpus founds many of the author's social observations, as here.

8. On "semblance," see "Translator's Notes," point 6, *infra*.

9. Robert Marteau (1925–2011) was a French poet who moved to Québec and became a Canadian citizen. Some of his books, like *Mont Royal* (Paris: Gallimard 1981), are haunted by the devastation of the first peoples of North America.

10. Deguy coins *anemomene* (borne by the wind) on the model of *anadyomene* (borne by the waves).

11. Augustin Berque (1942–) is a thinker published by Deguy in his collection *L'extrême contemporain* with Belin editions. A distinguished expert on Japan and a theorist of cultural geography within a phenomenological perspective, Berque has elaborated a thinking of the *Ecoumène* (Paris: Belin 2006) that resonates strongly with Deguy's intensifying eco-poetics. A book of his writings, *Thinking Through Landscape* appeared with Routledge in 2013.

12. The unattributed quotation, "*cet oeil d'eau morne*," comes from the poem by Arthur Rimbaud, "Mémoire." Wyatt Mason translates the formula as "this sad watery eye" in *Rimbaud Complete* (New York: Random House coll. The Modern Library Classics 2002) 131. In *A Man of Little Faith* Rimbaud is a more discreet presence than Mallarmé or Baudelaire but is occasionally, as here, a source of striking images and citable, renewable metaphoricity for Deguy (35, "Memoire"; 72, "The Drunken Boat"). In terms of the latter's thinking of poetic modernity, Rimbaud's articulation of a "fatal inability" (48) connects to Mallarmean intuitions of failure, to what Deguy discusses at the beginning of his "Motifs Towards a Poetics": "Contemporary poetry . . . far from glorifying the 'lyrical illusion' and from favouring 'romantic' identifications with heroes standing 'alone against all,' that madness of a subject believing himself to be the only exception to the law, had in fact to tone down its song, had to pull down its hopes, had to interiorize its failures in order to turn them into paradoxes. . . . What failures? The failures of the poets who thought they were failing. Contemporary poetry has therefore to meditate the different figures of paradoxical failure (the failure that is no way a simple failure); namely, to distinguish the failure of Baudelaire from that of Rimbaud, from that of Mallarmé . . ." (MOTIFS, 55). With respect to religious faith, Deguy will sometimes deploy Rimbaldian "Illuminations," the title of a collection of prose poems, as an alternative to religiously framed "revelation," as in the section of *A Man of Little Faith* entitled, "Revelation, continued . . ." (118). The emphasis there is placed by Deguy on the maintenance or paradoxical reestablishment of illusion after disillusion (ie, on the *little* faith). The alterity at the heart of subjectivity, the *wholly other* or the *third party*, so frequently interrogated in these pages and elsewhere by Deguy,

draws sometimes on the Rimbaldian source of "I is another" in the correspondence known as the *Lettres du voyant* [The Seer Letters] (139; see Mason, *op. cit.*, 364–370).

13. Deguy's thought of "the cultural," a substantification of the adjective that he forged as a neologism in the 1980s is discussed in more detail in the Introduction, see *infra* xxxviii and xliv n. 67.

14. Deguy makes a reference to Guillaume Apollinaire's "*La Jolie Rousse*" half-heard here: "*la bonté contrée énorme où tout se tait*" [goodness, the enormous country where all is hushed]. Deguy has written occasionally on Apollinaire, his "*Colchiques, encore*" (CPAC, 66–73) is a striking rethinking of that much commented-upon poem. Without a doubt, however, the poetic quasi-manifesto cited here, "The Beautiful Redhead" from *Calligrammes*, with its explorations of the tensions within poetry and within cultural tradition between "order and adventure," and with its pre- or simply *non*surrealist evocations of the deep resources of the nonconscious, is the key Apollinairean reference point in Deguy's lineage of poetic modernity. See Guillaume Apollinaire, *Calligrammes Poems of Peace and War* (1913–1916) tr. Anne Hyde Greet intro. S.I. Lockerbie, commentary Hyde Greet and Lockerbie, (Los Angeles: UCLA Press 1980) 345 for "The Beautiful Redhead."

15. Hence tramps (upon) rather than tramples.

16. MD note. Mark Anspach, *A charge de revanche*, Seuil 2002, 232.

17. The reference is to *Arrêts fréquents* (Marseille: Anne-Marie Métailié 1990). This theme is treated extensively and with numerous references in "To Conserve while Leaving Behind: Michel Deguy's Palinody," *infra.*

18. Deguy makes the cases agree with his syntax, perhaps indirectly suggesting an ironic aestheticism (truth of splendor vs. splendor of truth); it is of course a case of just what he goes on to discuss, an inverted comparison of splendor and truth, making reference to *Veritatis Splendor*, an encyclical from Pope John Paul II promulgated in August 1993.

19. Behold the man (John 19:5). Also on this page: *aere perennius* [more lasting than bronze] and *Anch'io son' pittore* [I too am a painter. Coreggio is said to have uttered this exclamation upon seeing the work of Raphael.]

20. MD note. I have proposed the definition: the essence of the host = we do not know who it is. [He is restating the ambivalence of *hôte* in French that designates both guest and host.]

21. *Letters 1925–1975 Hannah Arendt and Martin Heidegger* ed. Ursula Lutz, trans. Andrew Shields (New York: Harcourt 2004).

22. MD note. *Heidegger en France* Paris: Albin Michel 2001 t.1, 388.

II. NOTEBOOKS OF DISBELIEF

1. MD note. As for the question of whether one can not know what one knows, it will be necessary to await the Freudian exploration of the unconscious, then the Lacanian one, to hear it.

2. MD note. The risk run by this attitude is that of misology [Plato's term for the hatred of thought].

3. Todorov's preface is to be found in the French translation of *Le Grand Code* (Paris: Seuil collection Poétique 1989).

4. One of Deguy's most extensive examinations of the fruitful connection between his own poetics and Derrida's antinomies occurs in relation to Derrida's essay on European cultural identity, *The Other Heading* (tr. Pascale Brault and Michael Nass Bloomington: Indiana University Press 1992; originally published as *L'Autre cap* Paris: Editions de minuit 1991), and is found in Deguy's 1991 essay, "De la contemporanéité" GCD, 73–86.

5. Deguy has informed me that he was thinking here of a reference to Marguerite Yourcenar made in the Israeli poet Israel Eliraz's works.

6. One of the manifestations of the poet and intellectual's vigilance in Deguy's career has been his perspicacious attention to figures who later prove to be determining in contemporary thought and literature. The first critical essay on Derrida, early attention to Claude Simon, and early and sustained engagement with René Girard are key examples of this. Deguy co-edited, with Jean-Pierre Dupuy an early collection of texts on Girard (*René Girard et le problème du Mal* [Paris: Grasset 1982]) in which his own roadmap of engagement with Girardian thought may be found, "*Onglets de la lecture*," 61–87.

7. The stele in Tipasa, Algeria commemorates Albert Camus's essay, "Noces à Tipaza" [Nuptials at Tipasa] and reads: "*Je comprends ici qu'on appelle gloire: le droit d'aimer sans mesure.*" Camus is buried in Provence in the village of Lourmarin.

8. Deguy refers to critic and poet Marcelin Pleynet's essay, *Poésie et "Révolution": La révolution du style* (Paris: Editions pleins feux 2000).

9. MD note. I recopy the famous incipit: "Good Sense is, of all things among men, the most equally distributed; for every one thinks himself so abundantly provided with it, that those even who are the most difficult to satisfy in everything else, do not usually desire a larger measure of this quality than they already possess. And in this it is not likely that all are mistaken: the conviction is rather to be held as testifying that the power of judging aright and of distinguishing Truth from Error, which is properly what is called Good Sense or Reason, is by nature equal in all men." (*Discourse on the Method*, tr. John Veitch, Edinburgh and London 1873 p. 45.)

10. *Noeien* and *legein*—Thinking and Saying, the activities corresponding to *noos* and to *logos*.

11. Primo Levi, *The Mirror Maker*. (tr. Raymond Rosenthal) (London: 1990 Methuen Books), p. 138. Additional quotations from Levi are unattributed by Deguy and come from other sources.

12. MD note. "Auschwitz and Hiroshima were only the forerunners of things still to come. It will be so if science and only science are held to be of value. But to what else can we attach value? This is not easy to say. It is precisely all of that which scientists try to set aside, to abstract and to destroy: everything which has its origin elsewhere [. . .] All words have been discredited and those which have not yet been discredited will be soon. Whoever tries to grasp this other conception through the scientific method will lose it" (*Science nazie, science de mort*, Odile Jacob 1989).

13. MD note: One will read the fine book of poems by Jean-Charles Vegliante, which appeared under this title in the collection, "*L'extrême contemporain*" (Belin 2000). We have this common nothing in common.

14. In his general discussion of secularism and French *laïcité*, Deguy here refers to the *Loi du 9 décembre 1905 concernant la séparation des Eglises et de l'Etat*, which

is considered the key historical moment in the evolution from broad Enlightenment and Revolutionary principles of the separation of Church and State to a true Republican neutrality and full disengagement of the State and Churches within society.

15. Deguy refers to Theodor Adorno's title (*Minima Moralia: Reflections from Damaged Life* (London: Verso 1996), which plays on the disputed Aristotelian text, *Magna Moralia.*

16. MD note: "*Seul un dieu peut nous sauver*" Heidegger interview avec *Der Spiegel*, 1966 (*Réponses et questions sur l'histoire et la politique* Mercure de France, 1977). [The English version of the text, "Only a God Can Save Us: *Der Spiegel's* Interview (September 23, 1966)," may be found in *Martin Heidegger: Philosophical and Political Writings* ed. Manfred Stassen (New York: Continuum 2003) 24–48.]

III: SIMONE WEIL FROM MEMORY

1. Michel Deguy quotes from the Gallimard Folio Essays collection edition of *L'Enracinement*. I align his brief quotations with the Harper/Colophon Books edition of *The Need for Roots* (New York: 1952/1971). The original and the translation are given in the footnotes.

2. MD note. "*Pour être établie en toute rigueur, cette liste (des devoirs éternels) doit procéder par analogie*" (p. 13). *Plus loin*: "*D'une manière analogue, même au moment du sacrifice total, il n'est jamais dû à aucune collectivité autre chose qu'un respect analogue à celui qui est dû à la nourriture*" (p. 16). "In order to be absolutely correctly made out, this list ought to proceed from the example just given by way of analogy" (6). Further along: "Similarly, even when a total sacrifice is required, no more is owed to any collectivity whatever than a respect analogous to the one owed to food" (9).

3. *C'est une obligation éternelle envers l'être humain de ne pas le laisser souffrir de la faim quand on a l'occasion de le secourir. Cette obligation étant la plus évidente, elle doit servir de modèle pour dresser la liste des devoirs éternels envers tout être humain*" (13). "So it is an eternal obligation toward the human being not to let him suffer from hunger when one has the chance of coming to his assistance. This obligation being the most obvious of all, it can serve as a model on which to draw up the list of eternal duties toward each human being" (6).

4. Deguy refers the reader to p. 21 of the Gallimard edition. In the English translation we find the passage on p.12: "needs are arranged in antithetical pairs and have to combine together to form a balance."

5. See Alexander Isaevitch Solzhenitzyn's 1976 essay, "Repentance and Self-Limitation in the Life of Nations" in *From Under the Rubble* (Chicago: Regnery Gateway 1981).

6. MD note. Ernst Bloch. [*The Principle of Hope*. Three volumes MIT Press 1995.]

7. MD note. And the stepping-back of Professor Testard belongs to this terrible fear; as very likely do "fundamentalisms," even the most obscurantist, of which the most radical came, let us not forget, out of the forced Westernization of Iran by the Shah; they draw back in terror and fury from the accelerated profanation. [Jacques Testard, who successfully performed the first in vitro fertilization in France in the 1980s has famously taken a stand for a moratorium on genetic manipulation,

calling out for a citizen science, explicitly fearful of the acceleration of technoscience and its alliance with neoliberal economism.]

8. It is from a play by the painter and writer, Gilles Aillaud, "Vermeer et Spinoza" (Christian Bourgois 1986). Cited in *Ateliers: Esthétique de l'écart* by Armelle Auris, (Paris: L'Harmattan 1994) 92.

9. "It is not difficult to define the place that physical labour should occupy in a well-ordered social life. It should be its spiritual core." Weil, *The Need for Roots, op. cit.*, 304.

10. "Calendary" referred for the Romans to the first day of lunar cycles.

11. *ama et quod vis fac*—Augustine. The correct version is *Ama et vis quod fac*: Love and do whatever you wish. Deguy might simply be perpetuating a common misquote.

IV. JEWISH HUMANITY

1. MD note. *Lettres à l'opinion éclairée* Seuil 2002, 2e lettre.

2. MD note. *De quoi demain*, dialogue with Elisabeth Roudinesco, Fayard, 2001, p. 183.

3. Ibid.

4. MD note. *Restitutions. Unité et totalité chez F. Rosenweig. Etude sur l'architecture de "L'Etoile de la Rédemption"* Vrin 2001, p. 264–265.

5. Deguy refers here to the last lines of Jean-Paul Sartre's *Les Mots* [The Words].

INDEX